# THE MANY FACES OF APPALACHIA:
## Exploring a Region's Diversity

*Proceedings of the
Seventh Annual
Appalachian Studies Conference*

Edited by:
SAM GRAY

Managing Editor:
JACQUELINE STEWART

# APPALACHIAN CONSORTIUM PRESS
## Boone, North Carolina

    The Appalachian Consortium Press is a division of the Appalachian Consortium Incorporated, specializing in the publication of carefully produced books of particular interest to Southern Appalachia. The Press is controlled by the Publications Committee and the Board of Directors, the members of which are appointed by the Chief Administrative Officers of the member institutions and agencies of the corporation.

The member institutions of the Appalachian Consortium are:

Appalachian State University
Blue Ridge Parkway
East Tennessee State University
First Tennessee-Virginia Development District
Mars Hill College
Mountain Regional Library
U. S. Forest Service
Warren Wilson College
Western Carolina University
Western North Carolina Historical Association
North Carolina Division of Archives and History

ISBN: 978-1-4696-3684-9

Copyright © 1985 by the Appalachian Consortium, Inc. all rights reserved.

# Table of Contents

INTRODUCTION, *Sam Gray* ............................... vii

I. NORTHERN GEORGIA EXCEPTIONS: POLITICS
   The Reconstruction Careers of Joseph Brown and
   Benjamin Hill, *Derrell Roberts* ..................... 1

II. APPALACHIAN HANDICRAFT: COMMERCIALISM
    AND AUTHENTICITY
    Nineteenth Century Quilts in Macon County, North
    Carolina, *Laurel Horton* ........................... 11

III. INTERPRETING THE MOUNTAIN WOMAN'S
     EXPERIENCE
     Emma Bell Miles, Pioneer Folklorist of Appalachia,
     *Grace Toney Edwards* .............................. 23

     The Science Poetry of Marilou Awiakta, *Parks Lanier* . 29

     Going Home, *Ron Willoughby* ....................... 37

IV. SOCIAL THEORY AND SOCIAL LIFE IN
    APPALACHIA: A PANEL
    A Contribution to the Critique
    of Political Economy,
    *Allen Bateau* ...................................... 41

V. CURRENT RESEARCH IN COMMUNITY ISSUES
   Households and Families in Eastern
   Kentucky in 1900, *Thomas A. Arcury and
   Julia D. Porter* .................................... 47

VI. PRE-COLUMBIAN CHEROKEES
    Pre-Columbian Cultural Contact Between
    Chibchan and Iroquoian Linguistic Groups,
    *David K. Evans* .................................... 57

VII. NORTH GEORGIA WRITERS—PAST AND PRESENT
These Also Climbed Parnassus:
An Overview of Georgia Mountain Authors,
*Paul McClure* .................................. 71

VIII. THE BUSINESS OF TRADITION: TRADES,
HANDICRAFTS AND HOUSEHOLD ENTERPRISES
The Shell Button Industry in Appalachia,
*Cheryl Claassen* ................................ 77

IX. REGIONAL POETRY
Faces of Appalachia in Poetry,
*Bennie Lee Sinclair* ............................ 89

X. COMMUNITIES: PARTICIPATION OR RETREAT
Progress Is Our Most Important Product:
Decline in Citizen Participation and the
Professionalization of Schooling in an Appalachian
Rural County, *Tom Boyd* ........................ 107

XI. ECONOMICS I: MACRO
Surviving the 1990s: Inter-Regional
Variation in Economic Problems,
*Thomas R. Shannon* ............................. 125

Historical Perspectives on Energy,
Industrialization and the Shaping of
Appalachia, *Ted Couillard* ..................... 139

XII. NORTH GEORGIA MUSIC
North Georgia Musicians and Groups in the
1920s and 1930s, *Gene Wiggins* ................. 147

XIII. HISTORICAL DIVERSITY IN APPALACHIAN
COMMUNITIES
Diversity in Antebellum Mountain Life:
The Towns of Western North Carolina,
*John C. Inscoe* ................................ 153

XIV. THE THREE R'S:
RESEARCH, RESOURCES, RECORDS
The Great Smokies: Diverse Perceptions
of the Park as a Resource,
*David Carpenter* .................................. 169

XV. TOURISM THEN AND NOW
A Plunge into the Past:
Henry Ford and Friends
Tour the Southern Appalachians,
*Charles Gunter* .................................... 183

XVI. MOONSHINE AND BEYOND
A Touch of Mountain Dew:
Art and History of Whiskey-Making
in North Georgia, *Ray Rensi
and Leo Downing* .................................. 195

# Introduction

In March of 1978 the first Appalachian Studies Conference was held at Berea, Kentucky. My memories of this event are surprisingly clear—the weather was fine, the company congenial and the energy, drawn from diverse places and personalities, was sharply focused. I recall that many individuals who have remained involved in the Conference over the years were instrumental in shaping with their words and concerns, the issues of that first conference and much of the agendae of those to follow.

There were no papers read at Berea, instead, committees were formed upon an ad hoc and voluntary basis. The committees were actually discussion groups based on the various academic disciplines embraced by the notion of Appalachian Studies: Natural History, Literature, Geography, Folklore, History/Political Science, Economics, etc. The committees were supposed to distinguish and elaborate the issues and themes of Appalachian Studies and articulate intentions and strategies for the development and exploration of these issues. The eventual reports of the various committees were rendered on a Saturday afternoon too lovely for remaining indoors. These reports ranged from a somber call for a new text of Appalachian History to be written by the history committee to a delightful piece of impromptu theater (in verse no less) offered up by the literature committee. From these reports and the plenary session the following Sunday morning emerged certain ideas, issues and positions that were to become the durable content of each annual Appalachian Studies Conference. Three content areas can be identified from these 1978 Berea sessions. (1) A dichotomy between what was later designated "the action people and the creative people." At Berea, I believe two groups were designated, "the political types and the academic types," and the issue was which group would dominate the Appalachian Studies Conference. Neither ever did and the polarity has dimmed through the years for want of energy. This issue nevertheless serves some adaptive function for the continuation of the conference and is renewed annually.

(2) A second theme that was evident at Berea in 1978 was the purposeful inclusion of women, workers, and minorities in the design and function of the ASC and in our political and cultural analysis of the region. This theme, related to the first, has also undergone a slight shift in energy levels through the years. It would be hard to imagine any conference or convocation of educations and students in the 1970's that could ignore this crucial issue. The difficulty has been in determining as a conference, the appropriate practices to address the issue.

(3) Appalachian identity and regional autonomy constitute a third thematic current that has run strong in all the years of the conference. This complex of ideas and issues concerns the Idea of Appalachia itself

and the various textures and perspectives that contribute to that idea. The long march of regional definition antedates the conference and will doubtless continue for as long as there are minds to reflect on the meaning of mountains.

Some time near the end of that long day of words that began the Appalachian Studies Conference in 1978, Gurney Norman, native son and constant defender of the divine right of cultural deviancy, delivered a short, rambling address that delighted many, satisfied none and in a subtle way planted another thematic seed within the conference. Gurney's narrative that afternoon at Berea, like his novel, stories, and autobiography was a rich and varied amalgam of ideas, suggesting that regional identity, autonomy, institutions, images and issues are more diverse that homogeneous, more complex than simple and intricately connected to distant regions and institutions. This theme of cultural pluralism, of regional diversity and variation, adumbrated in 1978, achieved overt expression in 1984 at the Seventh Annual Conference held at Unicoi State Park, Helen, Georgia.

Cultural diversity within a region that is presupposed to be a coherent whole is a theme that is difficult to access and delineate. It is one that moves sometimes in resonance with, and sometimes dialectically across the other established themes and issues in Appalachian Studies. The idea cultural diversity and interrelationship of social parts can be a useful intellectual tool. It is an idea designed to account for the complex textures of codes, texts, images, institutions, cultural and political transformations within the region, but one always in danger of evaporating into relativism or tautology. For better or worse, it is a part of the ongoing assessment of who we are and to whom (or what) we, as Appalachian people, are related.

The Seventh Annual Appalachian Studies Conference at Unicoi State Park adopted the idea of diversity as the Conference theme. The conference did, in fact, enjoy more variety in the number and types of organizations and individuals attending as well as in papers and presentations. Budgetary and editorial constraints allow here only a remnant of the conference's diverse doings. It is our hope that these will offer the reader a glimpse of the varied texture of the whole cloth.

Sam Gray<br>January, 1985

NORTHERN GEORGIA EXCEPTIONS: POLITICS
The Reconstruction Careers of Joseph Brown and Benjamin Hill
    Derrell Roberts; Dalton Junior College; Dalton, GA
North Georgia Politics: 1872-1880
    Ellen Garrison; East Tenn. State Univ.; Johnson City, TN
Aspects of 20th Century Politics in North Georgia
    Carl Ross; Appalachian State University; Boone, NC
    Convenor: Sam Dayton; Mtn. Regional Area Planning Comm.; Gainesville, GA

# The Reconstruction Careers of Joseph Brown and Benjamin Hill

by
*Derrell Roberts*

The New South as proclaimed by Benjamin H. Hill, a product of the Antebellum South, recognized the advantages of the economic and political concept of the northern states of the United States. Joseph E. Brown, son of the Georgia mountains and Civil War Governor, recognized the benefits of that system some years before. The differences in their backgrounds possibly explain why Brown accepted Reconstruction and the New South sooner than Hill. Even so, economics provided the central force that merged their ideas in the 1870's. Meanwhile, their personalities and political followers clashed on most issues prior to that time.

Born April 15, 1821 in the Pickens District of South Carolina, Brown's family moved to Union County, Georgia. In the community of Gaddistown, Brown worked on the small farm owned by the family and attended the rural school in the area. At the age of nineteen, he drove a team of oxen, given to him by his father, to the Anderson District in South Carolina. There he traded the oxen for room, board and tuition for a year to attend the Calhoun Academy. Back in Georgia, he opened a "three month school" where he taught and made enough money to return to yet another academy in South Carolina. Meanwhile, he paid off debts incurred in his first year.

He returned to Georgia and settled in Canton in January 1844 and took charge of the town academy. There he taught school in the daytime, and at night and on Saturdays, he read law without the benefit of an instructor. Financially, the year was a profitable one, since he cleared enough to pay his school debts.

During the next year, Brown spent more time reading law, for he had dropped his full-time teaching career and was teaching the children of a

Canton physician for his room and board. The doctor later sent Brown to Yale Law School. But before he went to New Haven, he passed the Georgia Bar examination in 1845. He was graduated from Yale after a year there and in 1846, he returned to Canton where he began a very successful law practice. Then in 1847, he married Elizabeth Gresham, whose father was a South Carolina Baptist minister. Elizabeth was a devoted wife to Brown and a marvelous mother to their eight children (6 sons and 2 daughters).

Benjamin Harvey Hill was born in Hillsboro, Jasper County, Georgia in 1823. His ancestry was traced to Ireland and Wales and his father, John Hill, moved to Hillsboro from North Carolina. Hill's father and family, though moderate in financial means, were influential people in their community of small farmers. Like many farmers of moderate means, the whole family worked on the farm and Hill worked alongside the family slaves his father had acquired. Meanwhile, he was reared with the common, positive concepts of education, religion (the Methodist Church), and temperance.

Like Brown, the Hill's family moved, when he was ten years of age, to Long Cave in Troup County near LaGrange. At age sixteen, he went to Meriwether County to study with a minister who had graduated from Yale College. After a year there, he entered the University of Georgia at age seventeen in 1841 as a sophomore. Graduated from the University in 1844, he read law in Heard County, Georgia for a year and passed the examination for admittance to the Georgia Bar in 1845. In that year he settled into a law practice in LaGrange after he married Caroline E. Holt of Athens. In 1867, the family moved from LaGrange to Athens. Then in 1872, he moved from Athens to Atlanta where he lived until his death. His family included his wife, three daughters and two sons.

In the 1850's, the careers of the two men began to parallel. Brown was elected to the Georgia Senate in 1849. Distinctive issues in those years included the Compromise of 1850, Georgia's state-owned Western and Atlantic Railroad and property rights for women. These issues still faced the General Assembly when Hill was elected to the State House of Representatives in 1851. Interestingly, both men served their terms and did not offer for re-election.

While Hill, always on the border of financial ruin, retired to LaGrange to concentrate on his law practice for a while, Brown chose to run for another office. Elected judge of the Blue Ridge Circuit, Brown presided for a two year term.

During that time, Brown remained a Democrat while Hill moved from the dead Whig Party to the Know-Nothing or American Party. By 1860, he was a supporter of the Constitutional Union Party. In any case, Brown was a consistent supporter of the Democrats (the major party) while Hill played a role as a member of the "opposition group." But there was another notable parallel in that in the national election of 1852, Brown served as an elector to the Electoral College for Franklin Pierce. In 1856, Hill was an elector for former President Millard Fillmore.

In an unusual turn of events, Brown became the Democrats' candidate for Governor of Georgia in 1857. A large number of well-known candidates for the nomination provided a dead-lock which led to the proposal by Linton Stephens that Brown be nominated. Stephens' motion was accepted and Brown was nominated at the state convention.

Meanwhile, Hill was nominated to oppose Brown by the American (Know-Nothing) party. The most significant issues for that election year involved national affairs. The Democrats were forced to endorse the Buchanan administration. At the same time, the state party platform condemned the territorial governor's activities in Kansas. On state questions, Hill and the American party members condemned the operation of the Western and Atlantic Railroad and advocated its sale, while the Democrats pledged to keep it and turn it into a profitable, effective operation.

Even then, Hill was skilled in the art of debate and Brown was inexperienced. On several occasions, Hill clearly defeated Brown so that when leaders of the Democrats (Howell Cobb and Robert Toombs) discovered what was happening, they halted the debate. Toombs took Brown on a campaign tour of south Georgia where he could be taught. Toombs was a capable teacher and in a short period Brown developed a distinctive, "homey" speaking style that served him well in the remainder of his political career.

The course of the campaign and the governor's election in 1857 developed an adversary relationship that continued between the two men for two decades. In that election, Brown defeated Hill by more than ten thousand votes while Hill carried two of the eight congressional districts. While Hill did not run against Brown again, he consistently opposed him and supported opposition candidates. For instance, by 1859, Brown was the undisputed leader of the Democratic party when he stood for re-election to the governship. Meanwhile, the American party was extinct and was replaced in Georgia by a state group known as the "Opposition party." Hill led the party but the candidate to oppose Brown was Warren Aiken of Cassville. Brown was easily re-elected in that campaign. He was also re-elected in campaigns against only nominal opposition in 1861 and 1863 and served as governor until June, 1865.

Hill was elected to the Georgia Senate in 1859 as a strong Unionist. Logically, he would have been more comfortable following or joining Georgians like Howell Cobb and Robert Toombs. After all, he was a product of the "cotton" area of Georgia, owned slaves and was attuned to the Antebellum South. But it would appear that Brown from the mountains would have been more likely to have been a Unionist or nationalist and much less a part of the "Old South."

The secession movement and convention in 1860 brought the two Georgia leaders to the arena in opposition to each other. Brown joined the majority of the Southerners in his support of John C. Breckinridge of Kentucky for the presidency of the United States. Hill and Alexander H. Stephens supported John Bell of Tennessee and the compromise platform of the Constitutional Union party. Hill made interesting attempts to lure votes from Breckinridge and Stephen A. Douglas to Bell, but to no avail. The eventual winner, Abraham Lincoln was not a factor in Georgia. Again, Brown's supporters with Breckinridge beat Hill's candidate by almost ten thousand votes in Georgia.

The next battleground for the two was a Georgia's Secession Convention in Milledgeville in January, 1861. By that time South Carolina, Mississippi, Alabama, and Florida had already seceded, which made Georgia a pivotal state in the formation of the Confederacy. Hill appeared before the Secession Convention and made an eloquent plea against immediate secession and any dangerous or precipitate action. Hill believed that if existing laws regarding slavery were scrupulously enforced, all the problems of the South would be solved.

Brown was not a delegate to the Secession Convention, but he was given a seat on the floor where he quietly went about his work promoting secession. If he had been true to his upbringing in the northern part of Georgia, he would have opposed slavery and secession, but to the contrary, he advocated both. Brown was partially responsible for showing the delegates from the mountainous part of the state the advantages of secession for their section, even though they had no slaves. He pointed out to them that if Georgia did not secede, the slaves would surely be freed, and the national government would reimburse the slaveholders for the loss of their slaves. That would cost the government about two billion dollars and result in higher taxes for everyone, including those who had not owned slaves. Brown said the slaveholder would use that money to buy up the land of small farmers, and the freed slaves would compete with poor whites for land and jobs. Another alternative was that slaves could be relocated which would cost even more tax money. Again, Brown's views won over Hill's ideas and secession was approved in Georgia by a vote of 208 to 89.

H. J. Pearce, Jr.,: "So Hill was again overborne. He had been overborne in 1855 by the Democrats in the Fourth Congressional District, when they elected Hiram Warner; he had been overborne in the presidential canvas of 1856, when Toombs and Stephens won the electoral vote of the state for Buchanan; he had been overborne by Brown and the Democratic onslaught in the gubernatorial contest of 1857; he had been overborne by the Breckinridge party in the presidential campaign of 1860; and now in the Constitution Convention (for secession) of 1861 he had been overborne while leading a minority fight. If any public man of note in Georgia was *not* responsible for secession, it was Hill. —Secession had come."

Once secession took place, Hill's role changed, and Brown, serving as Governor of Georgia adopted a strong "states rights" position. In that posture, Brown opposed all attempts to centralize the Confederacy in any way. He vigorously opposed the conscription of men for the Confederate Army by the Confederate Congress. In his view, the states of the Confederacy should have been asked by the weak central government to provide troops as needed. When the Congress persisted, Brown provided exemptions for large numbers of Georgians who would ordinarily have been conscripted. Predictable, he also objected to taxation by the Confederate government. His position was much like the advocates of the Articles of Confederation in the early development of the United States government. Needless to say, these and other positions led the Georgia Governor into direct conflict with Confederate President Jefferson Davis.

Hill, on the other hand, might have been expected to have opposed the Confederate government, too. He had counseled for union and moderation and had bitterly opposed secession. Yet when the Confederacy was formed, he accepted the election by the Georgia General Assembly and became one of the state's Confederate Senators in Richmond. In that position, he was a strong supporter of President Davis, and thus was in conflict with Brown again. Hill was the Georgia spokesman for the Davis administration, and carried out several "trouble shooting" missions to the state.

At the end of the Civil War, both men were arrested by Federal troops and imprisoned for a brief period. Hill was arrested in LaGrange and spent a short time at Fort LaFayette in New York Harbour. Brown was taken from the Governor's Mansion in Milledgeville to Carroll Prison in Washington, D.C. Upon their release, Hill returned to LaGrange to practice law and Brown settled in Atlanta where he was active in business and political affairs.

Between 1865 and 1867, the two men were relatively inactive on the political scene because of the Reconstruction measures and the occupation of the state by Federal troops. Meanwhile, they both attempted to develop their financial resources, Brown in law and business and Hill in law and agriculture. It developed that Brown was much better adapted and inclined toward the business world than Hill was to agricultural pursuits.

After his brief imprisonment, Brown returned to Georgia, moved to Atlanta and began to counsel acquiescence to the policies of President Andrew Johnson. Hill also accepted Johnson's plan of Reconstruction and pledged his support in his request for a parole from the President in July, 1865. Therefore, both men were relatively quiet during the first year and a half of Reconstruction.

In February, 1867, Brown made a trip to Washington, D.C. with some Atlanta business and political associates. During those days, the Congressional Reconstruction plan was under consideration. Also, impeachment proceedings against President Johnson were just beginning. On his return to Atlanta from Washington, he found a letter from businessmen asking him for an opinion on the situation in the nation. Brown counseled acquiescence to the unpopular measures of Reconstruction and his public career took an unusual turn.

The national and regional situation looked gloomy to him. Clouds covered the political scene and the Republicans were in a strong position in national affairs. The right to vote by freedmen had already been settled, he said. The only question now was whether or not former Confederate officials could vote. Therefore, suffrage for the freed slaves was a moot issue. Further, the Civil War had settled the secession question. Therefore, people from the North ought to be invited to bring their money to the South and help developments there. He said that the Fourteenth Amendment to the Constitution should be ratified immediately. Continued resistance might further endanger the enfranchisement of a greater number of Southerners and might eventually lead to confiscation of property. For all those reasons and more, Brown said that all Reconstruction measures should be accepted "without further hesitation or delay."

No public figure was more publicly villified than Brown after his public letter. But it was Benjamin H. Hill who helped to focus the hatred of the public on Brown. With his scathing tongue and marvelous speaking style and with his pen, he called attention to the poor arguments and loopholes in Brown's public utterances nad notices.

Between June and August, 1867, Hill wrote a series of articles for the *Augusta Chronicle and Sentinel* that he called "Notes on the Situation". Henry W. Grady called the "Notes" the "profoundest and most eloquent political essays ever penned by an American." In the first article, Brown was portrayed as one who had "urged us into secession as the only peaceful method of securing our rights; who afterwards led us to subjugation as the only method of escaping military despotism: and was then advising the acceptance "of proposed terms for a new Union."

In another "Note," Hill described Brown as an ambitious politician who supported Reconstruction measures only because of the strength of the Republicans. The sufferings of Southern people did not matter to Brown, he charged. The former Governor was looking for political power even at the risk of becoming a traitor to his state. His most scathing criticism of Brown came in a description of how he had met the train of the incoming Union General John B. Pope who commanded the army of occupation. That night at a banquet in honor of the General, the former Governor responded to a toast to the honoree. Hill thought that any ordinary citizen would have been nauseated and he thought that Pope was too.

Hill's "Notes" were very effective and were reprinted all over the state. They were widely discussed and quoted, and the general populance agreed with Hill. But Brown replied to Hill in a series in the Augusta paper he called "Review of Notes on the Situation". While the Augusta editor hesitated to publish them for Brown, he wrote a short preamble to the first one in which he explained that the *Chronicle* whole-heartedly supported the views expressed by Hill. Nevertheless, he was willing to open his column to Brown to give him a chance to redeem himself. The tone of the preamble indicated that he did not think Brown could redeem himself, though.

Brown began his rebuttal by calling attention to Hill's inconsistencies. He said that Hill started as a Democrat, then Whig, Know-Nothing, Opposition, etc., and then became a Unionist. As a Unionist, Hill urged disunion if Lincoln was elected. When Lincoln was elected, he opposed secession at Georgia's convention. Then he was elected to the Confederate Senate where he voted against conscription and then castigated Brown when he objected to the Confederate draft. On an occasion, he charged, Hill made an impassioned speech for the militia and enrolled in it. When the militia was activated, he claimed an exemption because he was a Senator.

Congressional Reconstruction, he said, was not important. Congress had the power to do whatever it wanted to do in the matter. Georgia should accept the fact and restore its members to Congress in less than two years. Brown also lambasted Hill's objections to the new Georgia constitution. Even so, Brown played a significant role in the new document.

Brown followed his "Review of Notes on the Situation" by continued political activity. In 1868, he identified himself with the Republican party, attended the national convention and spoke to the gathering. He went on to help elect Rufus Bullock the Republican Governor of Georgia. After Brown's unsuccessful campaign for United States Senator, Bullock appointed him Chief Justice of the Georgia Supreme Court. Otherwise, he made more public statements on Reconstruction and made a great deal of money in real estate, banking, Georgia mines, railroad investments and other enterprises.

Hill gained a reputation in Antebellum Georgia as a magnificent speaker and that talent soared to new heights in the Reconstruction period. With his great speaking ability, he scoured Brown even before the publication of "Notes on the Situation." In July, 1867, he delivered a stirring speech against Congressional Reconstruction, Negro suffrage and Brown at Davis Hall in Atlanta. General Pope attended the speech and thought it a good reason why the South should have been considered conquered land instead of reconstructable states.

Meanwhile, Georgia was reconstructed by a desegregated General Assembly, a Republican governor was elected and inaugurated and Hill and the majority of Georgia's white citizens were mortified. At a rally to support the national slate for the Democratic party in July, 1868, Hill delivered his "Bush Arbor" address. The rally took place in downtown Atlanta under the arbor to protect participants from the heat. He attacked the Republican Governor, the General Assembly and others who might have aided Bullock's election. Henry Grady remembered his boyhood sensation as he listened to the speech; watched Robert Toombs throw his hat in the air as a reaction; and Grady picked up Toombs' hat and returned it to him.

Suddenly late in 1870, Hill announced that he had changed his mind about the Reconstruction policy. Since it was inevitable, Southerners should go ahead and bow to it and get it over with and move on to other issues. By finishing the process Georgia could "regain control of her own affairs." Needless to say, Georgians were stunned at the announcement. If Brown had been a traitor in reaching those conclusions, then how much more was Hill? Brown thought that the statements Hill made did "not look like the productions of the same mind." There is another interesting irony in this period, too, involving the two men; Brown was a leader in the Republican party and Hill was a spokesman for the Democrats.

Another interesting announcement was made about the same time that Hill changed his political mind. It was reported that Chief Justice Brown had resigned from the Georgia Supreme Court to become the President of the Western and Atlantic Railroad Leasing Company. Further, one of the several stockholders in the venture was Hill. Brown successfully pursued the lease by underground politics and interesting alliances involving Hill and others.

The railroad prospered significantly under Brown's leadership and the stockholders were well rewarded. For the next ten years, Brown attended to economic affairs for most of the time. Even so, there were unusual political turns for him. In 1872, he led the Liberal Republican group in Georgia as they supported Horace Greely for President of the United States as opposed to President U. S. Grant. Then in 1876, he represented the Democratic party in Florida in attempts to turn the disputed votes there to Samuel Tilden. While he was unsuccessful in Tilden's behalf, he did manage to move smoothly back into the Democratic party.

Hill bought several thousand acres of farm land in South Georgia and made an attempt at farming. He did not make nearly the money that Brown made in his ventures even though he was paid legal fees for one case in the range of $50,000 to $65,000. His speaking ability remained his most distinguished attribute. Even after his infamous change of mind in 1870, he made his most memorable speech in 1871 to the University of Georgia Alumni. Known as Hill's "New South" speech, he held the audience spellbound while he dismissed the "Old South" and cried out for a "New South." Hill's version of a "New South" would make better use of modern agricultural methods and use natural resources more efficiently as he promoted education at all levels. His address pre-dated Henry Grady's "New South" speech by several years.

But Hill was not forced to remain in the political "dog house" as long as Brown. In 1875, he was elected as a Democrat to the United States House of Representatives to fill an unexpired term of a deceased incumbent. He was re-elected and served in the House until 1877. In the House, his most famous speech involved a debate with Rep. James G. Blaine in 1876. Blaine attempted to wave the political "bloody shirt" in the Congress. Hill, effectively defended Confederate President Jefferson Davis and the Andersonville tragedy. He accused Blaine of raising the issue to win the Republican nomination for President of the United States in 1876.

In 1877, Hill was elected to the United States Senate where he was joined by Brown in 1880. In a political arrangement between Governor Alfred H. Colquitt, General John B. Gordon with Brown, Gordon resigned the Senate seat, Colquitt appointed Brown to the Senate and Brown supported Colquitt for re-election as governor. Subsequently, Brown was elected to the seat by the General Assembly and re-elected in 1884 to a full term that lasted to 1891. In the Senate he advocated internal improvements within the states, statehood for Utah and silver money among other rather liberal issues, though he was a staunch conservative, otherwise. During those years, too, he became an educational philanthropist and an active leader in the Southern Baptist Convention.

In 1882, Hill died of throat cancer and Brown participated in a memorial service for him in Atlanta. Twelve years later, Brown died of respiratory problems. They are both buried in Oakland Cemetery in Atlanta. Hill made a great deal of money but spent it unwisely and indulged his family. He left his wife the house in Atlanta and ten thousand dollars. Brown left a fortune of one and one half million dollars at the least, but more probably several millions of dollars.

As one attempts to compare the lives of the two men, various stereotypes of Brown's mountain and Hill's "Old South" cultures may be applied. When one does that, it is amazing in how many ways their expected roles are reversed until the early Reconstruction period. In that era, economics became the great concern and in the end, the two old enemies joined together in business ventures and in politics.

Had Brown followed the stereotype of the nineteenth century mountain man, he would have clung to illiteracy as a way of life. There would have been a tendency toward clanishness and a reticence to leave the area of his birth. Religion would have been spasmodic and primitive in practice. Brown was the opposite of those and most of the other general characteristics of nineteenth century Appalachian Mountain folk.

With sixty-five slaves in 1860, Hill might have been more the "fire-eater" in preserving the culture in which he lived. He might have been much more "States right" oriented than he was before the War in Confederate affairs. Had he been more the "Old South" activist, he would have joined with Robert Toombs and countless others in "never giving up."

Historians ought to be pleased that the two men did not fit the mold that their communities cast for them. If it had been otherwise, Brown might have been a mountain school-teacher and sometime lawyer at best. There would have been no political career that spanned all branches of state government and into the United States Senate. Further, there might not be a Georgia State-owned railroad today, much less the great personal fortune he developed. For Hill, he might have died an embittered "Old South" lawyer and "hack" politician. There might not have been his greatest speech on the "New South." Without the Hill-Blaine Debate, the "Bloody Shirt" politics might have been much worse.

In closing, let us all be thankful for leaders who are willing to step out of the stereotype and the molds into which they are placed. The willingness to do that is one of the several attributes of leadership.

APPALACHIAN HANDICRAFT: COMMERCIALISM AND AUTHENTICITY
Toward a Definition of Folk Art
 Mildred Dunevant; Appalachian State University; Boone, NC
The Penland Family of Potters
 Terence Painter; Maggie Valley, NC
Nineteenth Century Quilts in Macon Co., North Carolina
 Laurel Horton; McKissick Museums; Univ. of South Carolina; Columbia, SC
Jewel Waters, North Georgia Woodcarver
 Bob Hughes, Pat Meisel; Georgia Southern College; Statesboro, GA
 Convenor: Bob Conway; N. C. Div. of Archives & History; Asheville, NC

# Nineteenth Century Quilts in Macon County, North Carolina

by
*Laurel Horton*

One of the major tasks of present-day quilt historians is the examination of generally accepted assumptions about American quiltmaking traditions. In the Southern Appalachian mountains, that study is complicated and obscured by widely believed and exaggerated romantic notions of mountain life generally. As with most stereotypes these may be based on some truths, but the problem is that they obscure other truths which reflect the real variety of experience within mountain culture.

The stereotyped picture, in its extreme form, goes something like this: That the Southern mountains were settled by refugees and misfits from Tidewater culture; that these unfortunate folks took advantage of the mountainous terrain to escape from authority in its various forms, so that they could make their moonshine, shoot their neighbors, and marry their cousins; that they avoided with suspicion any contact with the outside world, and consequently, had to grow or manufacture everything they needed to live, including all food, clothing and shelter; that as a result they were completely ignorant of events and products of the civilized world; that because of their isolation and remoteness, they preserved their backward self-sufficiency *unchanged* well into the twentieth century, and to hear some people, if you go back into the hollers far enough, you can still find people untouched by the outside world, sitting in their log cabins, speaking pure Elizabethan English, singing ballads, and making baskets and quilts. We can laugh at this exaggeration, just as we laughed at the distorted view of mountain culture when we used to watch "The Beverly

Hillbillies." Still, we have never examined the assumptions behind the comedy. We assumed that there was some truth there without question.

Two groups are partly responsible for purveying these distortions. The first group are the travellers, local color writers, and tourists who have flocked to the mountains in great numbers since the railroads arrived in the late 1800's. They saw what they had planned to see, spectacular natural beauty and people living as they imagined their pioneer forebears had lived. Because they were mostly urban dwellers, their first close look at rural America convinced them that they were travelling backward in time, visiting their "contemporary ancestors," and "yesterday's people."

The second group were Northern social workers who sought to improve the life of the mountaineers. Some did this by recruiting laborers for the growing number of cotton mills in and around the mountains. Others, who wanted to preserve the picturesque aspects of the area, taught mountaineers to weave coverlets, to make baskets and quilts, and to carve little wooden animals, all to sell to tourists. This is an oversimplified explanation of why we associate crafts with the Southern mountains.

Several years ago at the North Carolina Quilt Symposium, a midwestern quilter told me she would be driving back home through the mountains and could I please tell her where she could stop off to see mountain ladies quilting. She had just spent three days with hundreds of quilters from all over the country, but she assumed that mountain quilters would be different, somehow pure and unaffected, and that they would be on display, perhaps under glass.

These stereotypes prevent us from seeing the wide diversity that has always been a part of Appalachian life. The new field of Appalachian Studies has encouraged dozens of scholars to produce volumes examining the myths and realities of Southern mountain history and culture. For my part in this work I have chosen to study quilts made in one North Carolina mountain county prior to the crafts revival of the twentieth century, with particular emphasis on the changing range of fabrics available to quiltmakers. Fabric selection is possibly the single most important element influencing the way quilts look.

To take a fresh look at mountain quilts, we'll start with geography. The Appalachian range *is* mountains, including foothills, plateaus, and six thousand foot peaks. Where there are mountians there are also valleys carved out by creeks and rivers. Some valleys are narrow, carrying fast-moving currents, some are wide and fertile. Between the mountains are gaps, formed by wind and water, through which animals and, later, humans, made trails.

The Southern Appalachians are recognized by biologists and ecologists for the abundance and diversity of plant and animal life. The Cherokee Indians recognized the area as a good place to live when they came from the North and drove out the earlier inhabitants. The Cherokee established small villages and a system of agriculture that supported their basic needs. A system of trails linked these villages to each other and to other tribes along the Atlantic coast, several hundred miles away, with whom the Cherokee traded for shells and for leaves of the Yaupon holly (Ilex vomitoria) which they used to prepare their Black Drink for ceremonial occasions.

These trails also brought the first white explorers beginning with DeSoto in the 1600's, and followed by geographers, artists, botanists, and speculators, and especially trappers and traders. Early white traders introduced the Cherokee to aspects of their civilization. Some, such as small pox, had devastating effects. Others were considerably more welcome. Imagine being an Indian woman responsible for taking stiff raw deerhides and other furs and skins and making clothing for a family. Imagine a moment of realization upon seeing for the first time brightly colored cloth carried or worn by a white trader, then to discover that the price of this wonderful, labor-saving stuff is to be paid with those very pelts and hides they would replace. This represents a very major cultural innovation.

Lest we tend to view such exchanges as accidental, haphazard, or infrequent, we must note that by 1707, the trade between the Cherokee and other tribes and white entrepreneurs operating out of Charleston, South Carolina, had reached such proportions and had become so lucrative that the colonial government of that state formed a Board of Commissioners to regulate the trade and license the traders. In 1716, this Board formed an official commercial treaty with the Cherokee Nation. John Henry Logan, in his *History of the Upper Country of South Carolina*, recreates a trading scene from this period:

> The smoke from a hundred campfires curls above the thick tops of the trees and the woods resound with the neighing of horses, and the barking of hungry Indian dogs. A large supply of goods has arrived from Charleston, and every pack-saddle came down from the Nation loaded with skins and furs, and these being now displayed to the best advantage, the work of barter begins.
>
> In the open air and in the trading-house are congregated a motley assembly of pack-horsemen, traders, hunters, squaws, children, soldiers, and stately Indian warriors—some silent and grave, seemingly uninterested in the scene; but the greater number loudly huxtering, and obstinately contending over their respective commodities in trade, in many barbarous tongues.
>
> The hunters from distant wilds want a supply of powder and ball, each squaw fancies some bright-colored fabric for a new petticoat or dress, while the warriors and old men eagerly demand guns, ammunition and blankets.

The clamor begins, however, presently to subside, and at length the last bargain has been struck, and the goods and peltries have alike changed hands. The packs are once more made up; the goods for the Indian towns, and the skins for the market on the seaboard, and everything is again ready for the trail . . . The trains enter the narrow paths, and are soon far on their way, leaving the garrisons and agents of the posts to the dull monotony of the wilderness till their next visit. (1)

Not all of the treaties made between the colonial and state governments and the Cherokee Nation were commercial. In a series of treaties the Cherokee ceded large portions of their land, in the vain hope that white settlers would be satisfied and would leave them the rest. Usually the land they gave up was already occupied by illegal white settlers. In 1817-19, the Cherokee ceded to the State of North Carolina the section which includes present-day Macon County. About this time Jacob Siler and William Brittain came into the area, bought an Indian cabin, and set up a store, to carry on trade with the Indians and to supply the needs of earlier settlers and the growing swell of newcomers, now that settlement was legal. Siler and Brittain hauled their wares by wagon and horseback over the mountain trails, from lowland trading centers to the south and east. Their wares would have included many of the same items earlier traded to the Indians, including iron cooking pots, guns and ammunition, blankets, and fabrics.

The first settlers in Macon County claimed large tracts of fertile flat land along the Little Tennessee River and larger creeks. They selected the site of the old Cherokee town of Nikwasi for their own county seat of Franklin. Later arrivals took up the remaining available land on smaller creeks and in the steeper coves. Within a few years the larger landowners had established flourishing farms. They produced a wide variety of agricultural products and hauled their surplus grain, fruit, and livestock to market towns in the low country where they traded for a wider selection of goods than was available at local stores. Roads were poor in the mountains during the nineteenth century, just as they were nearly everywhere in rural America at that time. Passage over the mountains was slow so travellers expected their market trips to take many days.

These well-to-do landowners formed a middle-class within the stratification of mountain society. Ronald Eller, in his book *Miners, Millhands, and Mountaineers: The Modernization of the Appalachian South, 1880-1930*, describes this group in this way:

> Usually the first to arrive on the land, such families had acquired large land holdings and by 1830 had emerged as a resident ruling class. More noticeable in the larger valleys and county seat towns, these wealthier families provided the political

leadership in the mountains and often controlled local commercial enterprises. Their descendants, having access to resources and educational opportunities in the flatlands, became merchants, teachers, and lawyers. (2)

To illustrate this point, here is a portion of a letter written by Laura Siler, a Macon County girl, to her favorite cousin, in which she entertains him with an ironic description of her boarding school experience in Asheville, which is 70 miles from Franklin and would have represented a journey of at least two days over two major mountain ranges:

September 29, 1847
Dear Cousin Leon,
    Well as you are aware I am settled in for the present in the notable city of Asheville. A place *unsurpassed* in the known world for the *intelligence, refinement, correct taste, generosity* and *hospitality* of its inhabitants, qualities that could not but endear them to so warm hearted a creature as I, especially when with that extra warmth of heart is united a *mind* and *taste so fully capable of appreciating* the many excellencies enumerated. Hah! (3)

The middle-class in Macon County formed a minority within the population, but its influence was felt by all. Even the residents of small farms higher in the coves would have been aware of this group as fashion setters in architectural styles, clothing, and politics.

A middle-class household inventory in the mid-nineteenth century would have included looms and spinning wheels to produce home furnishings and everyday clothing for the family and any servants or slaves. Macon County farmers raised sheep, consequently wool was available for clothing and blankets at little cost.

As we are now beginning to realize, quilts were not as commonplace in early America as was once thought. Until the widespread availability of inexpensive manufactured fabric in the second half of the nineteenth century, there simply wasn't an abundance of desirable fabric scraps. Most quilts which remain from that period are well-planned with the same fabrics throughout. We used to assume that there must have been large numbers of utilitarian scrap quilts that supplied the bedding needs of most of the population and that these quilts were worn out long ago, leaving no trace. But upon close examination it appears that in Macon County, as elsewhere during the early nineteenth century, blankets were cheap and available and quilts were special creations. A woman planning to spend the time and effort to make a quilt was likely also to have gone to the expense to purchase fabric especially for that quilt.

The Siler family in Macon County, like most of their neighbors, had little access to cash money. They bartered and they maintained charge accounts with local storekeepers which were settled once or twice a year. A record of the Siler family account with T. C. Bryson's store for 1849 survives in the Siler Family papers in the Southern Historical Collection. This account shows us what was purchased during that year and the prices paid. Among other items are included the following:

| | |
|---|---|
| 10 yds linen | 40 p yd |
| 1 doz buttons | 10 p dz |
| 1½ yd swiss muslin | 60 p yd |
| 2 pr ladies hoes [sic] | 40 p pr |
| 1 pr bl kid gloves | 1-00 |
| 1 card hooks & eyes | 10 |
| 10 yds calico | 15 p yd |
| 6 yds domestic | 15 p yd |
| 1 peice [sic] wadding | 5 |
| 1 tooth brush | 15 |
| 1 cake almond soap | 10    (4) |

We know that the Silers were a well-to-do family. Laura Siler married a doctor who later was elected to the State legislature. Not everyone in the mountains could afford to buy almond soap and black kid gloves, but these existed side by side with home-made lye soap and hand-knitted mittens. The availability of goods and the steady commerce in and out of the area affected everyone. Every family had to come into town from time to time and country people were aware of what merchandise was available even if they couldn't often afford it.

Some people have characterized the pre-Civil War and pre-industrial period in the mountains as a kind of golden age of comparative prosperity and well-being. The Civil War, the slow economic conditions and uncertain political situations afterward, followed by the exploitation of timber and minerals by outside interests and the advent of tourism in the late nineteenth century drastically altered the mountain region and its people. Traditional family life, agricultural patterns and the economic base were irrevocably changed. The problems which emerged during this period were not the result of the region being isolated from the outside world, but of the impact of modernization imposed by these outside interests. While there were places within the mountains that were at times comparatively inaccessible, there was never a period when mountain people were "cut off from the outside world." The trails and roads that brought people into the area didn't somehow close up behind them.

Having dealt with the myths of isolation and self-sufficiency, we now have a proper framework through which to view the quilts. I am indebted to Laura Nelle Estes of Franklin for locating these quilts and arranging interviews with their owners.

*Rose of Sharon*—made by Aunt Matt Anderson
Circa 1860—83" x 85"

A *Rose of Sharon* quilt was made, according to family tradition, by Aunt Matt Anderson, who worked as a live-in seamstress hired in the fall and winter to sew family clothing for Dr. and Mrs. A. C. Brabson and their eleven children. The Brabsons lived in the Riverside community south of Franklin in a large frame house which still stands. The fine work and precision reinforce the implication that this quilt was made by a professional seamstress. The seeming incongruity between the red and green fabrics in the blocks and the blue and tan tones in the border is attributable to fading of the cretonne prints of the latter. The batting in this quilt is wool, which is unusual for Southern quilts generally, but which may have been more available than cotton in the mountains. (5)

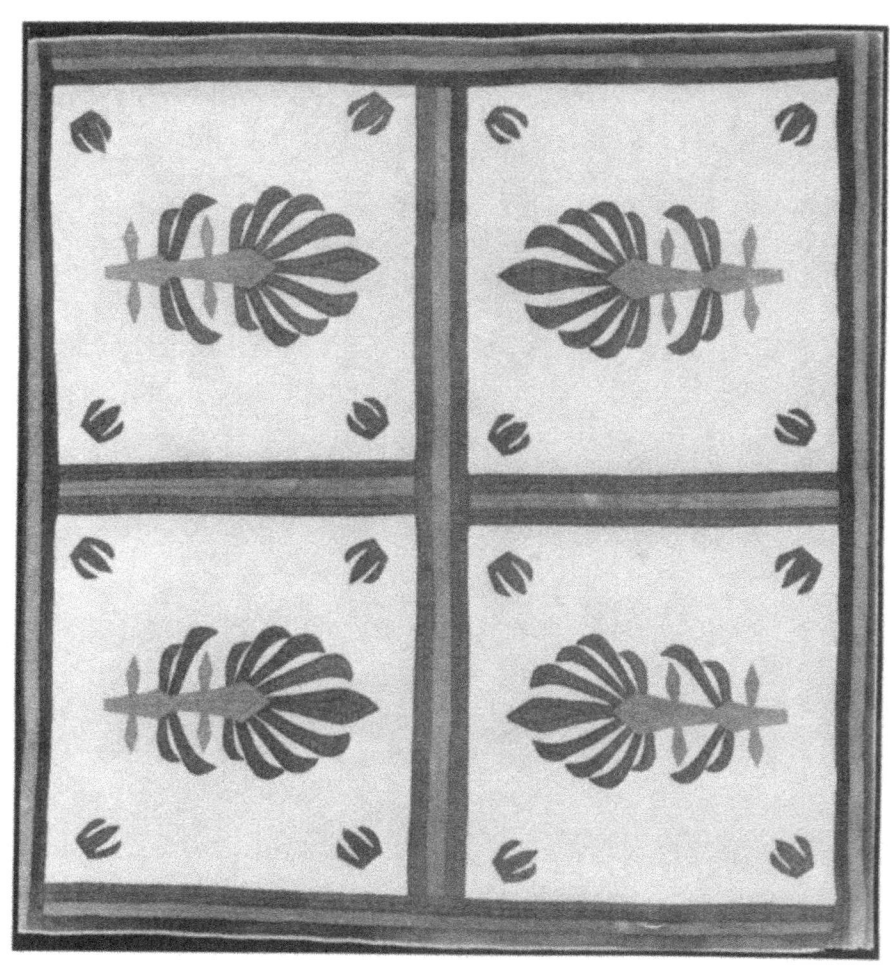

*Cotton Boll—made by Elizabeth Sanders Morrison
Circa 1864—63½" x 80"*

A *Cotton Boll* quilt was reportedly made by Elizabeth Sanders, who was born in 1833, married William Morrison, and died in 1864. The present owner is the quiltmaker's great-granddaughter and still has the Bible that Elizabeth Sanders received for her eleventh birthday. The applique design is similar to a quilt owned by the North Caorlina Museum of History. The four-corner arrangement is fairly uncommon, more often associated with very large applique motifs. The applique has been sewn on a machine, so it appears that there were sewing machines in the mountains at an early date. (6)

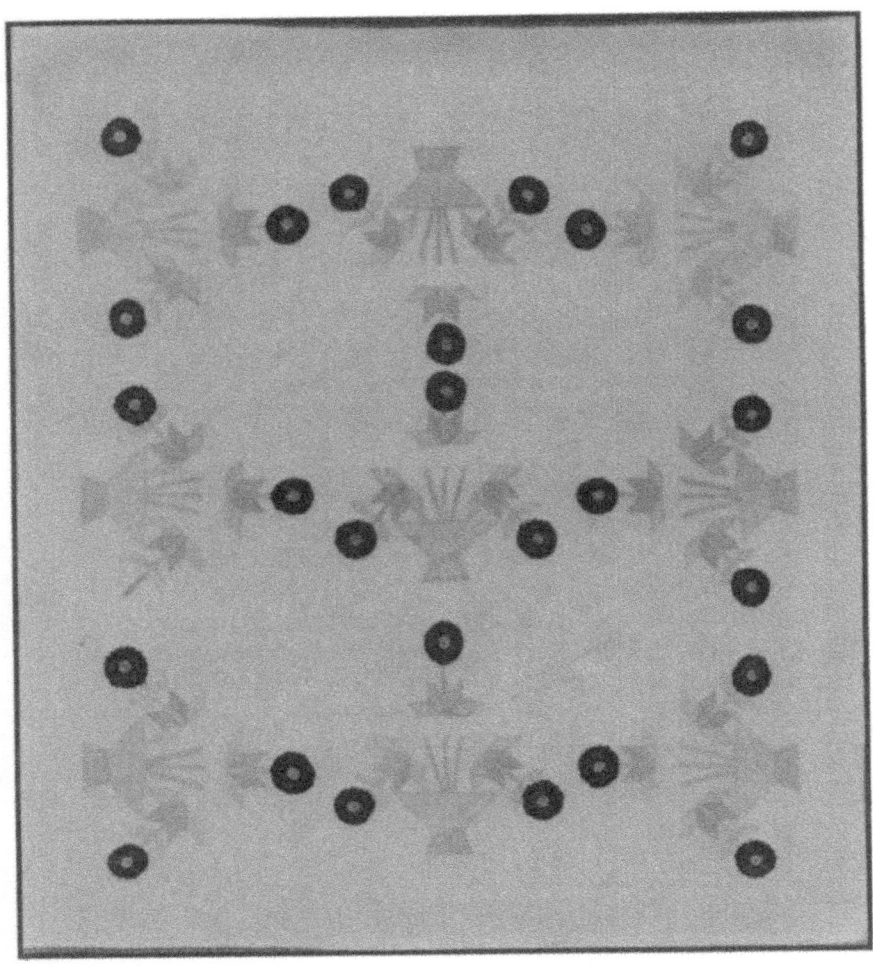

*North Carolina Lily Variation—made by Margaret Gillespie Slagle
Circa 1880—66½" x 75"*

An unusual quilt (7) was reportedly made by Margaret Gillespie as a young girl before her marriage to Henry Slagle in 1888. She was the granddaughter of Jesse Siler, an early Macon County resident, and the mother of the present owner. This quilt is a variation of the *North Carolina Lily*. The stems were apparently green originally but have now faded to tan. The most striking feature is the red gathered and appliqued "dahlia" flowers. One is missing, leading to speculation that someone at some point took it apart to see how it was made.

*Star Quilt—reportedly made by Mary Morrison Bryson*
*Circa 1880—62" x 76½"*

A *Star* quilt was reportedly made by Mary Morrison Bryson, who was born on May 10, 1841, and died on May 10, 1918. She married Samuel Byers Bryson, who died in 1895. They had ten children, one of whom, Robert T., was the father of the present owner. The maker of this quilt was related to the husband of the woman who made the *Cotton Boll* quilt. Four corner pieced arrangements are even less common than in applique. Perhaps Mary got the idea from her in-law. The quilt contains an unusual combination of printed fabrics in red, white, pink, and blue prints, but as the fabrics are consistent throughout, this appears to have been intentional. (8)

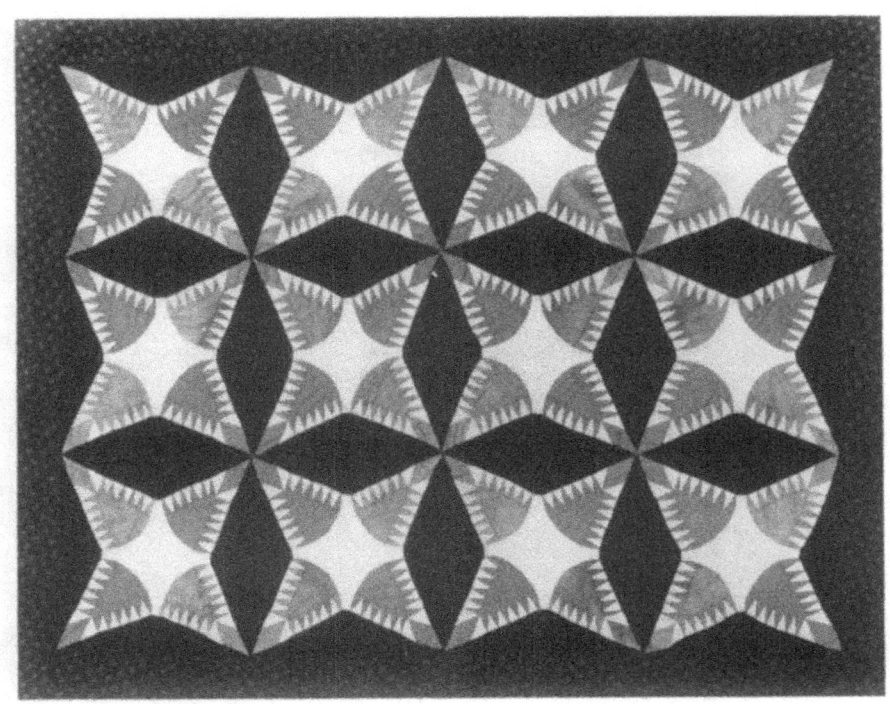

*Pine Burr—made by Harriet Love Anderson Stallcup
Circa 1880—69½" x 75½"*

A *Pine Burr* quilt was reportedly made by Harriet Love Anderson Stallcup, who lived in Tennessee, was widowed there, and moved to Macon County with her second husband just after the Civil War. Harriet Stallcup was the great-grandmother of the present owner's husband. The fabrics in this quilt are typical of the late nineteenth century, although the blue, pink, and green combination is uncommon. By alternating two colors in the same block the maker has created an even more complex design than usual.

In conclusion, these quilts made by early Macon County residents and handed down within their families do not fit the stereotype of isolation and self-sufficiency usually associated with mountain culture and mountain crafts. Doubtless there were quilts made from remnants of homespun, home-woven fabrics, and scrap quilts from more homely fabrics, but it seems there were also, at the same time, women who selected and purchased fabric in order to make formal, planned quilts. It is possible that these special quilts were the rule rather than the exception. These quilts are in many ways similar to nineteenth century quilts made elsewhere in the country. Since these are truly "mountain quilts" we must now expand our definition of that term to include them.

## Notes and References

(1) Logan, John H., *A History of the Upper Country of South Carolina*, S. G. Courtenay & Co., Charleston, and P. B. Glass, Columbia, 1859, (The Reprint Co., Spartanburg, 1960), pp. 251-252.

(2) Eller, Ronald D., *Miners, Millhands, and Mountaineers: The Modernization of the Appalachian South, 1880-1930*, The University of Tennessee Press, Knoxville, 1982, p. 11.

(3) Ms. letter, Laura Siler, September 29, 1847, in the Lyle and Siler Family Papers (#1818), Southern Historical Collection, Library of the University of North Carolina at Chapel Hill.

(4) Ms. store account record, dated August 11, 1849, in the Lyle and Siler Family Papers (#1818), Southern Historical Collection, Library of the University of North Carolina at Chapel Hill.

(5) Applique quilt, *Rose of Sharon*, made by Aunt Matt Anderson, Macon County, N. C., c. 1860. In collection of Betty Ann Bryant.

(6) Applique quilt, *Cotton Boll*, made by Elizabeth Sanders Morrison, Macon County, N. C., c. 1864. In collection of Sue Waldroop.

(7) Pieced and applique quilt, *North Carolina Lily* variation, made by Margaret Gillespie Slagle, Macon County, N. C., c. 1880. In collection of Harriet Slagle Setser.

(8) Pieced quilt, *Star*, made by Mary Morrison Bryson, Macon County, N. C., c. 1880.

(9) Pieced quilt, *Pine Burr*, made by Harriet Love Anderson Stallcup, Macon County, N. C., c. 1880.

## Bibliography

Clark, Thomas D. *Pills, Petticoats and Plows: The Southern Country Store*. The University of Oklahoma Press, Norman, 1944.

Eaton, Allen H. *Handicrafts of the Southern Highlands*. Russell Sage Foundation, New York, 1937. (Dover, New York, 1973).

Eller, Ronald D. *Miners, Millhands, and Mountaineers: The Modernization of the Appalachian South, 1880-1930*. The University of Tennessee Press, Knoxville, 1982.

Logan, John H. *A History of the Upper Country of South Carolina, from the Earliest Period to the Close of the War of Independence*. S. G. Courtenay & Co., Charleston, and P. B. Glass, Columbia, 1859. (The Reprint Co., Spartanburg, 1960).

Lyle and Siler Family Papers (#1818) in the Southern Historical Collection, Library of the University of North Carolina at Chapel Hill.

Shapiro, Henry D. *Appalachia On Our Mind: The Southern Mountains and Mountaineers in the American Consciousness*. The University of North Carolina Press, Chapel Hill, 1978.

"Macon County" vertical file folder, Macon County Public Library, Franklin, N. C.

INTERPRETING THE MOUNTAIN WOMAN'S EXPERIENCE
Emma Bell Miles: Pioneer Folklorist of Appalachia
   Grace Toney Edwards; Radford University; Radford, VA
The Science Poetry of Marilou Awiakta
   Parks Lanier; Radford University; Radford, VA
Alma
   Kathryn Stripling Byer; Cullowhee, NC
*Going Home*
Ron Willoughby; Radford University, Radford, VA
Convenor: Nancy Joyner: Western Carolina University; Cullowhee, NC

# Emma Bell Miles
# Pioneer Folklorist of Appalachia
by
*Grace Toney Edwards*

Allow me to introduce you to, or perhaps renew your acquaintance with, a *woman* whose impact on Appalachia has been significant. Hers is not the impact of a thundering explosion or even a great shudder, but rather that of a gentle rain that comes and goes, leaving behind it a soil refreshed and renewed. I speak of Emma Bell Miles, of Walden's Ridge, Tennessee. Her span on earth was relatively short, from 1879-1919, and her public career as a writer was even shorter — a scant fifteen years, from 1904-1919. Yet in that brief moment she produced two published books of prose, two books of poetry, at least fourteen short stories, more than a hundred newspaper columns, a dozen magazine articles, five volumes of personal journals, and scores of letters. Alongside the written products I must point to her art work: drawing, painting, illustrating, wall murals, and even some interior decorating. And these feats she accomplished while bearing and raising five children, keeping house for her husband, Frank Miles, growing a garden to help feed the brood, scouting the woods for blackberries and wild grapes, etc., etc. Her familial and domestic chores were not unusual for a mountain woman around the turn of the century, but her creative writing and her artwork certainly were.

    Miles is one of many women writers who chose the mountains and mountaineers as their subjects about this time. But she had a unique view not matched by others of her genre or time: she was a local *mountain* woman writing about *her* people. Although not mountain born, she was primarily mountain bred. True, she came out of a different culture from that of the mountains; her family heritage and education were different from those of most mountaineers. She was an only child; her parents were school teachers; and she was widely read and well educated by them. But these facts of difference gave her the bases from which she would later develop her dual perspective on mountain culture: that of *outsider* and *insider*.

She was an insider by virtue of having lived on Walden's Ridge from the time she was ten years old and by virtue of having married a mountain man from one of the pioneer families and by virtue of having borne and raised a mountain family in a manner fairly typical of a Walden's Ridge lifestyle. She had five children over the course of seven years, starting with twin daughters in 1902. She lived in a series of small houses ranging from a tent to a tarpaper shack to a mountain cabin. She lived in poverty, for there was no way to make a living except through farming and occasional day labor; and Frank was not a steady adherent to either of those activities. Emma carried the burden of supporting the family through her writing and painting.

I am making a case for her as an insider, but of course, the writing, sketching, and drawing were not typical among the women in a culture where illiteracy was the norm and utilitarianism the dominant force. In fact, Emma's exercising of these talents raised real suspicion among her husband's relatives and other mountain neighbors. As Grandma Miles, Emma's mother-in-law, was to say: "These here writers and typewriters will do to watch!"[1] In a culture operating largely through oral communication and by traditional standards, such suspicion is understandable. Indeed, it was such conflicts as the role of artist as perceived by mainstream culture and the role of wife and mother as perceived by the mountain folk culture that forever complicated Emma Bell Miles' life and in turn added much depth of insight and feeling to her writings. And it was the richness of the oral tradition that she so often turned to as subject matter for her works.

Miles wrote a variety of types of things, as mentioned earlier, including both poetry and prose. Many of these works were filled with folklore of her own collecting, which she placed in context and analyzed according to quite modern trends touted by professionals today. She was nationally published in the popular magazines of her day and in her two books; the magazines carried her poems first, then an article on mountain music, and eventually her short stories. She was recognized in *Who's Who in America* and other leading biographies for several years. And yet she and her works virtually disappeared from the public mind for about fifty years or more after her death. Then in 1975 the University of Tennessee Press brought Miles' name back into the view of Appalachian scholars and followers by reprinting her 1905 book about life in the southern mountains. Although *The Spirit of the Mountains* revived her name, there are still many revelations waiting to be made about her total output of literary and artistic works.

I make a claim for her today as one of the earliest pioneer folklorists of the Appalachian region. By 1900 she had begun to note the speech, the stories, the songs, the customs of her Walden's Ridge, Tennessee, neighbors. Though she was not trained as a folklorist and would never have called herself that, she believed that somewhere there was an audience who would like to read about "her people" in southeastern Tennessee. In 1904 she found that audience through a national publication, *Harper's Magazine. Harper's* accepted her article entitled "Some Real American Music" and ran it in the June issue. The article began with these words: "It is generally believed that America has no folk-music, nothing distinctively native out of which a national school of advanced composition may arise." Two paragraphs later she contended: "But there is hidden among the mountains of Kentucky, Tennessee, and the Carolinas a people of whose inner nature and its musical expression almost nothing has been said. The music of the Southern mountaineer is not only peculiar, but, like himself, peculiarly American."[2] In the article Miles combined text, context, and analysis. She gave the words, and in several cases, music, for sixteen songs; she recounted the circumstances under which such songs might be sung and expressed the reactions of both performer and audience to the performance; she traced the lineage of several of the pieces back to their English, Irish, and Scottish roots; and she evaluated the significance of this mountain music in terms of the contribution it could make to a "national American music." One specific song which she gave "exactly as it was sung to me by two young girls in the mountains" began:

> It was a ladie bright;
> Each child she had was three;
> She sent them off to a Northern State,
> For to learn their gramarie.

Though she made no specific analysis of the ballad in this article, she introduced it by saying: "The mountaineers sing many ballads of old England and Scotland. Their taste in music has no doubt been guided by these, which have come down from their ancestors."[3]

One year later in the book, *The Spirit of the Mountains*, she expanded the *Harper's* article to become Chapter VIII, still entitled "Some Real American Music." Here she suggests that "it should delight the heart of the student of English to compare the following instance ['A Ladie Bright'] with 'The Clerk's Twa Sons of Owsenford' and 'The Wife of Usher's Well.'"[4] She also added a final variant stanza that she obviously had collected after she did the original research for the article.

To place the chapter on music into its larger context, perhaps an overview of her framework for *The Spirit of the Mountains* is appropriate. This book contains ten chapters about mountain life, any one of which can be pulled out and read separately as an essay complete in itself. The setting is not specified as to which mountains are being described, but internal evidence continually points to the Walden's Ridge culture as the model for the author. However, she does fictionalize places and people in the book. She is not attempting a strict ethnography but rather is writing in the *local-color travel book* genre popular around the turn of the century. (Wilma Dykeman calls this the "parlor tradition" in contrast to the "frontier tradition" from which Sut Lovingood springs.)[5] To follow the conventions of that genre, she must compare and contrast the folk culture she is describing with mainstream culture. That means approaching the subject from the outsider's view or at least from the outsider's standard of measurement. Thus, Miles adopts the persona of mountain school teacher for her narrator, which implies education in and exposure to mainstream culture. Yet she wants to build on her inside perspective and so establishes early in the book that she is *of* the mountains, that she attended the same log church school which she now teaches. She dots her writing with *we, us, our,* and even more blatantly, with *my people* or *my own people.* Unfortunately, this inclusion of self sometimes seems superimposed and may produce the opposite effect of that intended. Ultimately she balances the duality of inside and outside perspectives to produce a book that shows both the quaint and the ordinary, the pretty and the ugly, the romance and the realism of the Tennessee mountain culture in the early 1900's.

Let us pay attention again, now, to my claim that she was one of the pioneer folklorists for Appalachia. If one places Miles in the history of formalized folklore collecting in America, he finds that she was a very early collector and analyst who did all the right things according to *today's* standards: i.e. collected texts, provided contexts, and analyzed the function and place of the lore in the culture. Yet, as I said before, Miles would never have called herself a folklorist. She was a writer. Whether or not she was even aware of Francis James Child's mammoth work on *The English and Scottish Popular Ballads,* I cannot say. I can assert, however, that she gave the lie to Child's claim that all the old ballads were dead, for she had found several of them alive and well on Walden's Ridge, Tennessee— most specifically his #79, "The Wife of Usher's Well," sung to her as "A Ladie Bright."

At the time she was writing these things, the American Folklore Society was only fifteen years old. A few isolated reports of bits of folklore had come out of the Southern Appalachians, but nothing on any great scale. Cecil Sharp, who is generally noted as the discoverer of traditional ballads in the mountains, was not to be heard of before 1916. Yet Emma Bell Miles collected ballads and folksongs and reported them in *Harper's Magazine* in 1904. Moreover, she showed how and when they were performed by the mountaineer; she placed him on the porch of his mountain cabin; she analyzed why he sings one kind of song and not another; why, for example, humor was so important in his music. She distinguished between songs sung by mountain men and those sung by mountain women. She saw a marked difference between male and female personalities and influences. The men, she believed, belonged to the "*young nation,* the young America." Thus, they sang songs of rollicking adventure or fun-loving ditties. The women, on the other hand, were of the "old race" because they lived with things that were old: their furnishings, their houses, their utensils were passed down through the generations and all had long histories and old traditions attached to them.[6] The men came indoors only to eat and sleep and then were out again hunting, farming, sawmilling, whatever; but the women lived inside with the old things. Consequently, the women crooned the traditional ballads of death, desolation, and domestic problems while they worked at the loom or spinning wheel or knitting.

Along with her collection and analysis of songs, Miles undertook a similar task with tales and legends. Without realizing what she did, she presented an interesting case study of how a piece of folklore is transmitted through the years and generations. She related the story of old Joe Winchester's search for the lost Cherokee silver mine. This was a family legend among the Winchesters, who were the people of Frank Miles' mother. Emma stated that she first heard the story as a child sitting on a sheepskin in front of a roaring fire in somebody's cabin. From then to adulthood she heard it several times from different people but with little variation. After her marriage she heard the story most often from Grandma Miles, who had a real flair for storytelling. But Grandpap was such a realist that he often squelched Grandma when she began to tell tales of questionable truth. Thus, the Joe Winchester story had practically dropped out of Grandma's repertoire so that one avenue of transmission was being sealed off. But Emma Bell Miles herself had picked it up and relayed it in print, in *The Spirit of the Mountains,*[7] so that another avenue had opened up. And in all likelihood the legend was still alive in the oral tradition of other people on the Ridge since Miles had heard it from various sources. In such a fashion, then, is folklore transmitted—sometimes moving from oral tradition into print and then back out again, but continuing to live through the ages.

In *The Spirit of the Mountains* Miles also discussed mountain dialect, proverbs, rhymes, superstitions, the supernatural, religion and a number of other topics revealing mountain culture. But the point I would leave you with is the significant contribution Miles made as one of the earliest folklorists, whether she knew it or not, in the Southern Appalachians. Long before Cecil Sharp, or Richard Chase, or Leonard Roberts, or Frank C. Brown, Emma Bell Miles was collecting and analyzing the lore of the mountains—all part of the oral tradition which she correctly saw as a valuable component of American literature, and certainly of American culture.

And for this atypical mountain woman, it was the typical mountain experience of home and family that gave her the stuff of which her contribution was fabricated: she took it from her children, her husband, her relatives, her neighbors, the Ridge itself. She told her own story almost eighty years ago; and even though her voice was silenced much too early, at the young age of thirty-nine, today we are the heirs to this remarkable woman's legacy, Emma Bell Miles.

## Notes

[1] Emma Bell Miles, Unpublished Journal, Vol. II, MS, 2 June 1912. This and volumes I, IV, and V of the personal journals are in the possession of Judith Miles Ford of Aline, Oklahoma. The manuscript of volume III is missing; however, typescript versions are held by the Chattanooga-Hamilton County Bicentennial Library and by the Tennessee State Library and Archives.

[2] Emma Bell Miles, "Some Real American Music," *Harper's Monthly Magazine*, June 1904, p. 118.

[3] Miles, "Some Real American Music," p. 121.

[4] Emma Bell Miles, *The Spirit of the Mountains*, A Facsimile Edition (Knoxville: The University of Tennessee Press, 1975), p. 163.

[5] Wilma Dykeman, "Appalachian Literature," in *Appalachia in Perspective*, Series of Videotaped Lectures from the Stokely Institute for Liberal Arts Education, University of Tennessee, Knoxville, Tennessee, Summer 1983.

[6] Miles, *The Spirit of the Mountains*, pp. 68-69.

[7] Miles, *The Spirit of the Mountains*, pp. 88-97.

# The Science Poetry of Marilou Awiakta

by
*Parks Lanier*

Cartoonist R. Hansen once drew a creature part woman, cockatrice, butterfly, and scorpion—beautiful but bizarre—demurely confessing to a curious little cupid, "My mother never speaks of that particular orgy." One can only feel sympathy for her, which is exactly how one feels when someone tries to discuss the paternity of science fiction. Like success, it has many fathers. Science fiction is a beautiful but bizarre creation, the result of a literary orgy which, some say, has been going on for thousands of years, at least since *Gilgamesh,* if not before.[1] And the orgy is all the more interesting if one remembers science fiction's twin— or clone— science poetry.

Science poetry is narrative poetry of estrangement set in an alternate world where the workings of science—biology, chemistry, physics, engineering, etc.—are a major cause or effect.[2] Like science fiction, science poetry turns upon what Darko Suvin calls the "novum" or "novelty." "Now the novelty in SF," he says, "can either be a new locus, or an agent (character) with new powers transforming the old locus, or a blend of both."[3] Earthlings may travel through time or space, or creatures from other times or other places may travel to earth. Science makes that possible. Science also makes possible "new powers transforming the old locus" without anyone going anywhere in space or time. Like science fiction, science poetry is attentive to change or transformation. For example, in her poem "The Planet," Josephine Jacobsen takes us to the moon's Sea of Tranquility, from which we view beautiful earth with "green fields, green fields/ocean of grasses, breakers of daisies" (ll. 9-10).[4] With a similar image of green grass in mind, Knute Skinner, in "Imagine Grass," invites us to journey to "a far-flung star/of an unnumbered magnitude/Mount Palomar has never viewed," (11. 10-12), but before we leave he reminds us:

> The planet that we plant upon
> rolls through its orbit of the sun,
> bending our grass upon the breeze.
> While far away the galaxies
> in a decelerating pace
> reach for the outer edge of space.[5]
> (11. 1-6)

Such a cosmic view, such a dramatic and sublime change of locus, is always thrilling. But so, too, is a transformation wrought on this earth, "the planet that we plant upon." Marilou Awiakta has taken such transformation as her subject in her collection of science poems *Abiding Appalachia: Where Mountain and Atom Meet*.

Oak Ridge, Tennessee, 1942: first there was the mystery, "new powers transforming the old locus," as Darko Suvin expresses it. Marilou Awiakta says that when she was a child of seven living in Knoxville, city of her birth, she realized that,

> ... a few miles away, we had a new frontier.
> Daddy went first, in '43—leaving at dawn
>     coming home at dark
> and saying nothing of his work except,
> "It's at Y-12, in Bear Creek Valley."
> The mystery deepened.
> The hum grew stronger.
> And I longed to go.
> Oak Ridge had a magic sound . . . .[6]

In a recent article for *MS.* magazine, Marilou expands on this story. Her father did not even know how his job fit the mysterious work going on at Oak Ridge. He could go only to his place of employment, not to "the most secret part" guarded by a maze of fences. What lay within that area he did not know. He saw "long, heavy trucks coming in. What they're bringing just seems to disappear. Somebody must know what happens to it, but nobody ever talks about it."[7] Something alien was being built, but not by aliens. A transforming force had come to Oak Ridge. "I can't imagine what," Marilou's father said. "I couldn't either," she says. "But I could feel its energy like a great hum."[8]

The writers of science fiction had "imagined what." The "fact" of atomic energy and the atomic bomb became one of the strongest claims for the predictive aspect of science fiction.[9] John Campbell, editor of *Astounding Science Fiction* magazine, received a visit from government agents in 1944 after publishing a story about the use of an atomic bomb.[10]

Lester Del Rey recounts that after his story "Nerves" appeared, a story about "an accident in a nuclear power station,"[11] copies of *Astounding Science Fiction* which appeared at Oak Ridge were "immediately stamped secret, and the research workers were refused permission to read it unless they had top clearance. They had to go outside the government plant to buy the issue from the newstands, where it was freely available."[12] Another editor, Philip Wylie, "received a similar visit [from government agents] in 1945; [also] . . . two comic-book stories featuring Superman were actually suppressed."[13]

The predictions were coming true, and Marilou was attracted to the alien city where gigantic bulldozers were leveling mountains or making new ones:

> So I kept listening to the hum, and longing . . .
> Mother said we'd go someday, in the fullness of time.
> And when I was nine the fullness came,
> exploding in a mushroom cloud that shook the earth.
> ("Genesis," 11. 52-55)

Nothing was ever to be the same again. Marilou Awiakta quotes Einstein who, after the bombing of Hiroshima, said, "The unleashed power of the atom has changed everything save our modes of thinking, and thus we drift toward unparalleled catastrophe."[14] To change "our modes of thinking" is one of the functions of Marilou's science poetry, something which her work has in common with the very best science fiction.

For critic Darko Suvin, the essence of science fiction is estrangement. Science fiction, he says, is "the literature of cognitive estrangement";[15] that is, it has "a different space/time location or central figures for the fable, unverifiable by common sense."[16] There is something alien or unknown. But the aliens, says Suvin, "utopians, monsters, or simply differing strangers [as they were at Oak Ridge] are a mirror to man just as the differing country [into which Black Oak Ridge was transformed] is a mirror for his world. But the mirror is not only a reflecting one, it is a transforming one, virgin womb and alchemical dynamo: the mirror is a crucible."[17] This precisely is the metaphor which fits not only Marilou's subject, but her work as well.

First the mirror showed destruction, the carnage of Hiroshima and Nagasaki. What was unknown and unseen "suddenly . . . had an image: the mushroom cloud. It had a name: the atom."[18] Looking west from Knoxville, Marilou had been lured by the hum of energy. "The atom was poetry in my childhood," she says, "images, rhythms—a presence beautiful, mysterious, dangerous . . . like the mountain. And I loved them both. Then the atom went awry . . . was alien" (*Abiding Appalachia*, p. 79).

The mushroom cloud was not its only image. The cow in the next field, as docile as Keats's garlanded heifer "lowing at the skies" became an emblem of the atomic nightmare. A sacrificial beast, she was familiar but alien:

> She'd like to be a friendly cow, I know,
> But she's radioactive now and locked
> behind a fence . . .
> . . . . . . . . .
> . . . It hurts my heart
> that I can't even stroke her head
> but as mother said,
> radiation's just not friendly.
> ("Test Cow," 11. 1-3; 7-10)

The cow might as well be from Jupiter, or fallen out of one of the terrible Martian machines in *The War of the Worlds*. She is an alien mirror to man, and the reflection is ugly and scary. But, as Suvin reminds us, it is also transforming.

As so often happens in science fiction, what first is alien and "awry" becomes familiar and comprehensible. The beast becomes beautiful. "I also saw the immense nurturing potential of the atom," Marilou says. "Terminal cancer patients came from everywhere to the research hospital. I especially remember one newspaper photograph of a man with emaciated hands reaching for the 'atomic cocktail' (a container of radioactive isotopes). His face was lighted with hope."[19] Once again Marilou felt the poetry of the atom, an experience she records in "Star Vision":

> In my hand lying prone upon
> the grass I could see
> each atom's tiny star—
> minute millions so far-flung
> so bright they swept me up
> with earth and sky
> in one vast expanse of light.
> ("Star Vision," 11. 6-12)

No longer is she apart; she is a part. From her Cherokee foremother she had learned "this firm step of mind/that seeks that whole/in strength and peace" ("An Indian Walkes in Me," 11. 25-27). Admirers of Frank Herbert's *Children of Dune* will no doubt liken Marilou's experience of communing with her Cherokee ancestors to that of the twins Leto and Ghanima who were "born with a totality of genetic memory, a terrifying awareness which set . . . [them] apart from all other living humans."[20] Marilou's experience, however, is unifying and consoling, a healing vision which is also a record of poetic rebirth that Marilou has commemorated by adopting a Cherokee surname, Awiakta.

"The atom has found its poetry again and I can feel love once more for its image and its sound," she says (*Abiding Appalachia*, p. 79). In addition to adopting a new name, for her life and work Marilou created an emblem of "the sacred white deer of the Cherokee, leaping in the heart of the atom....The reverent hunter evoked the white deer's blessing and guidance."[21] The deer is a symbol of reverence for life,[21] the nurturing, mothering aspect of the atom. The little white deer is also a symbol of hope. "There will be no sign of hope," Marilou says, "except deep in the invisible, where the atom's mother heart—slowly and patiently—bears new life."[22]

Darko Suvin spoke of the alien mirror as "virgin womb and alchemical dynamo." Scientists at Oak Ridge had also perceived the powers of the virgin and the dynamo, calling the reactor " 'The Lady' and, in moments of high emotion, [they] referred to her as 'our beloved reactor.' "[23] She inspired them to poetry. "In the control room," Marilou says, "they left a poem, 'To a Loyal Lady,' inscribed as 'thoughts from many hearts' " (*Abiding Appalachia*, p. 83). Marilou herself came to think of the nuclear reactor as a regal sister:

> In a nearby valley
> a new queen reigns.
> She is a deep pool
> clear and still
> and from the slender cylinder
> of her heart
> a blue glow rises
> a glow they call
> Cerenkov's fire . . .
>
> (*Abiding Appalachia*, p. 87)

When her father told her that the graphite core was black, Marilou imagined "a great black queen, standing behind her shield, holding the splitting atom in the shelter of her arms."[24] The maternal image is not unlike the iconography of Leonardo's *Madonna and Child With St. Anne,* where the Child emanates from the lap of the Virgin, who in turn sits upon her mother's lap. First there is Mother, then Daughter, then Cosmic Son.

Like the backgrounds of Leonardo's paintings, the background of *Abiding Appalachia,* for all its atomic science, remains essentially pastoral. This other world is symbolized by the childlike language and unsophisticated memories of Oak Ridge's wooden boardwalks in "Beneath My Feet": "Dryin' out you smell so good/I like to lie against your wood" (11. 13-14). Darko Suvin feels that "the pastoral . . . is essentially closer to SF [than to fantasy]; . . . SF has much to learn from the pastoral tradition," he believes, "primarily from its directly sensual relationships which do not manifest class alienation."[25] The worlds of the pastoral and science fiction are alike, he says, in "[offering] no assurances as to the outcome of the protagonists' endeavors."[26] In the unpredictable pastoral world, Marilou remembers her mother's advice:

> ... always test the 'seems' of things—
> briars may lurk in the dew-drenched grass
> and jagged glass in heaps of leaves.
> The toughest sole can't bear these
> without a wound.
> (Mother's Advice While Bandaging
> My Stubbed Toe," 11. 5-9)

Perfect advice for anyone undertaking atomic research, or for living in a world transformed by it, is her grandfather's advice, "Be plucky, like an Indian."

At the beginning of *Abiding Appalachia*, Marilou evokes memories of the Trail of Tears and the martyrdom of "Tsali, his brother, and all his sons save one" (p. 21) who gave their lives that a remnant of the Cherokee might continue to live in their mountain fastness. Over and over her poems raise the haunting question, "If our atomic present —or future— becomes our Trail of Tears, will we, too, be 'plucky like an Indian'?" We can be if we let the Indian in Marilou become the Indian in us, and if we resolve as she did, "And no more/could I follow any rule/that split my soul" ("An Indian Walks in Me," 11. 20-22).

Fusion. Harmony. This is what explodes from the crucible that is the poetry of Marilou Awiakta. She says, "Mother had already taught me that in the holistic philosophy of my Cherokee ancestors, beyond surface differences, everything is in physical and spiritual connection—God, nature, humanity. Harmony. All are one: a circle. It seemed natural for the atom to be a part of this connection."[27] In *Abiding Appalachia*, she says, "The language of science is coming round. The atom has found its poetry again and I can feel love once more for its image and its sound" (p. 79). Her phrase "coming round" suggests not only accommodation but also her sense of the sacred circle, symbol of unified life.

Darko Suvin might see Marilou's reaching toward myth, folklore, or fairytale, expressed in Awi Usdi, small chief of the deer, as "committing creative suicide,"[28] for he cannot bear that impulse in science fiction. Such transcendence antagonizes him, yet in science poetry, it seems to me, it is the perfect way to express that yearning which Suvin recognized as lying behind all great science fiction, "a hope of finding in the unknown the *ideal* environment, tribe, state, intelligence, or other aspect of the Supreme Good (or ... a fear of and revulsion from its contrary)."[29] If it is "creative suicide" for science fiction to turn toward the mythical, the religious, the fairytale, in expressing hope of finding the ideal, it is quite the opposite for science poetry, since all poetry springs from an impulse that is essentially "mythical." As a fitting conclusion for her work, Marilou's final poem, "Where Mountain and Atom Meet," invokes "an aura from the great I Am/that gathers to its own/spirits that have gone before" (11. 6-8). It is precisely at that point of gathering, and at that point only, "where mountain and atom meet," and where we, too, may enter the sacred circle ourselves.

## NOTES

[1] Lester Del Rey, *The World of Science Fiction, 1926-1976* (New York: Garland Publishing Co., 1980), pp. 12-13.

[2] The term "science poetry" is my own. The definition, however, is modeled on Darko Suvin's definition of science fiction in *Metamorphoses of Science Fiction* (New Haven: Yale University Press, 1979), p. 4.

[3] Suvin, p. 79.

[4] Edward Field, ed., *A Geography of Poets* (New York: Bantam, 1979), p. 327.

[5] Field, p. 32.

[6] Marilou Bonham Thompson, *Abiding Appalachia: Where Mountain and Atom Meet* (Memphis: St. Luke's Press, 1978), p. 48. All citations in the text are to this edition.

[7] Marilou Awiakta, "What is the Atom, Mother? Will it Hurt Us?" *MS.* (July 1983), p. 47.

[8] Awiakta, p. 47.

[9] Peter Nicholls, ed. *The Science Fiction Encyclopedia* (New York: Doubleday, 1979), p. 432.

[10] Del Rey, p. 108.

[11] Nicholls, p. 432.

[12] Del Rey, pp. 108-109.

[13] Nicholls, p. 432.

[14] Awiakta, p. 48.

[15] Suvin, p. 4.

[16] Suvin, p. 18.

[17] Suvin, p. 5

[18] Awiakta, p. 47.

[19] Awiakta, p. 47.

[20] Frank Herbert, *Children of Dune* (New York: Berkley Publishing Corp., 1976), p. 4.

[21] Awiakta, p. 48.

[22] Awiakta, p. 48.

[23] Awiakta, p. 47.

[24] Awiakta, p. 47.

[25]Suvin, p. 9.
[26]Suvin, p. 19.
[27]Awiakta, p. 47.
[28]Suvin, p. 8.
[29]Suvin, p. 5.

# Going Home

by
*Ron Willoughby*

"And God saw everything that he had made, and behold, it was very good." from Genesis 1:31, KJV

"But it's the truth even if it didn't happen." *One Flew Over the Cuckoo's Nest.*

I try to talk my mother out of going, but it doesn't do any good. Pardee is the place where she grew up and she wants to see it, or what's left of it, or the place where it was, one more time. So we drive over there, one hundred and fifty miles of four lane road that bulldozes its way across country, then up the narrow hollow on seven miles of one and a half lane humpbacked road that squirms through the woods, following the creek the way a puppy follows its mother. On the other side of the creek a railroad track tags along silently, only occasionally visible through the trees. On both sides of the hollow strip mine high walls follow the contours of the ridges as precisely as lines on a topographic map. We pass through Dunbar, where we lived for a while, where the company sold its houses to the miners, who fixed them up and settled down. Dunbar, population seventy-five, more or less, with no store, no post office, not even a gas station. Nothing but people and their homes. And the mountains.

Two miles above Dunbar is Pardee, the end of the line, the head of the hollow lying in the lap of Pine Mountain. Here the road is still in use only because there is a stripping operation going on above Pardee. The blacktop is slowly crumbling and disappearing from the outside edges toward the middle, like a scab on a healing cut.

We cross the creek and the railroad tracks, round one last bend, and are in Pardee. The hollow is little more than one hundred yards wide at this point. The road runs along the base of one ridge, and to our left is the creek, the railroad track and the opposite ridge. Once there were thirty or so houses lined up facing each other across the tracks, white as healthy young teeth. Now there are two teeth left, slowly rotting.

The first building we come to is the old church, which stands apart between the creek and the road. It had been a little white clapboard building with a high peaked roof topped by a homemade wooden cross, and served as the center of social life in Pardee. Now it is being razed, and only the front wall is standing.

I pull off the road in a cleared space beside the church. A bulldozer is already parked there, a giant yellow eraser waiting to finish rubbing out the last smudges of what had once been Pardee.

I look at Mother. She is looking intently at the remains of the church, already back in a time and place that no longer exists. Eventually she nods. "I remember when your daddy and I came to Sunday school and church here," she says. "That was before we were married, mostly. After we were married we lived in Dunbar and Appalachia, and we only came here when we were visiting. Your daddy taught Sunday school some, and there was a piano. We'd sing hymns and have a big time." She is smiling. "And before that, when I was a little girl, we had square dances and parties here. And there was a Christmas program every year. One of the men would dress up like Santa Claus and give us paper bags full of fruit and nuts and hard candy."

We stand silently for a minute longer, then turn away, clunk across the creek on the old wooden-decked bridge, and walk slowly along between the rusty rails of the railroad track. The ditches and the old house sites are overgrown with weeds and blackberry bushes. The two remaining houses are both in the row away from the creek. We stop in front of the first one. The steps are gone and the boards are missing from the floor of the porch. There is no door, and the windows don't even have frames, much less glass. A few shreds of clear plastic hang in the windows and occasionally twitch in a passing breeze. Behind the house the wooded ridge rises steeply, waiting patiently to reclaim its own. The old house is too tired to resist. It sags like a man who has spent twelve hours at the coal face with a pick in his hands.

"This is the house where Olin and Glad lived," Mother says. "I'm sure of it." Glad was one of mother's older sisters. She died in 1943 of a kidney infection. A few months after she died penicillin was introduced, and that same kidney infection would have been cleared up in ten days, without going to the hospital. Or so the story goes. I wonder how mother can be so sure this is the house.

"And after Glad died, Mary and Rich moved in here." Mary is another of mother's older sisters. She lives by herself in the Wildcat near Big Stone, where she and Rich and several of their children moved in the early fifties. They bought a house and a little piece of land with the insurance money that they got when Johnny, their second son, was killed in Korea in 1950. Right after his eighteenth birthday.

"And right over here," she points, "is where we lived."

I shake my head. I vaguely remember what the house looked like, but there's no house there now, and I'm still not sure she can recognize any of these places with certainty. But it doesn't matter. She's certain.

"Poppy used to work a twelve hour shift as the tipple foreman," she says. "We had a nicer house than most because he was a foreman. We had this beautiful white trellis in our front yard—do you remember it?—and Poppy told me after your daddy and I ran away to Harlan to get married that he had hoped the two of us would get married at home. We would have stood under the trellis. Said I was his last girl, and all the rest had run off to get married, and he'd hoped I would get married at home." She fell silent.

I remember some other stories about Poppy Hall. About how he'd had a lot of money and property at one time, but had let his brother hoodoo him out of it a little at a time while he was drunk, so that in the end Poppy wound up as a mine foreman, and died in a rented house in Norton, while great-uncle Ben ended up rich.

Or about how Poppy loved cars, used to buy a new one every year and keep it all shined up. My daddy told me about being with Poppy in his car once with Ray and Shine, two of mother's brothers. They'd just finished shining up the car and the windows were as clear as spring water. So clear that Poppy thought the window was down and spit a great gob of tobacco juice all over it. Daddy said that they were afraid to laugh out loud, so they nearly died because they swelled up ready to burst with all the laughs they swallowed.

And mother told me about the time Poppy came home drunk, and for some reason got upset with Mary and tried to throw her out the window of the upstairs bedroom. Mommy Hall ran into the room and started pulling at him, and he turned and hit her. And then he fell down on his knees and cried out, "What have I done?" And after that Poppy never took another drink. Or so the stories go.

Mother turned and pointed again. "Over there," she says "was the superintendent's house." This time I know she's right, because I can see the long flight of steps—there must be forty of them—leading up to an empty flat spot on the lower flank of the ridge. The house sat looking out over the rest of the camp like a corporate Big Brother, or so it must have seemed when the union and the company cops came into the hollow. Looking at the empty space at the top of the steps I have an eerie, childish thought: If I walked up those steps to the top, and if I stepped off onto the spot where the house had stood, would I disappear?

We wander on up the railroad track toward the remains of the tipple near the head of the hollow, crossing the creek again by stepping from tie to tie. The water is visible about five feet down through the gaps between the ties, and I remember how terrified I was as a child to make this same crossing. The water seemed to be thirty feet away then, but I made the crossing anyway because I was even more terrified of being called "chicken" by my friends.

We come to the company store a couple of hundred feet after crossing the bridge. "This is the new store," mother says. "I remember when the old one burned, and I remember them building this one. I loved that old store. Your daddy lived in a room on the second floor when he came up here to teach school. He and his roommate, the doctor, used to sit up at night and read Shakespeare aloud to each other."

Like most of what mother was saying today, I had heard this before, and my mental image of this scene is from outside, down the hollow from the building. It is dark, and the stars are visible if you look straight up. The only other light is in the window of Daddy's room, a dim yellow glow in the blackness of the ridge in the background. In the earth's guts thirteen year old boys pick and shovel coal and breathe coal dust, while the words of Shakespeare drift like thin morning mist over the hollow. But some thirteen year olds didn't go underground, and Daddy was proud of the letters he got from his students, even decades later, thanking him for being here when they needed him. Even though he gave up teaching in his early thirties to take a job where he could earn a living, men and women who were his students in Dunbar and Pardee were still writing him when he died at sixty-nine. He left two children, two grandchildren, and a wife who had been his student in the seventh grade.

We mount the steps to the porch of the "new" store, whose claim to fame is that some scenes from "Coal Miner's Daughter" were shot here, and look through the big windows. The plate glass lies in shards inside, and here and there among the debris is a baseball-sized rock. We turn away and look back down the hollow, where we can see all that remains of Pardee. The two decaying houses, the front of the church standing like the facade of a movie set, the long steps leading nowhere. In a moment I look at Mother. She has the relaxed face and unfocused stare of a newborn baby. In her mind she is building her own reality, with the creative power that is a wavering image of God, a deep Presence glimpsed in a wind-ruffled pond at dusk. Her faded blue eyes are the windows of a house in winter, and inside a young girl presses her nose to the frosted glass, looking out and listening to the faint voices outside. Perhaps one day Mother will become that young girl again, will open the door and go outside to become once more a part of that earlier time. But now, nearing seventy, she can only look through the girl's ageless eyes at the reality she has made. So she stands on the uneven boards of the porch, looking at what is, while the young girl presses her face to the window and sees what used to be.... and behold, it is very good.

SOCIAL THEORY AND SOCIAL LIFE IN
APPALACHIA: A PANEL
Presenters:
    Mary Anglin; New School for Social Research; New York, NY
    Alan Batteau; Committee on Institutional Cooperation; Evanston, IL
    Bill Horton; Abingdon, VA
    Jim Foster; Emory and Henry University; Emory, VA
Discussants:
    Tom Plaut; Mars Hill College; Mars Hill, NC
    Tom Shannon; Radford University; Radford, VA

# A Contribution to the Critique of Political Economy

by
*Allen Bateau*

Unless they are connected with protest potential from other sectors of society no conflicts arising from ... underprivilege can really overturn the system—they can only provoke it to shape reactions incompatible with formal democracy. For underprivileged groups are not social classes, nor do they ever even potentially represent the mass of the population. Their disenfranchisement and pauperization no longer coincide with exploitation, because the system does not live off their labor. They can represent at most a past phase of exploitation.

Appalachia has been studied for a variety of reasons: Some seek a romantic escape from urban society in the construction of Appalachian folk; others look for a laboratory within which to perfect tool for the improvement of society at large. Others have hoped to discover amidst the oppression of the coalfields seeds of the eventual transformation of American society. In all cases there is the presumption that in some manner Appalachia is exceptional, even as its boundaries are artificially drawn to preserve that exceptionality.

Yet every study of Appalachia contains within it assumptions about the nature of American society that belie this exceptionality. To the extent that one mis-understands American society, or is unclear on his or her assumptions, the resulting statements made about Appalachia will be misleading, romantic, or irrelevant. William G. Frost made such a mistake, being uncomfortable with the cultural pluralism in America, and thus blind to the ethnic diversity within Appalachia. Jack Weller made such a mistake, ignoring the macro-political and -economic bases of Appalachia's situation.

My study of Appalachia has been motivated by the observation that conditions there present in unusually dramatic form processes of exploitation and oppression found in many corners of American society. One can observe there processes of oppression which, while not qualitatively different from those underway elsewhere in America, nevertheless are cast into sufficiently high relief to permit one to view a structure that elsewhere is rather opaque. The opacity of these processes in our everyday lives is what makes them work. This opacity derives from the fact that in most cases people are controlled and manipulated not through force and fraud, but through the manipulation of consciousness. I have been trying for several years to understand how this manipulation of consiousness occurs in a variety of places in American society; in the process I have arrived, I hope, at some new understandings not only of the quality of oppression but also at the structures through which people and groups are oppressed.

I should first state some of the assumptions that have informed my study of Appalachia. I can reduce these to four statements, which after stating I will take the liberty to elaborate on.
1. America is a capitalistic society.
2. America is a continental society, embracing and assimilating to an unusual degree regional, ethnic, and other forms of diversity.
3. In America, the state—meaning the political and governmental apparatus at both federal and sub-federal levels—is large, powerful, and partially autonomous.
4. The dominant framework for authority in America is bureaucratic; in America, every form of large-scale organization, from corporate enterprise to religion to the state, is bureaucratized.

If one takes exception to any of these statements, we are in trouble, for I have deliberately chosen those that seem to me to be least exceptionable. One may be uncomfortable with some of them, particularly with the emphasis they suggest; but such discomfort does not per se discredit the statements or their logical implications.

To say that America is a capitalistic society means that it is divided by class, that surplus appropriation is a central dynamic, and that certain classes aggrandize themselves at the expense of others. For anyone who has taken a passing glance at the coal industry in Kentucky, such observations are commonplace. But (and this is a major qualification) if we must continually hark back to the coal industry to validate our statements about class, we are on shaky ground, particularly with regard to those districts and periods of Appalachia outside the coal industry's domination. I attempted to see how this would work for certain non-industrial spheres in eastern Kentucky, and suggested in an article in the *American Ethnologist* some revisions of our understanding of class.

The observation that America is a continental society is hardly novel; yet it suggests some interesting problems. Continental societies are rather unusual—there are only four of them in the world (five if you count Canada) and they are all marked by a heightened tension between strong centripetal government and the centrifugal tendencies of linguistic, cultural, regional, religious, and ethnic diversity. This is not a particularly trenchant observation, yet it creates some difficult issues for those interested in the first: For the models we have—both conservative and radical, I might add—of capitalism and class struggle were derived from societies where this sort of diversity was less of an issue, and hence could with some plausibility (and arrogance, one might add) be dismissed as "false consciousness" or "bourgeois nationalism," or "traditional survivals." In the last thirty years, however, we have seen that nationalism—with the linguistic, religious, ethnic, and other affinities from which it is built up—is a revolutionary force. A major intellectual task is squaring such an observation with some of our assumptions about the workings of capitalist society. In a world context, American society is unusually assimilationist, managing to a far greater degree than nearly every other society to integrate these forms of diversity with minimal violence. Given the relative political salience of ethnic and class loyalties in different contexts, these assimilationist tendencies also suggest some problems for understanding American class structure.

Now a major issue for us is whether these various non-economic affinities are reducible to distinctions of class or other economic relationships, or whether they are in their own right autonomous and alternative forms of consciousness. I'll return to this in a moment.

The observation of a large and powerful government and political apparatus in America, and that of its legal-rationalistic structure, is also rather pedestrian. The crucial question is what significance one attaches to these facts. Is a large government merely a tool of capital, or does it represent an independent sphere of action? Is bureaucracy an instrument or a form of domination? While these questions might seem to border on the Thomistic—kind of like asking how many civil servants can dance on the header of a computer tape—they have serious implications for how one seeks to improve the lives of one's fellows, whether in the office or in the hollers.

I began with the question of the role of human consciousness in the manifest processes of oppression. It is a metaphysical question that we cannot resolve here whether or not human consciousness is autonomous of or shackled to economic interests and domination. It is a metaphysical question, and no amount of professorial fudging ("partly yes, partly no") or dialectical backflips ("mutally reactive autonomous forces") will solve the problem. I will have to explain that I find the former assumption, of the autonomy of consciousness, more interesting, more plausible, and more productive for devising political strategy. Others may differ.

But once I've taken this step, several interesting possibilities are opened up. One can discover a diversity of semantic values in economic processes; one can better explain ethnic and religious affinities; and one can suggest new political strategies.

When we talk about how consciousness works, we are talking about forms, media, and contents of communication, about symbolic forms such as myth, ritual, and narrative, about processes such as persuasion, identification, faction, and sacrifice. All of these are symbolic processes, yet are very real in their political results. There is a well-developed literature of the systematic ways in which these symbolic processes work. I will elaborate on this in the discussion, commenting here only that they are irreducible to economic processes as one normally understands them.

With an understanding of consciousness as an autonomous agency, we also find new ends of action beyond simply economic aggrandizement. Individual identity and group solidarity, for instance, are created through symbolic processes which are irrational from an economic standpoint. The symbolic bases of ethnic and religious affiliation are more understandable if one assumes that they are partially independent of economic interests.

I would suggest also that with an understanding of these symbolic processes one arrives at a better understanding of ethnic and religious oppression, and ultimately at a new map of the class structure of American society, A paradox for me is how people who are well-fed and secure in their livelihood can feel oppressed. The answer of academic social science is to retreat into "relative deprivation." This suggests that nearly everyone can find an excuse to identify themselves as oppressed. But suppose we assume that people have an interest in more than just their economic and political situation; that they have an interest in such irrational matters as autonomy, identity, and group affiliation. Then anything that threatens these—threatens them symbolically, I should underscore, for that is how these things work—will be experienced as oppressive. Protestant fundamentalists find threats in sexual license, for such unpunished sin questions some of the axioms of their existence; most ethnic groups find stereotyping immediately offensive, not because it deprives them of their livelihood (although it can be used for that purpose), so much as because it stigmatizes and fragments their identity.

For every act of oppression there is an oppressor; yet in a rational society, what drives the shaming, stereotyping, and fragmentation of this symbolic oppression? In a brief article I wrote a few years back, I suggested that in the kind of society we have today, "intangibles such as health and personal identity have become resources, placed on the market, and made into resources for surplus appropriation." Elsewhere I have suggested that some of the shaming rituals that Sennett described for the workings of bureaucracy were means by which those with relative power could "accumulate economic, political, and psychological capital at the expense of the inferiors."

If you have indulged me thus far, you may think that this is an interesting metaphor, an extension of the meaning of surplus and capital into non-economic spheres. My intention however is literal, not metaphorical. You see, the genius of capitalism is that it continually places new segments of human experience on the market and extracts surplus value out of them. Three hundred years ago, before the industrial revolution, the notion that there might be a market in human labor was an outlandish one. A hundred years ago any notion of buying and selling human consciousness would seem pretty extravagant—yet now we have large advertising agencies engaged in just such a business. And if you think that identity is not for sale, then you haven't been to Bloomingdales.

That which can be sold is alienable; that which is alienable is a prime target for the workings of a capitalist market. If one can move beyond the simple economistic view of capital, and see that capital can take on a variety of forms, then one is permitted a conception of "human capital" as those intangible, infungible, yet accumulable resources an individual or a group possesses. These resources include such matters as skills, social relationships, group solidarity, individual identity. Through their accumulation the individual achieves a degree of autonomy in the face of capitalist predation. Yet one of the critical issues we see in the workings of capital today is the appropriation or destruction of the diverse forms of human capital.

Capitalism has been around for hundreds of years. It existed before the industrial revolution, and it will continue to grow even as industrial production employs ever-decreasing fractions of the American labor force. Bureaucracy has been around for thousands of years, and continues to grow and sequester new areas of human activity. If one is willing to abide by the evidence of states that have undergone socialist revolutions, then bureaucracy seems to be more durable than capitalism. The two have in common the facts of the oppression they create, albeit for at times dissimilar ends. The prospects for a revolution in this country leading to more equitable social forms rests more on messianic hope than on sober assessment of current possibility. Short of this, one can in fact find means to limit the encroachments of capitalism and bureaucracy. This requires a willingness to engage in confrontation and negotiation, rather than a retreat into sectarian avoidance; it requires not only knowing on which side (of several fences) you stand, but also who stands there with you and who your potential allies are.

I began this discussion with an epigraph which I think is suggestive of the political significance of processes of oppression in Appalachia. The epigraph is not from any "post-industrial theorist" such as Daniel Bell, but from Jurgen Habermas. Habermas, in "Toward a Rational Society" is attempting to locate the zone of conflict and protest in a society where legal-rationalistic structures have broken out of their traditional restraints and have usurped the very framework of the society. He suggests that student protest may provide the zone of conflict he seeks. His conclusion here is based partly on an assumption that may have seemed plausible in 1968 that student activists were less directed toward professional careers than other students.

In 1984 one despairs the protest potential among professionals or the proto-professionals found in most universities. Although one should not look for new ideas for fundamental change in the society from such classes, in certain kinds of situations they do represent potential allies for those who have worked out their own political agenda. Such negotiations with other classes and the powerful institutions of this society will always be like a card game in which the rules are biased in favor of your opponent—you can win at such games, if you know what you're playing for and are at times prepared to break the rules.

If one is convinced that the only solution lies in revolution, then this will certainly sound like I am trying to lure the proletarian sheep into the den of capitalist wolves. The motive of seduction, however, is not mine; it is rather one of the important dynamics of how the system works. In American society, the sheep are continually lured into the wolves' den, and their (seemingly) voluntary participation in their own oppression is essential to the workings of the system. No one is coerced into purchasing his or her identity at Bloomingdales; few feel the immediate spur of poverty and hunger as motives to sell their labor; most could survive in comfort (if not security or prestige) with far less income than they currently have. But the American economy continues to work, consuming far more labor, creating far more environmental spoliation, producing far too many useless goods, accumulating destabilizing surpluses, because the overwhelming majority of the society has bought into its myths of happiness through consumption and upward mobility.

These beliefs are essential to the survival of advanced capitalism. Finding an alternative yet equally persuasive set of beliefs, a new form of consciousness, if you wish, is a precondition and not a consequence of its demise.

CURRENT RESEARCH IN COMMUNITY ISSUES
Households and Families in Eastern Kentucky in 1900
  Thomas A. Arcury/Julia Porter, University of Kentucky;
  Lexington, KY
Poverty, Race and Class in Appalachian Cities
  Mike Maloney/Elizabeth Lilly; Appalachian Peoples Service
  Organization
The Graying of Central Appalachia
  Rosemary Goss, Virginia Tech.; Blacksburg, VA
Framework for Teaching Human Service Professionals About
Appalachian Communities
  John McNutt/Marcia Barron, Tusculum College; Greenville, TN
  Convenor: Aaron Hyatt; Western Carolina University; Cullowhee, NC

# Households and Families in Eastern Kentucky in 1900*

by
*Thomas A. Arcury and Julia D. Porter*

Figure 1: Percentage Distribution of Household Population by Age and Sex, Pike County and Ashland Samples, 1900

The purpose of this paper is to describe and compare the composition of rural and urban Appalachian Kentucky households in 1900. This task is undertaken for two reasons. First, for much of this century the composition of the traditional Appalachian family and household has been the center of attention for both scientific and popular analysis. While several analyses of the Appalachian family have been presented since the 1940s (Brown, 1952a, 1952b; Stephenson, 1968; Hicks, 1976; Bryant, 1981; Batteau, 1982; Ford, et al, 1983), little quantitative or qualitative data have been presented for earlier periods. The second reason for analysis of Appalachian data from this period is that it allows an examination of the effects of rapid industrialization and urbanization on the household composition of a region in which subsistence agriculture had dominated previously. Beginning shortly before 1900 areas of Eastern Kentucky became involved in the large scale commercial exploitation of the region's vast coal reserves.

The present study is the result of a preliminary investigation of household composition during this period. Data are abstracted from a sample of households listed in the 1900 census enumeration schedules for two communities: Ashland, the only city in Eastern Kentucky in 1900, and one rural enumeration district in Pike County.

## Traditional Appalachian Kentucky Household Composition

This study is concerned with the eastern one-third of Kentucky included in the Southern Appalachian Region (see Ford, 1962). Little is known about this region's family and household composition at or before the beginning of the twentieth century. Research on the history of any component of the region's social organization has been limited. Eller (1982) provides a valuable analysis of Southern Appalachian economic change between 1880 and 1930 due to industrialization, particularly the commercial exploitation of the region's timber and coal resources. But his discussion of micro-level sociocultural change is limited. Campbell (1921) describes some specific examples of Appalachian households, but his concern is more with lifestyle than with the analysis of social organization. Due to the dearth of published historical material, ethnographic analogy is used to provide some background on turn of the century Appalachian household composition.

Brown's research on rural Beech Creek, Kentucky (Brown, 1952a, 1952b; Brown, et al, 1963; Schwarzweller, et al, 1971) is the most completely documented study upon which ethnographic analogies are made. Brown found that the household consisting of a conjugal family, a husband, a wife and their dependent children, was the dominant form of household organization. These nuclear family households represented about 75 percent of all households in Beech Creek, with another 16 percent including a married couple with no children, and five percent including an additional family. Only three percent of all households did not contain a family.

Marriage was almost universal among this rural Appalachian population. Age at first marriage was at about 23 years for males, and 18 years for females. Often a new couple stayed for about one year in the dwelling of one of their families of orientation, usually that of the husband. This accounts for all of the households with an additional family. Often the newlyweds first child was born before they established their own household. Within eight to ten years after marriage, the average couple in Beech Creek had 3 or 4 children. When the wives were from 37 to 45 years of age household size was at its maximum; most contained at least four children, and many had six or more children.

The nuclear family household was the basic unit of production and consumption. Such families owned and farmed their land, made most of their tools and consumption goods, and were almost totally self-sufficient (Eller, 1979; Precourt, 1983). Labor differentiations were along age-sex lines, and there were an interdependence of age-sex roles. As the family worked the mountain homestead, economic roles and family roles could only be separated analytically (Brown, 1952a, 1952b).

The ideal of the separate, self-reliant nuclear family household meant the extended family household was rare. The presence of the household head's siblings or other relatives only occurred in situations of extreme old age or youth when the individual could not care for himself. Most older couples lived alone, or if a spouse died, in a single person household, maintaining a separate household as long as possible. The aged parents of a household head or his spouse resided in his household only in cases when the parents could no longer care for themselves. Often in these cases, the younger family would come to live in the parental household. Nonrelatives were also rare in the rural Appalachian household.

While the extended family household was a rarity in rural Appalachia, the extended family network was still an important part of the social organization. Several households containing related families usually lived in close proximity. This extended kin network, also called a "set" (see Batteau, 1982; Bryant, 1981, 1983), could be counted on in time of crises. The help of these kin also allowed aged and other disabled individuals to maintain separate households.

Ethnographic analogy with studies of more contemporary rural Appalachian households can be used to present some background on rural 1900 household composition, but similar research is not available for industrial Appalachian households. While this study examines the population of Ashland, Kentucky, it should be noted that this community does not totally reflect the rural Appalachian industrialization experience. Ashland existed as a city before commercial timber and coal extraction began. Most of the industrial workers did not live in cities, but in rural communities and company towns nearer to the mines. Oral history interviews and some published materials do indicate some changes in household composition. Native men who worked in the mines often moved their families to company towns or stayed at boarding houses.

**Methods**

Data for this study consist of a total of 300 households randomly selected from two localities in Appalachian Kentucky. The two localities were purposefully selected as representative of the two extremes of industrial and urban development present in the region in 1900. As the more industrial locality, the city of Ashland was selected. A census enumeration district in Pike County (Magisterial District 2), as totally removed from commercial coal production as possible, was selected as the traditional non-industrial locality. A total of 150 households was randomly selected for each locality from the 1900 census schedules. For the specific Pike County area only the single enumeration district was sampled. For Ashland, all three of the city's central precincts were included.

The four household structural types used in this study are adapted from those developed by Hammel and Laslett (1974): (1) nonfamily, (2) nuclear family only, (3) extended family, and (4) multiple family. Some variable definitions are dictated by the way they were recorded in the 1900 census. The ability to read and write was recorded instead of educational attainment. Literacy is defined here as the ability to both read and write. Migration can only be defined in terms of an individual's state or nation of birth.

In this study we use a rough measure of the number of nearby households containing relatives. Similar to the method used by Smith, et. al. (1979), this method involves examining the ten households which precede and the ten which follow each sampled household on the enumeration schedules, and recording the number of households which contain the same surname as that in the sample household.

## The Household Population

A comparison of the sample household populations neatly summarizes the differences between the two communities: one, Pike County, with a stable, homogeneous agricultural population; the other, Ashland, an industrializing, heterogeneous population in a state of flux. The age-sex pyramids (Figure 1) portray their differences. The Pike County pyramid indicates a population growing with high fertility. There does appear to

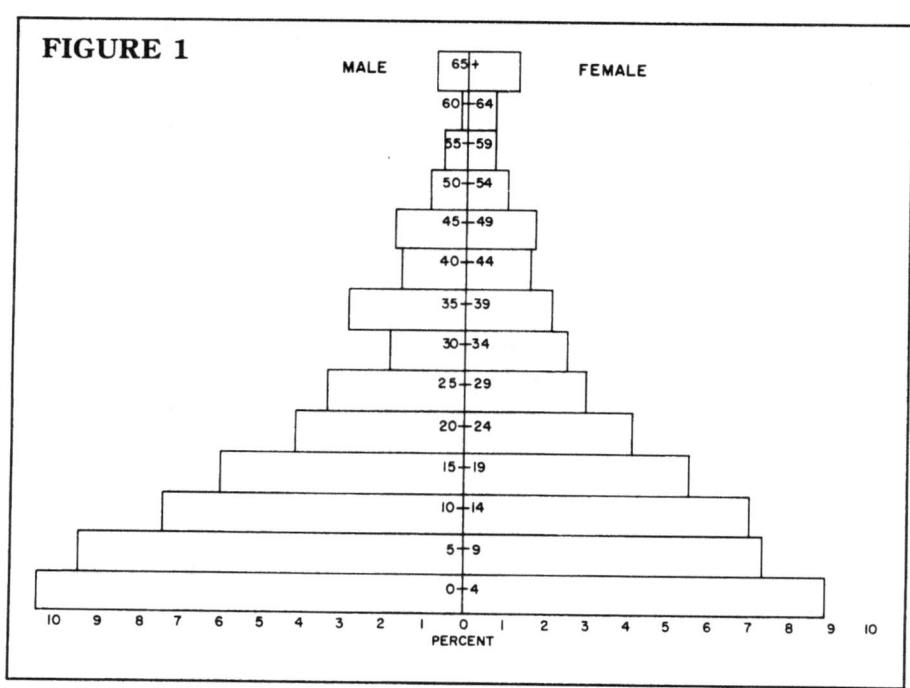

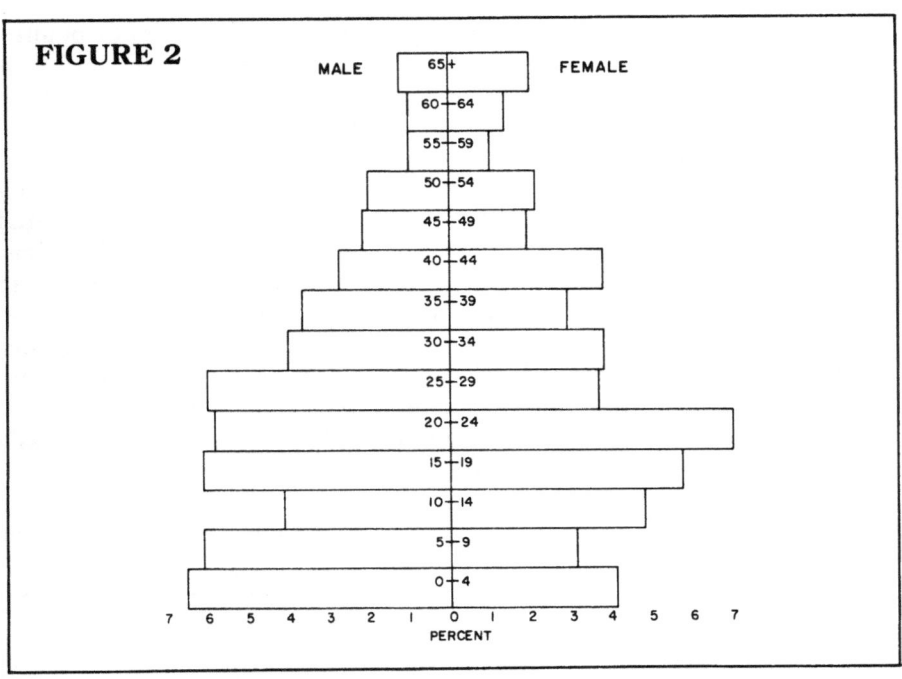

**FIGURE 2**

| TABLE 1. State or Nation of Birth and Race of Sample Household Population by Residence ||||
|---|---|---|---|---|
| State or Nation of Birth | Rural | | Urban | |
| | N | % | N | % |
| Kentucky | 799 | 89.0 | 445 | 63.1 |
| Ohio | 0 | | 92 | 13.0 |
| Virginia | 55 | 6.1 | 58 | 8.2 |
| West Virginia | 7 | .8 | 30 | 4.3 |
| Other U. S. | 36 | 4.0 | 50 | 7.1 |
| Foreign born | 1 | .1 | 30 | 4.3 |
| Missing | | | (5) | |
| Total | 898 | 100.0 | 705 | 100.0 |
| Race | | | | |
|   White | 898 | 100.0 | 665 | 93.7 |
|   Black | 0 | | 45 | 6.3 |
|   Total | 898 | 100.0 | 710 | 100.0 |

be some outmigration of young adult males in the Pike County population, but there does not appear to be any significant inmigration. The bulge in the 15 through 34 age cohorts for Ashland indicates a population being affected by substantial inmigration. Fertility in the Ashland population also is relatively low.

The lack of inmigration in the rural Pike population and the strong influence of inmigration in the urban Ashland population is substantiated when place of birth within the population is examined (Table 1). The great majority (89 percent) of the rural population is Kentucky born. Less than two-thirds (63.1 percent) of the urban population were born in Kentucky. A significant number of the urban population were born in the neighboring states of Ohio and Virginia/West Virginia, in other parts of the U.S., and even outside of the country. In addition to the ethnic heterogeneity of Ashland, there is also some racial variety. About 6 percent of Ashland's population is black; the entire rural Pike population is white.

The rural sample is employed almost entirely in agriculture: 75.1 percent of the work force are farmers (Table 2). The only other significant

TABLE 2. Occupations and Literacy of Sample Household Population by Residence

| Occupation | Rural | | Urban | |
|---|---|---|---|---|
| | N | % | N | % |
| Professional, Technical; Managers & Administrators | 1 | .6 | 24 | 9.8 |
| Sales and Clerical | 1 | .6 | 25 | 10.2 |
| Craftsmen | 4 | 2.5 | 38 | 15.5 |
| Operatives | 0 | | 42 | 17.2 |
| All Laborers | 31 | 19.3 | 86 | 35.1 |
| Farmers | 121 | 75.1 | 4 | 1.6 |
| All Service | 3 | 1.9 | 26 | 10.6 |
| Missing | (2) | | (18) | |
| Not in the labor force | (735) | | (447) | |
| Total | 161 | 100.0 | 245 | 100.0 |
| Literacy | | | | |
| Read and write | 300 | 53.9 | 500 | 90.6 |
| Read only | 61 | 10.9 | 8 | 1.4 |
| Neither | 196 | 35.2 | 44 | 8.0 |
| Missing and Children | (341) | | (158) | |
| Total | 557 | 100.0 | 552 | 100.0 |

occupational group consists of laborers (19.3 percent), with most of these being farm laborers. The urban labor force is distributed among all the occupational groups with a significant proportion in each group except farmers.

Finally, there is a large difference in the level of literacy of the two populations. Ninety percent of the urban sample can both read and write. In the rural population only 53.9 percent can read and write, with an additional 10.9 percent who can only read.

### Household Composition

The characteristics of all Appalachian rural and urban sample households differ significantly on each dimension measured. The differences in the distribution of household types (Table 3) are the smallest of any variable. The rural population has a slightly greater proportion of nuclear family, and the more complex extended and multiple family types. The major differences in structural types is the proportion of nonfamily households: only one such household (.7 percent) is present in the rural sample, but nonfamily households constitute 7.4 percent of the urban sample.

A further difference is represented by the number of generations which the households span. In Pike County 10.7 percent of the households span one generation, and 18 percent span three or more generations; in Ashland, 18.1 percent of the households span one generation and only 9.4 percent span three or more generations.

Another major difference between the rural and urban Appalachian households is the number of persons resident, and some specific characteristics of these persons. The median number of persons in the rural

**TABLE 3. Distribution of Household Type by Urban-Rural Residence for Total Sample and Native Kentucky Subsample**

| Household Type | Rural | | Urban | |
|---|---|---|---|---|
| | N | % | N | % |
| Nonfamily | 1 | .7 | 11 | 7.4 |
| Nuclear Family | 113 | 75.3 | 107 | 71.8 |
| Extended Family | 23 | 15.3 | 15 | 10.1 |
| Multiple Family | 13 | 8.7 | 16 | 10.7 |
| Total | 150 | 100.0 | 149 | 100.0 |

$X^2 = 10.488$     df=3     $P<.05$

households is 6.4, while in the urban households the median number is 4.8. A large proportion of the inhabitants in the rural households are young children of the household head. The median number of children under the age of 18 in rural households is 3.8. Only 20.8 percent of the Pike County households have no children under 18 present, while 34.2 percent have five or more children under 18 present. Far fewer urban households have young children of the head resident; the median number of children under 18 is 1.6. Of the urban households, 36.9 percent have no children under 18 present, while only 5.4 percent have five or more children under 18 present. Unexpectedly, a significantly greater proportion of the urban households have older children of the head present.

The specific composition of the rural and urban households can be further illuminated by examining the distribution of relationship to the household head by the sex of the residents (Table 4). A greater proportion of the urban population (both males and females) have the status of household head or head's spouse than does the rural population. Conversely, a greater proportion of the rural population have the dependent statuses of child or grandchild. A higher percentage of the urban population includes siblings or siblings' children of the head, as well as there being more nonrelatives in the urban households. Females are twice as likely to be heads in urban households as they are in rural households.

Rural households appear to have a much greater tendency to have relatives living in nearby dwellings. Fewer than one-third of the Pike County households have no nearby households which do not share the

TABLE 4. Relationship to Household Head by Sex by Urban-Rural Residence

| Relationship to Household Head | Male[a] | | Female[b] | |
|---|---|---|---|---|
| | Rural | Urban | Rural | Urban |
| Head | 141  30.3 | 128  34.9 | 11  2.5 | 20  5.9 |
| Spouse | | | 132  30.5 | 120  35.6 |
| Child | 275  59.1 | 183  49.9 | 247  57.0 | 151  44.8 |
| Grandchild | 29  6.2 | 12  3.3 | 13  3.0 | 4  1.2 |
| Parent/Grandparent | 2  .4 | 4  1.1 | 13  3.0 | 12  3.6 |
| Sibling/Sibling's Child | 7  1.5 | 16  4.4 | 8  1.8 | 12  3.6 |
| Not Related | 11  2.4 | 30  6.5 | 9  2.1 | 18  5.3 |
| Total | 465  99.9 | 373  100.1 | 433  99.9 | 337  100.0 |

a $X^2 = 29.601$    df=5    $P<.05$
b $X^2 = 23.031$    df=6    $P<.05$

head's surname, while 82.5 percent of the Ashland households have no same surname households nearby. Of the urban households with nearby same surname households, most have only one such neighbor. Almost one-fifth of the rural households have four surname neighbors, and another one-fifth have three such neighbors.

## Interpretation and Conclusions

The data indicate differences in household composition are largely the result of industrialization in urban Ashland. The charateristics of 1900 rural Pike County households are very similar to those described since 1940 for more isolated traditional Appalachian neighborhoods (Brown, 1952a, 1952b; Bryant, 1981; Batteau, 1982). These characteristics include the presence of a large number of children, the infrequency of co-residing nonrelatives, the infrequency of co-residing siblings and other collaterals, and the tendency of relatives to live nearby. The 1900 Pike County data also indicate that children married young and left the parental household soon after marriage, and that older parents maintained separate households as long as possible.

The differences found to exist in the household composition of the rural and urban samples suggest two general conclusions. First, intraregional variation existed in Appalachian Kentucky as early as 1900, a period when the region is considered to have been relatively isolated from the mainstream of American society. The second conclusion is that Ashland's experience is a forerunner of household composition change in many rural Appalachian communities with the coming of industrialization, particularly commercial coal production. The exact nature of household and family change in the rural industrializing communities deserves further investigation.

*This project was supported by an Appalachian Studies Fellowship from the Appalachian Center, Berea College, Berea, Kentucky.

## REFERENCE

Batteau, Allen
    1982 Mosbys and Broomsedge: The Semantics of Class in an Appalachian Kinship System. American Ethnologist 9:445-466.

Bryant, F. Carlene
    1981 We're All Kin: A Cultural Study of a Mountain Neighborhood. Knoxville: University of Tennessee Press.

    1983 Family Group Organization in a Cumberland Mountain Neighborhood. In Allen Batteau, ed., Appalachia and America: Autonomy and Regional Dependence. Lexington: University Press of Kentucky.

Brown, James S.
   1952a The Farm Family in a Kentucky Mountain Neighborhood. Kentucky Agricultural Experiment Station Bulletin 587.

   1952b The Family Group in a Kentucky Mountain Farming Community. Kentucky Agricultural Experiment Station Bulletin 588.

Brown, James S., Harry K. Schwarzweller, and J. J. Mangalam
   1963 Kentucky Mountain Migration and the Stem-Family: An American Variation on a Theme by LePlay. Rural Sociology 28: 48-69.

Campbell, John C.
   1921 The Southern Highlander and His Homeland. New York: The Russell Sage Foundation.

Eller, Ronald D.
   1979 Land and Family: An Historical View of Preindustrial Appalachia. Appalachian Journal 6:83-109.

   1982 Miners, Millhands, and Mountaineers: Industrialization of the Appalachian South, 1880-1930. Knoxville: University of Tennessee Press.

Ford, Thomas R., ed.
   1962 The Southern Appalachian Region: A Survey. University of Kentucky Press.

Ford, Thomas R., Thomas A. Arcury, and Julia D. Porter
   1983 Changes in the Structure of Central Appalachian Mountain Families and Households, 1958-1976. CDC Development Paper No. 19, Center for Developmental Change, University of Kentucky.

Hammel, Eugene A., and Peter Laslett
   1974 Comparing Household Structure Over Time and Between Cultures. Comparative Studies in Society and History 16:1, 73-109.

Hicks, George L.
   1976 Appalachian Valley. New York: Holt, Rinehart and Winston.

Precourt, Walter
   1983 The Image of Appalachian Poverty. In Allen Batteau, ed., Appalachia and America: Autonomy and Regional Dependence. Lexington: University Press of Kentucky.

Schwarzweller, Harry K., James S. Brown, and J. J. Mangalam
   1971 Mountain Families in Transition: A Case Study of Appalachian Migration, University Park: Pennsylvania State University Press.

Smith, Daniel Scott, Michel Dahlin and Mark Friedberger
   1979 The Family Structure of the Older Black Population in the American South in 1880 and 1900. Sociology and Social Research 63:544-565.

Stephenson, John B.
   1968 Shiloh: A Mountain Community. Lexington: University of Kentucky Press.

**PRE-COLUMBIAN CHEROKEES**
Pre-Columbian Cultural Contact Between Chibchan and
Iroquoian Linguistic Groups
  David K. Evans; Wake Forest University; Winston-Salem, NC
**Man of Lightning** (Film)
  Gary Moss; Georgia State University; Atlanta, GA
  Convenor: Theda Perdue; Clemson University; Clemson, SC

# Pre-Columbian Cultural Contact Between Chibchan and Iroquoian Linguistic Groups

by
*David K. Evans*

Nowhere in this paper am I suggesting that the ancestors of the people in the mountains of North Carolina today known as the Cherokee, came from Central or South America. What I am saying, however, is that there is ample evidence to strongly suggest that much of the cultural past of these proud people may indeed have found its way up from the South. I will suggest that the people contacted by the whites, and called Cherokee, may well have been several peoples at an earlier date, and that fate and fortune, coupled with time, had welded the various cultures into one by the time of the first European contacts. My evidence for making this assumption will be archaeological, historical, linguistic, and ethnographical.

If I were asked to say just when and where this research began, I would say it was in Amubri, on a June evening in 1972, after the arrival of the swallows, but before the bats. Amubri, a Bribri Indian settlement, has a Catholic Mission station on the plain at the edge of the mountains of the Talamanca rain forest in Southern Costa Rica.

In June the swallows come, every evening, just before sunset. They dart about, ingesting insects on the wing. As the sun goes down behind the mountains, everything, including the birds in zig-zag flight, is cast in shades of red, orange, and gold, from the spectacular sunsets common to the region.

Almost at once, when the light fades, the swallows vanish, and the bats appear for their share of the insects. For me the appearance of the bats was always a sign to pump up the gas lamps for the evening—so

I know this research began before the bats took over where the swallows left off because there was still enough natural light in the sky to read by.

My students, all team members of Wake Forest University's Overseas Research Center, were drifting back from the river, where they had bathed. My wife and one of the Catholic Sisters had gone to find a guitar string, and I had climbed the wooden steps to the upper balcony of the building that served as the church, the school, warehouse, lab for my students and home for the two German priests who presided over the mission.

For two summers, among other things, I had been collecting clan names among the Bribri Indians and their mountain neighbors (and liguistic kin), the Cabecar. In checking these names against earlier accounts by W. M. Gabb and other writers of the last century, I had found that many were now extinct and long forgotten by all but the oldest of the Indians.

That evening, as I climbed the steps to work on my data on the clans, Padre Bernado Drüg, a German priest in his sixties with a huge salt and pepper beard, was waiting for me with a surprise—an original copy of H. de F. Pittier's work on the language of the Bribri, published in Vienna in 1898. Padre Bernardo knew that I had tried in vain to obtain a copy of this work. Although relatively little has been written on the Talamanca tribes, most that has has simply quoted extensively from two sources, Gabb (1875) and Pittier.

Albeit slightly worm eaten and smelling of mildew, with ample evidence of having been wet at some time in its long existence, Pittier's work was indeed a surprise and a delight for me. And, as I sat in a hammock with the book in my lap, there was still enough daylight for me to read the names of the clans that existed in this remote part of Central America toward the close of the 19th century.

Almost at once, I read the name *Arauuak*. Pittier translated this to be *Die Donner Haus Leute,* or *"The Thunder House People."* At once I wondered if the *Arauuak* could have been the *Arawak,* first described by Columbus as being the tall, peaceful, light-skinned natives he found on the island of Hispanola—now Haiti and the Domican Republic.

One surprise followed another as I read Pittier that night, first in the fading light and later by the precarious glow of that spitting, hissing field lamp. For years I had wondered about the early accounts of the *Arawak* the Spanish had met during their first contacts in the islands of the Greater Antilles. I knew that *Canoa* was an island Arawak word, carried over into Spanish and picked up by English as *canoe.* And Pittier indicated that there once existed, among the Chibchan speaking Bribri I was studying, an ancient clan known as the *Kęnô-thŭk-wȧk.* This Pittier translated as *"die schiffer"* oder *"die seeleute"* (1898:30). In English, of course, this would be *The Shippers* or *The People of the Sea,* with Keno = boat, u = house, or clan, and wak = people or family.

This was my first inkling that at least some ancient Bribri clans may have been seafarers. This led me to ask if it was possible that not only the *Keno-thuk-wak* were sea people, but that the *Arauuak (Thunder House People* or *People of Thunder)* may have been mariners as well?

I felt, that evening, that there was a strong likelihood that the island *Arawak* encountered by Columbus, and the ancient Bribri *Arauuak* were the same people. Speaking of the island *Arawak*, the American archaeologist, Irving Rouse, writing about the aboriginal inhabitants of the Greater Antilles, had written that "Arawak culture was . . . oriented towards the sea" . . . he later noted that . . . "the Awawak were probably seafarers" (1951:260). One thing I thought was obvious, both the *Bribri* and the ancient *Arawak* of Columbus' time spoke the same or similar Chibchan dialect. The evidence for me, at that time, was the word *Keno* in Bribri, that Columbus rendered Canoa in Spanish.

This, more or less, is where, how, and when this particular research began—all because of a rare work printed in Vienna in 1898, and a chance reading of that work in a bush mission station in Costa Rica—this, plus something else that came drifting up from my memory that evening, something I had read in the 1875 writings by William Gabb. I searched through my field copy and there it was—page 571—where Gabb, perhaps puzzled, had written,

> ". . . a curious coincidence exists in the fact that in the island of Santo Domingo (the Hispaniola of Columbus), where there are no venomous reptiles, a poisonous plant, retaining its native name, is called by the people, ki-be."

Kebe, in Bribri, means snake, and Gabb had written the above as a brief footnote beside the word in this Bribri vocabulary. His "curious coincidence," to me of course, was now neither curious nor a coincidence, because I was beginning to believe that it was quite probable that at least some of the Caribbean inhabitants described by Columbus as Arawak were in reality "People of Thunder," and were, or had been at some time past, a clan of the Bribri.

## The Cherokee Connection

Long ago, the 19th century Cherokee Chief, William P. Ross, in discussing the mysterious origins of his ancient people, was quoted as having said:

> "No response comes down the gallery of time from the silent recesses of the past. Echo alone replies, where and whence came they" (1893).

That silence has puzzled me for the past decade or so, and this paper is an attempt to shed some light on the question, from "where and whence" came the Cherokee.

I am under no illusion that I have discovered an ethnographic or linguistic or historical fact that is new, but only wish to bring my data to the attention of others who may be better qualified than I to examine these ideas. I am aware that it has long been the custom of some to relegate data such as I present in this paper into the limbo of fairy tales. Nevertheless in the light of the data present here, I hope that perhaps, behind these artifacts, myths, and legends, there may well lie a grain or two of historical fact.

## Archaeological Evidence

There is today a great deal of archaeological evidence to support quite early migrations of people from the South into what is now Florida and the Gulf Coast.

It may well be that many different small groups of people came up either the Central American—Yucatan—Florida route, or by way of island-hopping to Cuba and then crossing the 96 mile channel to Florida. The fact is, we have historical evidence that the Florida channel was crossed by Indian canoes and apparently quite frequently. Peter Martyr recorded that "natives of the mainland were accustomed to visiting the Lucayas Islands (Bahamas) in order to take pigeons, returning with their canoes laden" (Sauer:189). Carl Sauer thought that it may well have been such seafaring natives who informed the Spanish of a fountain of youth to be found on an island known to the natives as Bimini (Sauer:190).

More solid evidence is to be found in archaeological sites such as Crystal River in Florida, where a temple site reported to be Mayan, dates to A.D. 440 (Bullen:861). And certainly the archaeology of Florida east of Pensacola Bay would seem to indicate that many groups may have visited the area more-or-less around the same point in time. Holmes tells us that, "The manner of occurence of the ceramic remains of the Gulf region is interesting. In many cases several varieties of ware are intermingled on a single site" (Holmes 1888:104).

Of special interest to the possibility that there may be a Southern, tropical origin of *some* Cherokee cultural traits, however, is what Holmes wrote on the next page. He wrote, "Strangely enough, in the national collections from southwestern Alabama there are a lot of sherds exhibiting typical features of the peculiar pottery of New York State, which seem to belong to the Iroquoian tribes."

Holmes went on the speculate, "that the museum record may be defective and that the association is accidental" (p. 105). It is possible, however, the Holmes' observation that Iroquoian-type ware was in the South is not "strange," nor is the fact that it associates so well with the North "accidental." It may well be that the museum records are in no way "defective," but that these records simply did not fit the preconceived notions of the archaeology of the 1880's.

Holmes had noted that here and there along the Gulf Coast are certain pieces of pottery that do not affiliate with the ordinary ware, yet at the same time appear to present closer analogies with the wares of Yucatan and the Caribbean islands. It was noted that on the Gulf Coast of Florida, at Point Washington site, just South of Jolly Bay, several "exotics," or non-local ware are found. The "exotics" are the stamped ware of the Appalachian district to the North. Holmes went on to say that the techniques used among some of this ware gives . . . "a striking effect and reminding one of Central American methods of treatment" (109).

What was so odd was that though typical of the Southern Appalachian mountains, homeland of the Cherokee, this stamped pottery was "seen at a glance to embody the commonest concepts of the Gulf Coast groups" (110).

Another intriguing bit of archaeological evidence that may directly link the Cherokee with the cultures of the South is that in one mound, believed by Thomas to have been the work of the Cherokee, copper bells were found. Thomas apparently did not credit the ancient Cherokee with the ability to produce such copper bells, for in writing about a number of small copper "hawk-bells" found with the skeleton of a child, Thomas observed,

> "They are precisely of the form of the ordinary sleigh bell of the present day, but with pebbles and shell beads for rattles" (p. 34).

He then added:

> ". . . that the bells indicate contact with Europeans must be conceded" (p. 35).

This strikes one as a rather strange conclusion for Thomas to have drawn, and can be challenged on at least two points:

1. If the bells were indeed European artifacts, why would the Indians remove the usual metal ball or clapper and replace it with clay balls or shell beads? And,
2. I have seen many of these same type copper hawk-bells, with clay balls or small rock clappers, dug from pre-Columbian sites on Roatán Island in the Western Caribbean, and I have seen gold bells of the very same type, again with similar clappers, from the Limón Coast of Costa Rica and from Bribri grave sites in the mountainous interior of the Talamanca rain forest.

Such bells are thought to have preceeded all known European contacts in the New World by centuries. In fact, Columbus reported such copper bells in the huge canoe he seized on his last voyage to the Indies in 1502.

## Linguistic Evidence

What I hope to do in this paper is simply list some of the data that supports my theory that some aspects of the culture of the Cherokee, found in the Appalachian Mountains when the Europeans first made contact in 1540, had been in some ways influenced by cultures from the South, and that the primary influence may have been from seafaring Chibchan speaking peoples from the Antilles and Central America.

We know, from early writers, that there were mysterious groups of people in contact with the Cherokee. One such people was known to James Mooney as the Taskigi. He wrote about them saying, "who or what the Taskigi were is uncertain and can probably never be known, but they were neither Cherokee nor Muscogee proper." He went on to add that . . . "It is not a Cherokee word, and Cherokee informants state positively that the Taskigi were a foreign people, with distinct language and customs" (389).

Another mysterious group, well-known to those who have studied the Cherokee, is the *Ani̊-kuta'ni*. Of them Mooney writes, "Among other perishing traditions is that relating to the Ani-kuta'ni . . . concerning whom the modern Cherokee know so little that their very identity is now a matter of dispute, a few holding that they were an ancient people who preceeded the Cherokee and built the mounds, while others, with more authority, claim that they were a clan or society in the tribe and were destroyed long ago by pestilence or other calamity" (392).

Joseph B. Mahan, Jr. writes . . . "Mooney continues to the effect that from the various statement, it would seem that the *Ani̊-kuta'ni'* were a priestly clan, having hereditary supervision of all religious ceremonies among the Cherokee. In consequence of having abused their sacred privileges, they were attacked and completely exterminated by the rest of the tribe, leaving the priestly functions to be assumed thereafter by individual doctors and conjurers" (184-85).

Hayword, in his *History of Tennessee,* quoted a Cherokee as saying that the ancient priests of the Cherokee had been destroyed (249), and John Ross spoke of the *Nicotani,* described as a mystical, religious body, of whom the Cherokee people stood in great awe. Where they came from is no longer known, and all that can be said for certain about their passing was that they were massacred by the Cherokee themselves because one or more of them interfered with the wife or wives of a prominent Cherokee. It was said, "His wife was remarkable for her beauty, and was forcibly abducted and violated by one of the Nicotani" (MacGowan 1866:139).

If they really existed, it would seem that Ross' *Nicotani* were probably the same *Ani:kuta'ni'* described by Mooney. But who were these ancient, mysterious and foreign people among the Cherokee, and from where did they come?

It is suggested here that they were Chibchan speakers, and that they had come, originally, from Central and possibly Northern South America, and had eventually reached the Gulf Coast and Florida via the islands of the Greater Antilles.

Mooney further tells us that the Cherokee call themselves *Ani-yunwiya*, and he notes that this means "real people" or "principal people." Bantram (297) spelled it *Ani kitu hwa*. Mooney tells us that no occasion the Cherokee referred to themselves as *Kitu'hwa*. He noted that this was an ancient settlement on the Tuckasegee river and thought this might have been ". . . the orginial nucleus of the tribe" (1900:15).

These bits of linguistic information from the Cherokee are of interest to my basic thesis that they, in their remote past, had been in contact with Chibchan speaking peoples from the South.

The Cherokee term *Ani,'* used as a prefix, would make perfectly good sense even today to the Bribri with whom I have worked in the Talamanca rain forest of Costa Rica. The Bribri use the identical prefix *Ani'* to refer to "we." In their Chibchan dialect the prefix breaks down into a' (you) and ni' (me) to mean "we" or "us" as opposed to others.

The suffix "wa" as found in the word *kitū hwa*, which Mooney tells us was also used among the Cherokee to describe a region, village and a dialect, as well as the people themselves, translates in Bribri to mean "people." The u sound, found in the middle of the Cherokee word *kitu hwa* translates into Bribri as "house" or "clan," and finally, *kit,* translates to mean a "cord" or a "vein" or "binding material" in Bribri.

The Cherokee *Ani:ū-wa*, taken together in Bribri, translates to mean "we people of the same house" and Mooney's "kit-ū-hwa" translates to mean "People bound together, or "people of the same vein," or perhaps "people of the same blood."

Bartram's spelling of *Ani-kita-hwa* would translate beautifully in Chibchan to this day, as *We people bound of the same cord* (297).

But if the Cherokee call themselves *Ani-kitu-hwa*, then what does the word *Cherokee* itself mean, and from where did it come? The name Cherokee has no meaning whatsoever to the people known today as the Cherokee. Why? The answer, I believe, is because the word *Cherokee* is Chibchan and not an Iriquois word at all.

Lying just to the South of the Bribri region in Talamanca, across the border in what is now Panama, there exists a large lagoon, known even today by its Indian name—*Chiriqui.* As with the Cherokee of Mooney's time, the Chibchan language lumped the inhabitants, the quiet bay, and other landmarks, as well as the entire region itself, under the term *Chiriqui*. Thus the people from this region were referred to as the *Chiriqui* (Sauer:127).

It should be pointed out, however, that the Indians of this region would not necessarily refer to themselves as *Chiriqui*, unless specifically asked, "from where do you come?" More than likely, the Spanish would have asked them their name or "what do you call yourself?" to which they would probably refer to their *clan* or *family* name.

It seems quite likely that something like this would explain why Columbus was so puzzled when he labelled all of the Indians of Haiti *Arawak* and then tried unsuccessfully to use them as interpreters on Cuba. The Spanish had asked them what they called themselves and they had replied Ará-ū-wak, *"Thunder House People,"* or *"People of the House of Thunder."* But Columbus had assumed that all Indians in the Antilles were *Arawaks* and spoke the same dialect and thus had run into translation difficulties later in Cuba.

In returning to our discussion of the Central American region known as *Chiriqui*, however, Peter Martyr recorded other people of this region who did not appear quite like their neighbors. He tells of the Spanish fighting against men as "bearded as any bearded Christian." The record reads, "In this Escoria there was a breed of Indians much larger than the others and better conditioned" (Sauer 271).

Apparently, these unusual Indians fought from mounds protected by palisades, the Spanish reported "forts made with two or three enclosures of timber and large trees and very great moat around" . . . and added ". . . these could well pass for good forts in Italy" (Sauer 271).

We hear again, some two centuries later, of the Indians in the region of *Chiriqui*. An Englishman, by the name of John Cockburn, published a book in London in 1779, entitled *"The Unfortunate Englishman"* in which he gives an account of having been marooned in this region and having walked northward seeking an English settlement. In his account he tells of tall Indians of light skin, fighting from well-made forts, who had the habit of painting their faces *red and black* before battle. He adds that they were called by others in the region the *Cherokee*.

Although Cockburn's *Cherokee* is simply an *anglicized* spelling of *Chiriqui*, it does present evidence that a people in that region of Central America were still being referred to by that name by others near the close of the 18th century (Cockburn 1779:147), *and*, that these people with the same name exhibited cultural practices of fighting from behind palisades with their faces painted, *red and black*.

At once this brings to mind the practice of the Eastern Cherokee of the Appalachians. We are told that ". . . an oration by the war speaker anticipated the formal departure of a war party. When they ventured forth, they were elaborately painted red and black" (Oswalt 1973:509).

Cockburn's account is intriguingly similar to a report written about the same time concerning Indians believed to have been the Cherokee in the mountains of Western North Carolina and Northern Georgia.

Heckewelder's encounter with the Cherokee, later described by Thomas in 1890, reads as follows . . .

> "They are said to have been remarkably tall . . . it is related that they built to themselves regular fortifications or entrenchments from which they would sally out."

Such fortification was described as "properly entrenchments, being walls or banks of earth regularly thrown up, with a deep ditch on the outside" (Thomas:12:13).

It becomes clear that in 1540 De Soto's chroniclers were accurate in their descriptions of the mounds they passed by in the mountains of North Georgia and North Carolina. They had noted that such mounds were not only fortified with huge timbers, but protected by vast moats as well. This all too well brings to mind not only fortified, moat-ringed, mounds described by Cockburn in the Central American region of *Chiriqui* but the great mound known as *Etowah* in the Southern Appalachians of North Georgia.

*Etowah*, likewise, is not a Cherokee word. However, following Pittier, one could translate *Etowah* as *Et-ū-wak*, meaning in Chibchan "that" or "it" "which was once of our people" (cf. Pittier:74). Again, if one considers the ancient name Mooney informs us the Cherokee used for themselves on occasion—*Kitū-wha*, and remember that in Mooney's day he found three dialects in use, it would seem possible that both words are of Chibchan origin and were perhaps introduced by those mysterious foreigners who for a time at least, resided with the Cherokee and were held by them in such awe (cf. Chiltoskey 1972:54).

If we add to the above, place names found in the Central American region of *Chiriqui* and in the Appalachian mountain homeland of the Cherokee at the time of contact, we have even more linguistic evidence of possible contact.

For example, Bartram notes that in 1777 he visited a war town called *Coweta*. He tells us the town was near or on the Chattahoochee River. On the Southeast coast of Costa Rica today, South of Puerto Limón and near the Rio Estrella, is located a town named after the Chibchan word for the district and an ancient Indian settlement. In Spanish this name has come down to us *ca-hui-ta*. A perfect English rendition of the Spanish is the name of Bartram's 18th century Cherokee war town—*Coweta!*

Moreover, as with the Chibchan language, Mooney, writing about the Cherokee language in 1894, tells us "It may be noted that as a rule the Cherokee and some other tribes have no names for rivers or settlements." Just as with the people of Central America, Mooney noted that in the past, among the Cherokee "... The name belongs to the district, and is applied alike to the stream and to the town or mountain situated within it" (1894:xxix).

My basic theory is that Chibchan speakers, at some time past, made their way northwards by sea, perhaps reaching the Gulf Coast and Florida as the archaeological record suggest. It is in this region that I am suggesting these Chibchan seafarers encountered Iroquois speaking Indians and, affiliating themselves with them, introduced words and cultural practices from the Antilles and Central America.

One such word, which seems to support my theory of ancient contact between the Iroquoian linguistic family (of which most linguists agree Cherokee is related) and the now extinct Arawak of the Western Antilles, is *"canoe."* As noted at the beginning of this paper, the English word *"canoe"* is clearly derived from the Spanish *canoa*, which was taken directly from the Arawak word *keno*.

I want to stress that this word was not only found among the now extinct island Arawak of Columbus' day, but is to be found today among both the Bribri of Costa Rica and the Northern Iroquoin speakers of New York and Canada.

Dr. Marianne Williams, a noted linguist specializing in the Iroquoian language, upon my inquiring, informed me that,

"... (concerning) ... the words boat in Iroquoian, in Northern Iroquoian it is a nice, clean cognate set."

|  |  |  |
|---|---|---|
| | Seneca | — Kaãwãa |
| | Cayuga | — Khá õ we |
| Five Nations | Onondaga | — kah' õ weh |
| | Mohawk | — Kahū we=yá |
| | Oneida | — kahūwakû |

It would seem at a glance that if one takes the Bribri word for boat *Kéno* and adds the Bribri suffix *uák* or *wák*, or *u-wa* to denote "clan," "tribe," or "people," then the Iroquoian word Kahõweh, with the proper tonal sounds, would be understood by the Bribri even today to mean *"People of the Sea."* It is probable that the non-seafaring Iroquois, simply transferred the entire name for the seafaring people they encountered into their language to mean boat.

One more bit of evidence to suggest that this is precisely what they did is the rather unusual word used by the Bribri to denote net or woven bags. They used this word from the tiny bags carried over the shoulder by jungle hunters to large cargo nets with straps to fit the shoulders and head. The Bribri name for such bags is *Chá'cara*, a most unusual word. This same word among the Iroquoian dialects has retained the Bribri meaning in its *entirety* as well. I am told by Dr. Williams that *Chácara*, the net carrying bags of the Bribri, would today among the Iroquois translate as "a container."

Frank G. Speck, writing in the 1920's, theorized that the culture of the Cherokee, and perhaps the Iroquois too, may have had their origins in the tropical rain forests of the South. In building his case, Speck noted that none of the Southern tribes except the Cherokees, and possibly the Catawbas, "rimmed their baskets with a thin oak loop bound fast with a hickory fibre withe."

He also noted that this particular characteristic of basket making is to be found in the Orinoco and Amazon basins. This is precisely from where many linguists and archaeologists think the original Chibchan language families dispersed northward (Speck 1920).

Consider yet more linguistic evidence linking the Iroquoian dialects with the Chibchan speakers in the South. As was noted above, one of the five Iroquois nations is the *Cayuga*. Today the word is used among the inhabitants of the Bay Islands of Honduras in Central America, and elsewhere in the Western Caribbean to mean an Indian dugout boat. On Roatán Island, if the dugout has been finished with decking and small motor, it is referred to by the English term "dory." If it is roughly finished, unpainted and without motor, being propelled by paddle and rude sail, it is known to this day as a *"cayuga,"* the very same word used today as the name of one of the 5 Iroquois Nations in New York and Canada (Evans:52).

I would like to end this paper with a look at historical and ethnographic accounts that would seem to link the Cherokee with Antillean and Central American cultures in times past.

At Puerto Limón, Costa Rica, the first Spanish landfall on the mainland of the New World, Columbus reported finding cloth made from the inner bark of certain trees. The Bribri call this cloth *mastate* (made from, among other species, the *Brosimum costaricensis* tree (Stone:22). There are many accounts of Cherokee bark cloth, the technique for making it, and its uses, and others before me have tried to link this cultural artifact with the South. And a Southern link seems also to be warranted to account for the method of poisoning fish, with the Bribri crushing the inner bark of the *Habillo* tree and the Cherokee poisoning their fish with toxin made by crushing horse chestnuts (Miling 1940:18).

Mention should perhaps be made at this point of the blow gun, known today among both the Bribri and the Cherokee. The blow gun is most certainly a tropical hunting weapon. And both the Bribri and the Cherokee support shoulder bags in association with the blow gun. The difference here is that while the Bribri carry in their bag clay pellets and several bones to smooth and calibrate the unfired clay balls to match the bore of their blow guns, the Cherokee missile is a dart, supposedly poisoned.

As for history, it too has something to add; for example, Carl Sauer, in his excellent account of the early Spanish Main, tells us that,

> "Dogs that did not bark were noted by Columbus. These were found throughout the islands, and later around the Caribbean and beyond. They were small, Las Casas said, the size of a lap dog, and were eaten—indeed were kept to be eaten" (1966:59).

Listen now to Mooney, as he reminds us that De Soto was welcomed among the Cherokee somewhere near what is now the Western N. C. mountain town of Murphy. He tells us the Spanish were greeted in 1540 by Cherokees with "a little corn and many wild turkeys, together with some dogs of a peculiar small species, which were bred for eating purposes and did not bark" (1900:25, see also Ranjel, in Oviedo, Historia General y Natural de las Indies, I, p. 652, Madrid 1851).

To go on now, and describe similar burial practices, similar medical practices, similar myths and artifacts, even a similar God in a similar heaven, would be possible but perhaps tiresome to the reader.

What I believe at this point in my research, is that in seeking the Cherokee's past only in the North with their linguistic kin, the Iroquois, we have been but seeking a part of their cultural past. And that by turning Southward we may, to misquote the Cherokee chief with whom I began this paper, find indeed that if we look hard enough, and listen well, some faint response may indeed come down the gallery of time from the silent recesses of the past, and that, little by little, we may discover from "where and whence came they."

## BIBLIOGRAPHY

Bartram, William
    1928 *Travels of William Bartram*, Mark Van Doren, ed., (N.P.), Dover Publishers

Bourne, E. G., Ed.
    1904 Narratives of the Career of Hernando de Soto, 2 vol. New York

Bullen, Ripley P.
    1966 "Stelae at the Crystal River Site, Florida" *American Antiquity*, Vol. 31, no. 6: 861-865, October

Cockburn, John
    1779 *The Unfortunate Englishman*, London

Columbus, C.
    1930 *The Voyages of Christopher Columbus*, Newly translated and edited by Cecil Jane, London

Conzemius, Edward
    1926 On the Aborigines of the Bay Islands (Honduras), Roma, atti del XXII, Congresso Internazionale degli Americanist: Settembre

Davidson, William V.
    1974 Historical Geography of the Bay Islands, Honduras, Southern University Press

Evans, David K.
    1966 The People of French Harbour: A Study of Conflict and Change on Roatan Island, Honduras. University of California, Berkeley, Ph.D. Dissertation Unpublished

Ford, James
    1966 "Early Formative Cultures in Georgia and Florida," *American Antiquity,* vol. 31, no. 6, October: 781799

Gabb, Wm. M.
    1895 *On the Tribes and Languages of Costa Rica,* American Philosophical Society, Vol. XIV, August: 483-602

Holmes, W. H.
    1903 "Aboriginal Pottery of the Eastern United States," 20th Annual Report Bureau of Ethnology, Washington, D.C.

Holmes, W. H.
    1888 "Ancient Art of the Province of Chiriqui," 6th Annual Report, Bureau of Ethnology, Washington, D.C.

MacGowan, D. J.
    "Indian Secret Societies" *Historical Notes and Queries concerning the Antiquities of America X,* (Morrisania, N.Y.: Henry B. Dawson)

Mahan, Joseph B., Jr.
    1969 *Identification of the Tsoyaha Waeno Builders of Temple Mounds,* (Ph.D. Dissertation, University of North Carolina, Chapel Hill

Mooney, James
    1894 "Administrative Report," 11th Annual Report of the Bureau of Ethnology (1889-90) Smithsonian Institution, Washington, D.C.

Mooney, James
    1900 *Myths of the Cherokee,* 19th Annual Report of the U.S. Bureau of American Ethnology to the Secretary of the Smithsonian Institution 1897-98, Washington, D.C.

Navarrete, M.F. De
    1825-32 Coleccion de los viajes y descubrimientos, que hicieron por marlos espanoles desde fines del siglo XV, 5 vols., Madrid

Oswalt, Wendell H.
    1973 "The Eastern Cherokee: Farmers of the Southeast," *This Land Was Theirs,* John Wiley and Sons, New York

Oviedo
    1959 *Historia general y natural de las India.* Bib. Antores Espanoles, vol. 67-71, Madrid

Pittier, H. deFabrega
    1898 Die Sprache der Bribri—Indianer in Costa Rica Sitzungsberichte, Band CXXXVIII, Wien

Ross, William P.
    1893 *The Life and Times of Honorable William P. Ross of the Cherokee Nation,* Mrs. Wm. P. Ross, ed., Fort Smith

Rouse, Irving
    1964 "Prehistory of the West Indies," *Science* 144:499-513

Rouse, Irving
    1966 "Mesoamerica and the Eastern Caribbean Area," *Archaeological Frontiers and External Connections*, Handbook of Middle American Indians, vol. 4, Robert Wauchope, ed., 234-242

Sauer, Carl O.
    1966 *The Early Spanish Main*, University of California Press, Berkely and Los Angeles

Speck, Frank G.
    1920 *Decorative Art and Basketry of the Cherokees*, Milwaukee

Stone, Doris
    1962 *The Talamancan Tribes of Costa Rica*, Peabody Museum of Archaeology and Ethnology, Harvard, Cambridge, vol. XLII, no. 2

Stone, Doris
    1966 "Synthesis of Lower Central American Ethnology," Vol. 4, Handbook of Middle America Indian, Robert Wauchope, ed., Austin

Thomas, Cyrus
    1890 *The Cherokees in Pre-Columbian Times*, N.D.C. Hodges publisher, New York

NORTH GEORGIA WRITERS—PAST AND PRESENT
These Also Climbed Parnassus
  Paul McClure; N. Georgia College; Dahlonega, GA
Works of Byron Herbert Reese
  Raymond Cook; Valdosta, GA
  Readings by Bettie Sellers; Young Harris College; Young Harris, GA
  Convenor: Julia Evatt; Ellijay, GA

# These Also Climbed Parnassus: An Overview of Georgia Mountain Authors

by
*Paul McClure*

Most of the acclaim that has come to Southern Appalachian writers has come to those from Kentucky, Tennessee, and North Carolina. Relatively little recognition has been achieved by writers from the mountains of North Georgia, but they too have contributed significantly to our mountain heritage, from the early nineteenth century to the present day.

Most nineteenth-century literature set in the Georgia mountains was produced by lowlanders, some of whom had at best an imperfect understanding of the region and its people. Probably the first of these was William Gilmore Simms, whose novel *Guy Rivers* (1834), involving frontier violence and intrigue in what is now the Cleveland-Dahlonega area, shows the influence of James Fenimore Cooper and Sir Walter Scott. However, it reveals little understanding of the Georgia mountains.

After the Civil War came Sidney Lanier, whose poems show a great love for nature and the land. Especially noteworthy is "Song of the Chattahoochee," which personifies the wild, uncontrollable river singing happily in its mad rush "out of the hills of Habersham/Down the valleys of Hall," answering the call of Duty to water the plain. As a result mainly of this one poem, Lake Lanier and many other things in northeast Georgia have been named for this poet.

Joel Chandler Harris is usually remembered as the creator of Uncle Remus, but he also wrote a few stories depicting north Georgia mountaineers. His long-short story "At Teague Poteet's," which appeared in a volume called *Mingo and Other Sketches in Black and White* (1884) reveals considerable insight into the hill-dweller's personality and lifestyle. The title character is so fiercely independent that he refuses to fight for either side in the Civil War. He shoots at recruiters for both sides when they approach his cabin. Later he gives the same treatment to "revenuers" when they approach his still. Another story, "Trouble on Lost Mountain," in the volume *Free Joe and Other Georgian Sketches* (1887), reveals the tragic results of the jealousy that separates two young mountain lovers because of the presence of a stranger in their midst, who, ironically, is unaware that he is the focus of the trouble until it is too late. The story presents all three characters sympathetically and ends on a note of pathos. Both these stories show Harris' keen ear for dialect as well as his understanding of human nature.

Roughly contemporary with Harris was his friend Harry Stillwell Edwards of Macon, whose story "An Idyl of Sinkin' Mountain" takes place near Tallulah Falls. First published in *Century Magazine* in 1888, it was later included in Edwards' collection *Two Runaways and Other Stories* (1889). It is the story of a young, poverty-stricken mountaineer in his search for true love and a decent living. He eventually finds both on his own farm—a mica deposit is discovered there, and he falls in love with an orphan girl whom his mother had taken in but he had heretofore regarded somewhat as a sister. The story suffers from some lack of realism and from the author's imitation of the characters and dialect of Mary Murfree. Edwards, who knew little of the mountains in the 1880's, came to know them better in the 1920's, when he wrote several newspaper sketches with a mountain setting.

The one native north Georgian to receive much literary fame in the nineteenth century was humorist Charles Henry Smith of Cartersville, known to his readers as "Bill Arp." He started writing in 1861 in the form of an "open letter" to President Lincoln, which he read to some of his backwoods friends near Rome, one of whom was named Bill Arp, who asked Smith what name he was going to use when he published the letter. Smith replied that he had not yet decided on a name. So Bill said, "Well, squire, I wish you would print mine, for them's my sentiments."[1] Smith continued to use the name "Bill Arp" in over 2000 informal essays published as "open letters" in Atlanta newspapers and elsewhere until his death in 1903. These "letters" were collected in several books over the years; three of the best-known are *Bill Arp, So Called* (1866), Bill Arp's Peace Papers (1873), and *The Farm and the Fireside* (1891). Over the years the *persona* of Bill Arp changed from that of a semi-literate backwoodsman to that of a cultivated Southern gentleman who used impeccable English. But the earlier sketches, which used mountain dialect and rough frontier humor, are more interesting.

In the early twentieth century, the most prolific of all Georgia mountain writers, Will N. Harben of the Dalton-Chatsworth area, wrote a number of novels and short stories which poignantly and faithfully depict the people of that region, although a few have their settings largely in other parts of the country. Although he published his first novel, *White Marie*, in 1889, he did not become really well known until his volume of short stories, *Northern Georgia Sketches*, appeared in 1900. It received favorable notice from William Dean Howells, who asked Harben for a novel to be published by *Harper's*. Harben's reply was the novel *Westerfelt*, which had been heretofore rejected but was published in *Harper's* in 1901. It is the story of "a common man dogged by guilt after the suicide of a girl who loved him hopelessly."[2] Altogether Harben wrote over twenty-five novels and other books before his death in 1919. Of these, *Ann Boyd* (1906) is usually regarded as Harben's most powerful work of fiction.

However, perhaps the most interesting of Harben's novels in terms of our Appalachian heritage is *Pole Baker* (1905). Though it begins slowly, it soon captures the reader's interest, not so much in the title character as in the whole cast, for it is more the story of a whole community than of one man. The irony is that Pole Baker, a poor, barely literate dirt farmer with a serious drinking problem, is throughout the novel a stabilizing influence on the rest of the community, including his wealthy friend Nelson Floyd. Floyd eventually emerges as the central character with an identity crisis to solve and problems in his love affair with Cynthia Porter, whose mother hates Floyd and tries both fair means and foul to separate the lovers. But with common sense and elementary investigative methods, Pole Baker solves Floyd's identity problem, brings the lovers together, and inadvertently finds a better life for himself as well. This novel, while somewhat inauspicious in terms of dialect and other local-color aspects, is more original in plot and characterization than most other mountain novels, especially those of the early twentieth century. It may be that Will Harben is one of the most underrated novelists of his age.

Around the turn of the century Corra Harris, who as a Methodist minister's wife lived in several communities in north Georgia, began to write stories and articles for various periodicals. In 1910 appeared her first and most famous novel, *A Circuit Rider's Wife*. It tells the story of Mary Thompson's trials and joys as a minister's wife in rural north Georgia. Though influenced by the author's own experiences, it is not predominantly autobiographical. It later served as the basis for the popular motion picture *I'd Climb the Highest Mountain*, which premiered in the early 1950's. There were also two sequels to this novel: *A Circuit Rider's Widow* (1916) and *My Son* (1921). Corra Harris also wrote a number of other novels, all highly popular in their day but usually criticized today for their overt didacticism. She also wrote a few satires on small-town politics and on the church hierarchy. Some of her later books, especially *My Book and My Heart* (1924), are more obviously autobiographical than her earlier works. During the last several years of her life she lived in a cabin near Pine Log Mountain in Bartow County and wrote a column called "A Candlelit Column" for the *Atlanta Journal*, until her death in 1935.

Her works were among the most wholesome and inspiring of popular fiction.

Tastes in literature began to change in the 1920's, and that change was reflected in the works of Lillian Smith when she began writing in the 1930's. Born in Florida, she moved with her parents to Clayton in her teens. There her father managed a hotel and a youth camp, which she herself directed for a time. Her first novel, *Strange Fruit* (1944), with its story of an interracial love affair, outraged most Southerners and was banned as obscene in some places. Nevertheless, it was so popular that a dramatized version was performed on Broadway for a time. She also wrote a half-dozen other books, but like *Strange Fruit*, they can hardly be called Appalachian literature on the basis of setting or theme. Lillian Smith can be called a Georgia mountain writer only by virtue of her having resided in the region for a number of years.

The first prominent Georgia mountain native poet was Byron Herbert Reece of Union County. A quintessential mountaineer, reared in the remote Choestoe Valley, he remained a dirt farmer as well as a poet his whole short, tortured life. Yet no poetry evokes the spirit of the mountains, of nature, and of the soil more than his. Though he published some poetry in obsure poetry journals as a youth, it was only after the encouragement and recommendation of Jesse Stuart that he received much notice. His first book of poetry, *Ballad of the Bones* (1945), was well received, as was his novel *Better a Dinner of Herbs* (1950). He served for a time as poet-in-residence at UCLA and later did the same at Emory, but ill health forced him to return home. For the last few years of his life he served as poet-in-residence and teacher at Young Harris College, near his home. His suicide in 1958 was a tragic waste of a prodigious talent.

Another Georgia mountain native who became a notable poet is Don West. Born in 1906 in a one-room cabin in the almost inaccessible Devil's Hollow in Gilmer County, he grew up with very little schooling, but showed early a great love for books. His uncle, who had fought in World War I, saw to it that he had a chance to enroll in the Berry School near Rome, Georgia. There he learned fast, but he left Berry in his junior year as a result of his stand in favor of a teacher who was fired. Thus began West's involvement in controversy, his championing of those whom he regarded as victims of injustice, which has marked his career ever since. After working for a few years, he enrolled in Lincoln Memorial University, where he became a friend of Jesse Stuart and later became involved in more controversy. As a graduate student at Vanderbilt he received a fellowship to study in Denmark. At Vanderbilt he wrote his first book of poetry, called *Crab-Grass* (1931). He also attended other institutions of higher learning, but, as he puts it, "My real education has been beaten into me by the everlasting toil and hunger I've seen, by the struggles in textile and coal-mining centers, where our people were tolled down from the hills with fair promises of a better life . . ."³ The poverty and oppression suffered by mountain people has been a major concern of his, and for this reason much of his poetry is anti-establishment. Its weakness is that it often sounds like propaganda, but some of his poetry rises to lyric heights comparable with that of the best mountain poets. During the last few decades he has lived mainly in West Virginia, where until recently he directed the Appalachian South Folklife Center. His principal books of poetry include *Clods of Southern Earth* (1946), *The Road Is Rocky* (1951), and *O Mountaineers* (1974).

Poetry continues to flow from the pens of north Georgians today. Bettie Sellers of Young Harris, whose first book of poetry, *Westward from Bald Mountain*, appeared about a decade ago, now has published several other works and is currently engaged in a highly ambitious series of poems. She is only one of several north Georgia poets who are gaining a reputation outside the region as well as in it. In addition, such nationally known poets as James Dickey have set a number of their works in the Georgia mountains.

North Georgians are continuing to produce prose, too. Terry Kay has written a delightful novel called *After Eli*, set in the Nacoochee Valley; Julia Evatt of Ellijay has attracted considerable notice with her "Leland Benjamin" stories; and Gloria Stargel of Gainesville has brought inspirational narrative back into vogue (at least in Georgia) with her autobiographical story *The Healing*. perhaps the most interesting contemporary prose writer in terms of our Georgia mountain heritage is Jimmy Townsend of Jasper, whose brand of homespun philosophy in *Mountain Echoes, Wait Jest a Cotton-Pickin' Minute*, and other works bears comparison to that of Mark Twain and Will Rogers. Still another prose writer of note is Lt. Gov. Zell Miller of Towns County, whose book *The Mountains Within Me* contains much of the essence of our Appalachian heritage.

In view of this continuing and ongoing production of literature by people from the Georgia mountains, this heritage seems in no danger of fading into obscurity. In fact, the literary future of the region looks bright.

## NOTES

[1] Joseph H. Baird, "Bill Arp's Humor in the Bleak South," *Atlanta Journal and Constitution Magazine*, Oct. 18, 1970, pp. 18-19.

[2] Robert Bush, in *Southern Writers: A Biographical Dictionary*, ed. Robert Bain et al. (Baton Rouge: LSU Press, 1979), p. 200.

[3] *In a Land of Plenty: A Don West Reader* (Minneapolis: West End Press, 1982), pp. 6-7.

THE BUSINESS OF TRADITION: TRADES, HANDICRAFTS
AND HOUSEHOLD ENTERPRISES
The Shell Button Industry in Appalachia
   Cheryl Claassen; Appalachian State University; Boone, NC
Oral Histories of Appalachian Craftsmen
   Mont Whitson; Morehead State University; Morehead, KY
Appalachian Ethnicity as Reflected in a Craft Cooperative
   Susan Keefe; Appalachian State University; Boone, NC
   Convenor: Gordon McKinney; Western Carolina University, Cullowhee, NC

# The Shell Button Industry in Appalachia

by
*Cheryl Claassen*

The major motivating factor for collecting freshwater shellfish in the Eastern United States during historic times was the shell button industry which flourished from 1891 until 1930 in most regions. The button industry derived its raw materials largely from local populations, working rivers and streams from Wisconsin to Texas and east to the Appalachians (Georgia to Pittsburgh) and including New York and New England. After 1855 the shellfish populations in New England and New York rivers declined due to overharvesting and the shelling center jumped to Muscatine, Iowa in 1891.[1] The rate of spread eastward from Muscatine toward Pittsburgh and the western edge of the southern Appalachian Mountains was directly related to the rate of depletion of shellfish bed in the Mississippi-Illinois River system.[2] Consequently then, the duration of the industry and the shelling activity shortens as one moves toward the Appalachians. Buttons were cut in Cincinnati and Cleveland by 1898 using Mississippi River shells.[3] By 1912, the income from this industry was greater than $6 million yearly. From 1930 to 1940 plastics came to replace shell as the major raw material for buttons ending what was in most places no more than a 20 year long industry. Most button factories closed while some converted to plastic or military button manufacture. The largest factory in Muscatine, Iowa continues today to manufacture shell buttons, the only producer of this product in the U.S.

A TVA warning of overfishing in 1933 apparently stopped the shelling on the Tennessee River but men returning home after WWII discovered the beds had recovered and shellfishing began immediately. Following a hiatus of over twenty years the Japanese demand for shell nacre revitalized the shellfishing activity in the Eastern United States. In the late 1950s, the cultured pearl industry of Japan got over 80% of its shell stock from the Tennessee River.[4]

Shellfishing activities resumed on the Ohio in Ohio in 1950. A single collector moved onto the Muskingum River in 1966, harvesting 35 tons of shell that year.[5] Today several companies employ men full time on a seasonal basis to dive for deeper shell beds in numerous Eastern rivers. Unlike the days of shell buttons when the term "prospecting" characterized the activities of shellers, today shellers or divers are told where to dive, what species to take and in what quantity. Company owned tractor-trailers buy the shell from the divers at company specified locations. Two years ago (1981), the Tennessee Shell Company (President is Latandresse) began culturing pearls at two locations in this country. This development should insure the future of commercial shellfishing in the Eastern United States.[6]

## Appalachian Shellfishing: Locations and Yields

Although the major impetus for shellfishing was the button industry, shellfishing for pearls preceded the commercial collection of shells on several Appalachian streams, particularly the Powell, Clinch and Holston Rivers. In 1909 a government sponsored button potential assay trip to these rivers found that the pearlers had no awareness of markets for shells or the button industry,[7] then 18 years old, in spite of factories as close as Clarksville, Kentucky and Knoxville. Pearling occurred primarily in the months of July, August, and September, used the same techniques for capture as were used elsewhere for shelling and relied on pearl buyers for marketing.

Huge piles of discarded shells were observed by the government party visiting the Clinch, Holston, and Powell Rivers. Mr. J. Beopple, the Bureau of Fisheries agent conducting the 1909 survey of these rivers and legendary father of the shell button industry in America, instructed the local pearlers and interested persons in the market value of certain species of shell for the button industry.

> The commercial value of such shells was explained to the pearl hunters, who were advised to seek a market for this material. It was learned that few pearls had been found during the preceding summer, so that a market for the shells was practically necessary to supplement the income from the yield of pearls.[8]

Under Boepple's influence, a single car of shells reached the market (place unspecified) late in the 1909 season. The following seasons, 1910 and 1911,

98 tons of shell from the Clinch and 56 tons of shell from the Holston were sold to button factories. Boepple rated the shells from the "Clinch and Holston Rivers as having the best mussels for buttons that I have seen in all my experience in the button business."[10] Neither the tonnage nor the earnings beyond 1913 are known for these rivers, where shellfishing lasted into the 1940s.

Pearlers had been in operation on the Cumberland River for at least 20 years when the government party of Wilson and Clark assayed the Cumberland shellfishery in 1914.[11] Few species were found living above Cumberland Falls but from the falls to Celina, Tennessee, a distance of 175 miles, considerable pearling was underway with the activity tapering off south of this area at Carthage. One hundred men were often pearling at one bed near Rowena and at one time, 150 men on a single bed. The Caney Fork was said to have the best pearls available. "Our own observations, as well as records of people engaged in the pearl trade, indicate that pearling was once an important occupation in the upper river."[12] Downriver from Carthage, pearling was a secondary activity to shelling.

The major southern Appalachian rivers exploited by shellers collecting shells for factory buyers were the Ohio, as early as 1908,[13] the Cumberland, and the Tennessee. Collection records from the Ohio River in Ohio from 1908 until 1963 (Table 1) indicate that the peak years of collecting activity were 1908 until 1922 with a hiatus from 1931 until 1950.

TABLE 1
Ohio River Basin Commercial Shellfish Catch—1894-1963
(Thousands of pounds—thousands of dollars)[15]

|      | Total Pounds | Total Value | Av. Price Per Ton (Dollars) |
|------|-------------:|------------:|----------------------------:|
| 1894 | — —          | — —         | — —                         |
| 1899 | — —          | — —         | — —                         |
| 1903 | — —          | — —         | — —                         |
| 1908 | 26,263       | 289         | 22                          |
| 1912-13 | 31,482    | 283         | 18                          |
| 1922 | 16,318       | 356         | 42                          |
| 1931 | 8,318        | 122         | 29                          |
| 1950 | 553          | 10          | 34                          |
| 1954 | 2,812        | 59          | 42                          |
| 1955 | 3,956        | 94          | 48                          |
| 1956 | 4,264        | 109         | 51                          |
| 1957 | 3,383        | 83          | 49                          |
| 1958 | 1,144        | 29          | 51                          |
| 1959 | 708          | 22          | 62                          |
| 1960 | 2,260        | 95          | 84                          |
| 1962 | 1,150        | 47          | 82                          |
| 1963 | 2,762        | 160         | 116                         |

From 17,000 to 31,000 pounds were taken each year during the peak period, 2054 tons of shell valued at $119,000 in 1912 alone.[14] In addition, in 1926, commercial harvesting in Ohio was recorded on 25 Ohio streams.

On the Cumberland in 1913, a catch of 1267 tons of shell valued at $22,000 was recorded. For the Tennessee River this same year, the figures are 906 tons and $11,000.[16] In neither case is it possible to determine the proportion of the catch that came from outside Appalachia. Shelling on the Tennessee reached a standstill in the 1940s.

Lesser regional rivers and creeks known to the author as shelling locations are the Scioto, Muskingum, Tuscarawas, Killbucks, Mohican, Sandusky, and Wills in Ohio,[17] Clear Fork, Big South Fork, Beaver Creek, Goose Creek, Obey River in Kentucky,[18] and the Holston, Clinch (particularly near Lone Mountain[19]), Power, Caney Fork, French Broad, and Stones River in Tennessee.[20] (See the appendix for a detailed account of shellfishing along the upper Cumberland.) Catch figures for several rivers and streams for the years 1912 and 1913,[21] 1926,[22] and the 1960s,[23] are to be found in Table 2.

### TABLE 2
### Catch Figures for Appalachian Streams

| Water Body | | Weight (ton) | Value-Shell | Value-Pearls |
|---|---|---|---|---|
| Muskingum | 1912[13] | 688 | $14,000 | |
| | 1926[14] | 36 | $ 1,800 | $ 65 |
| | 1966[15] | 35 | | |
| | 1968 | 90 | | |
| | 1969 | 417 | | |
| | 1970 | 650 | | |
| Tuscarawas | 1926 | 18 | $   935 | $ 30 |
| Killbucks | 1926 | 55 | $ 2,475 | $100 |
| Mohican | 1926 | 40 | $ 1,600 | $150 |
| Wills | 1926 | 19 | $   430 | $ 0 |
| Clinch | 1913 | 98 | | |
| Holston | 1913 | 56 | | |

## Methods of Collection—Preparation of Shellfish

In 1919, 70% of the shellfish gathered in the United States were taken by the Crowfoot bar, 5% by hand and 1% by dredge.[24] The popularity of the crowfoot bar was due to its adaptability to a variety of riverine conditions and its ease of operation for even the inexperienced. Developed in

1897, this method capitalized on the animals' instinct to clamp shut whenever disturbed. When dragging the foot over the bottom, any hooks that are caught between the values of the animal will be clamped down on. The crowfoot bar is raised periodically and cleaned of shellfish, then lowered again. The boat type most frequently employed in this operation is the john boat. Coker[25] describes numerous other techniques. In 1967, the methods of collecting and handling mussels had changed little since 1891.[26]

Appalachian pearlers seen in 1909 on the Clinch River had developed two unique techniques for catching shellfish.[27] One was the crude method of using an iron hook to pry the animal from the bottom and then push it into a tin can that was lowered to the bottom. The second innovation was to use a plow drawn by a strong team and working in 4 to 12 inch deep water, thoroughly plow up the bottom so that the mussels could be easily picked up.

At campsites along a river, sometimes after transfer to a flat boat, shellers "cook out" the animals. Campsites were chosen for proximity to a good shell bed and by convenience to shade and wood.[28] Tents or frame buildings were constructed. House boats or shanty boats are a common shelter. The cooker was frequently a vat 5' long, 2' wide and from 12" to 18" deep. It was suspended over a trench with a fire and fitted with a stove pipe to furnish draft. In many Appalachian areas this vat is similar to a molasses cooker.[29] Driftwood was commonly used as fuel. The vat was and is today, filled with mussels and a small amount of water and then covered with burlap or gunney sacks. Steam eventually kills the shellfish relaxing the hinge muscles that hold the paired valves together. The meat is cut out and it along with any unsuitable shells—those too small or endangered or inappropriate species—are discarded. The water in the cooker was strained to recover any pearls; meats were explored for the same reason.

### Shellfishers

More often than not shellers were and are today, itinerates living (then) on shantyboats or (now) in trailers or motels. Shellers worked an area either in an individual family group or formed a sort of camp town with a dozen or more families grouped together. Along the Cumberland River in Monroe County, an informant recalled seeing only Caucasian shellers.[30] Some had huge families and most returned summer after summer to the same river. The Rose family, with eleven daughters, moved their shantyboat into Monroe County each spring, "cooking out" on shore and cooking meals both on shore and on boat. They wintered each year near the mouth of Greesy Creek, subsisting, like many shellers, on fur trapping.[31] Other families covered greater territory. One family which reportedly began shelling "in the east" can be traced next to the Muskingum of Ohio, the Wabash in Indiana, the Ohio River and finally in Texas.[32]

Local people also shelled and pearled.

Many of the shellers are nomadic and therefore move readily with their launches from a region of poor fishery to a better locality. It is often the case however, that in times of low water, when the mussels are easily obtained, the farm hands, miscellaneous laborers, and others engage temporarily in shelling, using any kind of available equipment or collecting by hand.[33]

Although itinerants shelled the Cumberland in Monroe County, Kentucky, local people such as the young Hascill Haile and his brother gathered shellfish only to look for pearls, discarding both shell and meat. Every other day, in the summer during low water, the teenage brothers would collect shellfish with a crowfoot bar while checking the family fish traps. They usually spent the entire day doing this. Haile soon began buying pearls locally for another buyer who visited the area periodically from Salina, Tennessee. Haile reports that he made "a lot of money pearling, more than working by the hour." He has retained several pearls in a private collection. Currently he makes guitars choosing Arkansas shells for the enlay work.

Divers working for modern companies such as the American Shell Company of Knoxville or the Tennessee Shell Company of Camden, Tennessee, are only occasionally local people. As in earlier days the divers are itinerate, often traveling with their own and other families.[34]

## Marketing

Haile reports that buyers paid the itinerate shellers by the ton in the 1920s, then loaded the whole shells onto locally owned barges destined for a button factory in Nashville. Shells collected on the northern Clinch River near Lone Mountain were sold to factory buyers from Knoxville such as Patton's which closed in 1982. (In the mid 1930s the company had switched from the production of shell buttons to metal military buttons.[35]). Shells were transported to market on barges on the Cumberland, and by boxcar and wagon from the Clinch.[36] On the Tennessee River, in 1956, the shellers got $60/ton with the meat in and packed in 200 lb. boxes while middlemen such as Latandresse got $100/ton in the States and $480/ton in Japan.[37]

Known Ohio factories were located near or on the Ohio River. One factory was located between Ripley and Manchester,[38] one on Brush Creek,[39] and one in Manchester.[40] The Manchester factory sent buyers to "comb the country from the Appalachians to the Rockies and from the

Gulf to the Lakes to secure clam shells."[41] The advent of restrictive legislation necessitated a reliance on foreign shell. In 1949 they were cutting only shells from India and the Persian Gulf at Manchester. The blanks cut in Manchester were then sent to Amsterdam, New York, for polishing and finishing.[42]

A noteworthy difficulty encountered in many places in Appalachia was high transportation costs. In areas remote from manufacturing centers shellers might own a cutting machine so that the button blanks could be punched out for sale to a buyer and the excess weight discarded. A cutting machine in 1919 cost about $16.[43]

Shell companies today are highly competitive enterprises. During interviews with personnel at both the Tennessee Shell Company and the American Shell Company, requests for information on the number of divers, diving locations and average weekly income were denied. It was possible to learn a few facts about the modern operation, however. Raw shell is sent to Japan where it is contracted out to cheap labor for cutting and polishing in Hong Kong, Taiwan, the Philippines, and Korea. Shells are bought from the divers in 100 lb. lots and transported by tractor-trailer to the company.[44] The collecting season is usually March until November but in some areas of the South individuals are willing to dive year round. The American Shell Company exports "a container or two each week."[45]

## Discussion

Several aspects of commercial shellfishing suggest future research topics. The shell button industry was a short-lived capitalistic enterprise that could, because of the length of its duration, provide an excellent case study of industrial capitalism. The processes typical of industrial development are extremely contracted and complete in this example.

The itinerant life style of shellers has never been recorded or studied. Just how their ideological, social, and technological attributes compare with other American itinerant groups would be equally interesting.

Itinerate shellers were both local seasonal laborers and "foreigners" in an area. Similar seasonal wage labor was available in the lumber industry, beginning in the Ohio-Kentucky-Tennessee area in the 1870s suggesting it could have served as a model for seasonal, and part time shell collecting.

> At convenient intervals during the cultivating and harvesting seasons and during the winter, the farmers went into the woods to cut saw logs and to snake or haul them to the nearest tributary capable of floating to a raft yard . . . These farmer-loggers spent much of their time in the woods during summer months between 1870-1935 cutting on their own property or working for larger landowners or timber buyers.[46]

The economic impact of this activity during the first period of collecting on the lives of Appalachian citizens is quite elusive at this time. Shell prices per ton are the easiest to obtain. Table 1 gives annual prices and net value for Ohio River basin collections from 1908 to 1931. Boepple estimated the Clinch shells would bring $77 per ton. If this figure is correct, the 1913 market proceeds from Clinch River shell was approximately $7549 and $4312 for Holston River shellers.

The number of people involved is a very elusive figure for any area or time period. Oral interviews with buyers appear to be the only possible means of estimating the number of people involved and the amounts realized in any one community. These figures are equally elusive in this second period of shellfishing activity. Company personnel are candid in their refusal to release information on the number of divers employed or their catches. The number of collecting permits issued in those states requiring permits will give some indication of this figure. In 1966 the mussel shell harvest from the Tennessee River was estimated at 5,468,000 pounds valued at $577,161.[47] Unfortunately this figure includes areas outside of the Appalachian region.

It is most likely that shellfishing never exceeded the economic contribution of other part time labor in Appalachia. Pearling on the other hand, may have exceeded the earning potential of any other wage labor job available between 1890 and 1930. The highest price paid for a pearl from the Clinch River was $2,500, sometime before 1914. At Burnside, Tennessee, a personal collection of pearls valued at $20,000 was seen by Wilson and Clark. They also learned that one of the principal merchants in Carthage bought $15,000 worth of pearls every year. He generally paid between $20 to $300 for a single pearl in the years 1907-1909. Boepple's guide on the Holston River had found and sold approximately $14000 worth of pearls in that same time period. Hascill Haile reports making more money pearling than he ever did in wage labor.

Again, the number of men involved in this activity is difficult to estimate. Many shellfish beds in the upper Cumberland River and in the Holston and Clinch Rivers were fished to the point of exhaustion. As many as 150 men worked a single shellfish bed in a single season on the Cumberland near Rowena. In contrast, four pearlers were encountered working beds on the Clinch October 31st, 1909. Most likely, large numbers of boys and men probably pearled at least one season in their lifetime during the period 1900-1930.

The historical shell button and pearl industries are important from several standpoints. In both cases there are living participants who can provide much data on what are essentially unrecorded activities. These activities, in as much as they netted cash and facilitated the local participation in an expanding cash economy are unknown factors in the process of the mountaineer's acculturation. They also provided an avenue of exit from Appalachia for individuals and families. To what extent shellfishing influenced people in either regard is the major challenge of future research.

## FOOTNOTES

1. Irving Richman, *History of Muscatine County, Iowa* (S. J. Clarke, Chicago, 1911), p. 303.
2. Robert E. Coker, Freshwater Mussels and Mussel Industries of the United States. *Bulletin of the Bureau of Fisheries*, Vol. XXXVI 1917-1918, Document No. 865. (Government Printing Office, Washington, 1919), p. 32.
3. Clarence Clark, "Management of Naiad Populations in Ohio" in *Rare and Endangered Mollusks of the U. S.*, ed. S. E. Jorgensen and R. W. Sharp (1917), pp. 26-33.
4. Comments by Ben Jaco in *Rare and Endangered Mollusks of the U. S.*, pp. 57-59.
5. Clarence Clark, "Management of Naiad Populations in Ohio," p. 29.
6. John Latandresse, personal communication, Oct. 1983, Camden, Tennessee.
7. J. F. Boepple and R. E. Coker, Mussel Resources of the Holston and Clinch Rivers of Eastern Tennessee, *Bureau of Fisheries Document* No. 765, 1912. (Government Printing Office, Washington), p. 3.
8. J. F. Boepple and R. E. Coker, Mussel Resources of the Holston and Clinch Rivers of Eastern Tennessee, p. 9.
9. Ibid, p. 13.
10. Ibid, p. 11.
11. Charles B. Wilson and H. Walton Clark, The Mussels of the Cumberland River and Its Tributaries. *Bureau of Fisheries Document* No. 781, 1914. (Government Printing Office, Washington), p. 42.
12. Charles B. Wilson and H. Walton Clark, The Mussels of the Cumberland River and Its Tributaries, p. 44.
13. Clarence Clark, "Management of Naiad Populations in Ohio," p. 26.
14. Robert E. Coker, Freshwater Mussels and Mussel Industries of the United States, p. 40.
15. Table 1 taken from Ohio River Basin Comprehensive Survey, Appendix G, Vol. 8. U. S. Dept. of Interior, Fish and Wildlife Service 1960.
16. Robert Coker, Freshwater Mussels and Mussel Industries of the United States, p. 40.
17. Clarence Clark, "Management of Naiad Populations in Ohio," p. 26.
18. Charles Wilson and H. Walton Clark, The Mussels of the Cumberland and Its Tributaries.
19. Lewis Kalter, TVA *Island Wilderness Biological Survey* (1935), p. 52.
20. John Latandresse, personal communication, Oct. 1983, Camden, Tennessee.
21. Robert E. Coker, Freshwater Mussels and Mussel Industries of the United States, p. 40. Source for all 1912, 1913 figures in Table 2.
22. Clarence Clark, "Management of Naiad Populations in Ohio," p. 26.
23. Ibid, p. 30.

24. Robert E. Coker, Freshwater Mussels and Mussel Industries of the United States, p. 59.
25. Ibid.
26. Paul Parmalee, The Fresh-Water Mussels of Illinois (Illinois State Museum Popular Science Series, volume 8), p. 2.
27. J. F. Boepple and R. E. Coker, Mussel Resources of the Holston and Clinch Rivers of Eastern Tennessee, p. 10.
28. Robert E. Coker, Freshwater Mussels and Mussel Industries of the United States, p. 59.
29. Hascell Haile, personal communication, Oct. 1983, Tompkinsville, Kentucky.
30. Ibid.
31. Ibid.
32. John Latandresse, personal communication, Oct. 1983, Camden, Tennessee.
33. Robert E. Coker, Freshwater Mussels and Mussel Industries of the United States, p. 44.
34. John Latandresse, personal communication, Oct. 1983, Camden, Tennessee.
35. Paul Parmalee, personal communication, Oct. 1983, Knoxville, Tennessee.
36. John Latandresse, personal communication, Oct. 1983, Camden, Tennessee.
37. John C. Williams comments in *Rare and Endangered Species of the U. S.*, p. 51.
38. Robert Genheimer, personal communication, Oct. 1982, Cincinnati, Ohio.
39. David Brose, personal communication, Nov. 1983, Columbia, South Carolina.
40. Rendall Rhoades, "Clam Shells and Buttons," *Ohio Conservation Bulletin*, June, 1951, pp. 14-15.
41. Ibid.
42. Ibid.
43. Robert E. Coker, Freshwater Mussels and Mussel Industries of the United States, p. 44.
44. John Latandresse, personal communication, Oct. 1983, Camden, Tennessee.
45. Interview with an official of the American Shell Company, Knoxville, Tennessee, Oct. 1983.
46. William Lynwood Montell, *Don't Go Up Kettle Creek* (University of Tennessee Press 1983), p. 85.
47. Development of Water Resources in Appalachia. Appendix G, Fish and Wildlife Resources. U. S. Dept. of Interior, Fish and Wildlife Service 1969, p. 16.

## REFERENCES CITED

Boepple, J. F. and R. E. Coker
    1912  Mussel Resources of the Holston and Clinch Rivers of Eastern Tennessee. *U. S. Bureau of Fisheries*, Document No. 765, Government Printing Office, Washington.

Clark, Clarence
    1971  Management of Naiad Populations in Ohio. In *Rare and Endangered Mollusks (Naiads) of the U. S.*, ed. S. E. Jorgensen and R. W. Sharpe, (U. S. Dept. of the Interior, Fish and Wildlife Service, Bureau of Sport Fisheries and Wildlife Region 3. Twin Cities, Minn. 55111), pp. 25-33.

Coker, Robert E.
    1919  Freshwater Mussels and Mussel Industries of the United States. *Bulletin of the Bureau of Fisheries*, Vol. 36, 1917-1918, Document No. 865, Government Printing Office, Washington.

Kalter, Lewis
    1935  Island Wilderness Biological Survey. Tennessee Valley Authority.

Montell, William
    1983  *Don't Go Up Kettle Creek.* University of Tennessee Press, Knoxville.

Parmalee, Paul
    1967  *The Fresh-Water Mussels of Illinois.* Illinois State Museum Popular Science Series 8.

Rhoades, Rendall
    1951  Clam Shells and Buttons. *Ohio Conservation Bulletin*, June, pp. 14-15.

Richman, Irving
    1911  *History of Muscatine County, Iowa.* S. J. Clarke, Chicago.

U. S. Department of Interior
    1960  Ohio River Basin Comprehensive Survey, Appendix G, Vol. 8. Fish and Wildlife Resources. Fish and Wildlife Service.

    1969  Development of Water Resources in Appalachia, Appendix G. Fish and Wildlife Resources. Fish and Wildlife Service.

Wilson, Charles B. and H. Walton Clark
    1914  The Mussels of the Cumberland River and Its Tributaries. *U. S. Bureau of Fisheries*, Document No. 781, Government Printing Office, Washington.

**REGIONAL POETRY**
Reading by:
  Don Johnson; East Tennessee State University; Johnson City, TN
  Bennie Lee Sinclair; Cleveland, SC
  Thomas Crowe; Webster, NC
Convenor:
  Sam Gray, Western Carolina University, Cullowhee, NC

# Faces of Appalachia in Poetry
by
*Bennie Lee Sinclair*

The Blue Ridge escarpment of South Carolina, as well as similar terrain in neighboring Georgia and North Carolina, has furnished contrast for much of my poetry. Here where highland and lowland abruptly meet, the mountains ever looming blue to those dispossessed of them, the abundant lights of the fertile piedmont taunting those who would resist its lure, the conflict of a century-and-a-half old migration is keenly felt.

The necessary movement from hill country to mill country so typical of escarpment folk is subject of the following two poems. In the first the sustaining image, that of the radio, is particularly reminiscent of South Carolina where, in the late 1930's and early 1940's, the legendary Arthur Smith began his career playing bluegrass and country music on the state's first radio station WSPA, in Spartanburg. Hill-haunted listeners who cannot afford to move home again, though sometimes generations removed from the ridges, have continued to make that music the most popular in the area.

### BLUEGRASS
### & COUNTRY MADRIGALS

I.

Ours,
the hard-
scrabble land.
Out of the bones of mules

sometimes the green corn
grew, too late. Over-wet, or stony, or dry,
always there were fields
we could not negotiate—

until the mills opened up
new vistas, and we swarmed:
tuning the night's radio
for our lost and irregular

theme.

## II.

Listen!
Whenever a straw-and-wind fiddle
bends, bow to breast
in the deep fields of night,

a music begins—
a system of vibrating strings
that shakes the ruined valleys and hills
asleep under concrete or slag;

shakes awake
a diminishing vision
we only gather, like dew or kindling,
out of the windows of Greyhounds

or houses we left, as we pass.

## III.

Pressed by this wind, the guitar
(the poet's guitar
of rain)
descends in coded note-drops

through awnings and roofs of a city
until we also wake, children
bewitched under sheets of tin
to hear such music fall

freely, piercing the walls of our high-rise
down to that remnant of land
we hold buried, somewhere
beneath the sub-floor

under our realized dreams.

## IV.

And drowning this echo, the rain,
a broken voice
takes hold.
Our roused heart, like a maverick banjo,

sloughs up the mined-out steepsides
braying (as if we still climbed
a wilderness)
until, near the top, we look down

at our future, almost behind us
and relayed
in this system of strings—mere viscera
stretched and strummed

tight as our squandered soul,
on its frame.

## V.

Curtains
of rags
at the windows; rags
on the table

and doors; rags
into cracks
for the chinking; and rags
into rugs

for the floors;
hot mustard-pack rags
for the dying
of croup or flu or cold—

and yet, in the evenings, we sang:
the clear chorus of those open spaces
imbuing us, making us love them
no matter how far we remain.

## VI.

Surrounded by fresh, laundered linen
in our new rooms that are vaulted
like heaven, we wait
the thesis of displaced seed

or tuber: and in the darkness we hear
a gentle rain, yet intricate as math
far-fetched, fetched far and homeward
for us (who have paid our dues in the fields

gathering cotton, or wheat, or dust;
and no one ever to tell us
which are the roots that grow
or may blossom again)—

Listen!

The next poem had roots in the childhood experience of accompanying my father in his search for bootleg and music. Born at Fruitland, North Carolina, he was the first of his family to leave the hills, a move he always regretted. I remember our 1940's wanderings—in his 1940 Ford, a black cloth flapping where the shotgun window would be—and the toe-tapping music, the moonshiners' wild children my playmates for the evening. I envision the narrator of this poem to be my alter-ego Polly Esther, who sings with the Textile Boys band.

### THE FIRST TIME
### EVER I HEARD YOU, HONEY,
### AS A ONE-MAN BLUEGRASS BAND

The first time ever I heard you, honey,
as a one-man bluegrass band,
you were tuning it up
when the music started up,
coming right out of your skin:
and I couldn't keep still
and I couldn't say no
to a sound so good for my soul;
and I thought about my daddy
and his old Ford—

how we rode through the hills for a song—
and I couldn't give it up
and I wouldn't give it up,
I'd been looking for you so long:
a man who can make the banjo moan,
a man who can stroke a guitar;
a man who isn't afraid to sing

like a slow-moving rattle-freight car;
a man who can thump like a drum with his toes,
hold the mouth-organ right with his teeth . . .
you got me, honey, you don't even have to play
no more, tonight, oh please . . .

    A major asset of escarpment highlands is the plentitude of water that springs from the ridges. Gravity flow spring water is a luxury flatlander, with dug well, cannot envision. My husband, potter Don Lewis, remembered visits to his great aunt's home in the North Georgia mountains as the happiest times of his childhood. Especially splendid to him was the spring that supplied her family with water. As he and I searched for land years later, springwater was his main requirement. Then, shortly after we found and moved to our dream place (more than a hundred acres with more than a hundred springs) a terrible year-long drought, the worst in the area's history, dried up springs and creeks. He was deeply affected by the drought, a depression that resulted in an artist's block that lasted until the rains at last came again.

## LORD OF SPRINGS

The first day that we climbed our land
I stood at the uppermost spring
mesmerized, and it winter, by color:
my husband—red jacket, blue jeans—
kneeling amid stone gray, algae green,
to drink from that shining source;
and by how complete he seemed
rising satisfied like an animal or a god,
droplets gleaming from his brown beard
in that stark unscreened sunlight,
who had always, in our search,
considered water his Muse.

Here, on this one tract
wedged between mountains
and rivers the Indians named "Saluda"—
"Saluda": *Land Where the Green Corn Grows*—
we had found two good-sized streams, a dozen
lesser springs; the acreage itself
well-forested and intact:
and, though tin cans left by bootleggers
rusted in mulch at the rim,
and as we dug toward bedrock
we sifted precious birdpoints
the Cherokee had tossed in,
it seemed in the aeons of flow
few others had been,
the grade much too significant
for those just passing.


For him, not house site or tenable field
the priority, but days and weeks of his life
engineering that high water down—the line
an unwieldy plastic kink,
a half-mile-long black snake
recoiling and striking with strength—
until at last the grand rush came,
knocking the cup from my hand.
Triumphant, we settled in
accepting steadily rain, torrents, mists;
only occasionally did we labor
like pilgrims to that spring
along the singing creek
appositely: drought
was something we never dreamed.


Now, month after month, a year
without rain. Against a tolling heart
he climbs daily to that spring, a priest
fearful the flame to go out,
his water barely flickering.
I step across those streams
that once I could not leap,
wake abruptly in the night
escaping an ancient rite:
*blood for water, water for corn;*

and a persuasion of haunting voices
chanting their sibilant name, *Saluda.*

Am I as basic as they?
What wouldn't I do
to restore him?

Over the ridge, a fire.
In our cornfield parched stalks moan
from its wind, the brown leaves clattering like sticks
or primeval bones
applauding sacrifice.
Without, can it ever be
the same, that origin or measure
of his dreams, or mine of him?

A powerful, lithe man—dark, with
gifted hands—when he comes out of the shower
glistening, erect, and I prepare for him,
it seems to me this space—the dry creeks,
the pond, the lake—
should be shaken by that tide
his presence makes:
and I share what the faithful prayed
upon our mountain
offering quartz or blood
to the headspring:

*Downstream the river waits, Saluda:*
*downhill the seed corn holds*
*new life, and feast, and future:*
*but may all my blessings rise*
*just here, with you, forever*
*Lord of Springs.*

My father's parents, Effie Barton and Joseph Elim Sinclair, were eighth generation Southern Appalachioners: the Bartons, English who remain in the "Dark Corner" of South Carolina near Tigerville; the Sinclairs, Scots Highlanders who settled in the Bearwallow section of North Carolina. Because I am a writer, and interested, elders of both families (most now deceased) have over the years led me on lengthy tours of hillside farms and cemeteries, and told me family stories that will live only as long as someone remembers, or writes them down. In planning a poem about wildflowers, I was struck with a quote from Emerson (for whom my late father and brother, Waldo Graham Sinclair Sr. and Jr., as well as many of their Barton cousins, were named) that seemed a suitable epigraph for joining the images of flora and family.

## MY APPALACHIAN WILDFLOWERS

". . . whereby contrary and remote
things cohere, and flower out
from one stem . . ." Emerson

Exuding truth
these fragile flowers endure
delicate as tears
ten million years:

innocent of strength
appallingly they break
like knifeblades out of the graywacke,
a force like stars

glistening and complex: and yet
they do not last, but resurrect
haphazard in the fields
or on the steeps—

like ghosts they bloom:
faces we have known,
connecting us.

I.  In autumn, when the forest
    seems holding its breath,
    the spectacular lilac-blue gentian,
    its petals

vivid as bright paper wings,
glows along the brown creekbanks
triumphant as some wise shaman
instructing this student of flowers

its standard, against death.
Later, unravelling out of the snow,
the sweet arbutus clings
so tightly to the slope

no thaw may pry it loose:
its deceptive buds—little beads
of the purest pearlescence—
more persistent

than even the children
suffering rheum and phlegm
who shall not manage to stir
their hillside stones again.

How clearly their cycles reflect us!
Adorning cradle, altar, grave,
the softness of their designation
(Stellaria, Kalmia, Lobelia)

belying
though the mountains be slaughtered around us
these preglacial, anteholocaust flowers
will remain.


II. Their division
is magnificent:
from the sallow Indian Pipe, a saprophyte
illusory, ghostly white

shrivelling on its stem,
at zenith
an unnoticed skeleton;
to milkweed, in genesis

undistinguished, later undergoing
metamorphosis, bloom to chrysalis,
releasing at year's end
a silvery tuft, a lovely, flying skein

spun finer than any thread—the unknown
its seedbed.
Galax, toad flax: in summer
flowers strange as their names

like generations past
(remember "Aunt Kindness," and
"Pleasant," her brother—twin?)

come back to visit,
recognition guaranteed

of root or gene
however diverse or common
may seem the family.

III. Violets, for instance.
In merely one afternoon
I catalogue sixteen
explicit from one another

in color, shape, leaf;
and attend a clever neighbor
actually capturing them
in a bottle—so simple!—of jelly,

its lavender held to the light
astonishing;
then witness, at dusk, roadside,
a pencil-legged doe and her fawn

likewise feasting on violets (the halberd-
leaved, yellow ones)—
rolling the nuggets like butter
onto their tongues.

So much! And I have not even begun
Violaceaen taxonomy;
or the remedies, dyes, superstitions
the true student must learn of them.

IV. Sometimes, wading fields of cousins
these ridges have hemmed in
like daisies and mountains asters
of flu, the old wars, sin—

I think how the happenstance flowers
adapt and carry on
despite this constant winnowing
by heat, cold, drought, flood,

slide, gust, blade, rock,
flame, craw, mole's whim:

how again, and again each turning
bloodroot heralds spring

abruptly as new flesh,
pale stalk
a resilient green;
and rue anemone, its leafy fringe

poignant as old lace
whispers into bloom.
Whether camp or mine or town
has been, or been

moved on, the cabin gone,
indomitable as kin
these flowers peculiar to place
whenever we climb toward home

welcome us. Out of the evening mist
like ghosts they bloom:
faces we have known,
connecting us.

Like psalms they bloom:
music that we live,
uplifting us.

As a small boy my brother learned to gather Indian artifacts on a great-uncle's farm, site of an ancient riverside village. By the time he joined the Order of the Arrow at the Boy Scouts' Camp Old Indian in northern Greenville County, S. C., in the 1940's, he was already an accomplished and responsible scholar of the woodland Indian culture.

He had hiked the entire mountain range of South Carolina and chosen the area around Jocassee as his destined home. Here were the sites of two of the oldest Indian villages in the Southeast, Keowee and Toxaway, as well as some of the state's last virgin timber and great clumps of the rarest wildflower in the world, Oconee Bell.

When he learned that all was to be inundated by a nuclear power plant and lake, it seemed that all his dreams were devastated. His personal life had not gone well, but he had hoped for a new life in that beautiful place. Ironically, the last time that my husband and I spent with him, before his sudden death from cerebral hemorrhage at age thirty three, was in a melancholy combing of that doomed place for artifacts. The following became an elegy for the land as well as the man.

# THE ARROWHEAD SCHOLAR
# 1967

In laurel caves above the river
we hunt for arrowheads—
intently scavenging
for those lost cultures grounded

in this shelf of sand
and rock. Once, Siberian visionaries
(dreaming food)
hiked a sunken strait to forage, mutate,

settle this primordial basin. Now, a dam
begins to shroud it, locking in the secrets
of the Cherokee, and those tribes older
who survived prehistory

to civilize this valley—only
tenacious drifts of laurel
high, at the new crater's rim, hide
some final relic

for those who care to race
the drowning hour. For this, my husband and I
have as our guide
my brother, the Arrowhead Scholar,

who can discern out of earth
a handful of points, and each its story:
the type of rock, the age, the use
some hunter young and dedicate as himself

found of it in the laurel there, or lost,
of time and savagery,
beneath our feet. He leads us
with a ripened Eagle Scout's vision of sweet

water, virgin air, forests plentiful
of bone and wing
above these vanished towns
of Keowee, and Toxaway—

and it is reincarnate in his glistening face
as he steps among their leavings
stirring no more sound
than some ghost, until above us, in the greenery,

he begins to sing as he catalogues
our finds—a sentimental ballad
of the maid Jocassee
who went down here, swimming to her lover

(his wife merely chokes for him of cancer,
and disgrace)
and he repeats that song, our father's mistakes
with a constancy

that perplexes me. Last winter,
the doctors at the State Hospital
sent him home
(they said that he was sane)

and now his labyrinth has grown
until I could split my heart
and wrap the pelt around him, suffering
his long-ago face (and mine)

pressed against the glass on Sundays
(Daddy's visiting day)
until our hope was passed. Instead,
my offering is this redemptive afternoon

in which he can forget that it has come again
(the Sabbath)
and his own son waits.
This brutally uprooted past depends

on his wandering hand to salvage
while I and my husband (his keepers, and more— as
long as we are in sight he believes
in happiness)

follow the tentative trail he makes through laurel and
sawbrier, aware
of the dizzying rim
whenever the dark leaves part, before him.

## 1970: ENVOI

The dam arcs
gently as a bird's great wing
(the buzzard of Cherokee legend, whose span
erupted these hills)

and a shimmering Visitor's Center, impressive,
of concrete and steel,
welcomes my husband and me
to a hydroelectric saga, the Story

of Nuclear Energy woven of films, recordings,
animation—but little is said
of what once was here;
of our lost Indian villages, only

the names. From a crowded terrace we stare
the freshly-reflected expanse where drown
a thousand forest colors
and, on the farther bank,

I see my brother's sweat-curled hair
flashing black
amid the green, until the vision splinters
into a flock of displaced, shrieking

crows, and I remember
his burst brain. Of that other, nothing remains
except a sack of flaked stones
gathered by that young man marked of scars

some unhonored gambling debt
had got him: yet, when I saw him last, laid out
for Intensive Care with a towel
loincloth, his reserve

was a fine as any warrior's
who might have carried them. I do not know
what could have been. When Daddy failed us, we said
it was the times

were hard (so many dreams misplaced
of dust and joblessness)

and yet, our faith in better days
turns out the same. Waiting outside those
honky-tonks

(the River Street Bar and the Dixie Grill, with Mama)
to remind a staggering man
of our claim; and later, when we buried him,
I vowed myself out of soap opera

while my brother—God knows—
must have mistaken the role
as freedom. Whatever, I shall not repeat this
pilgrimage, for him. Technology

has done this place in, in trust
of the future, but I know
(of the Arrowhead Scholar)
that the past must be suffered again

as it is today,
in my brother's form,
moving with his magnificent grace
among the laurel there, which is no more.

Acknowledgements:
"Bluegrass and Country Madrigals appeared in *San Jose Studies: Poems 1976;* "The First Time Ever I Heard You, Honey, As A One-Man Bluegrass Band" appeared in *The North Carolina Arts Journal;* "The Arrowhead Scholar appeared in *The South Carolina Review*. All were included in the book THE ARROWHEAD SCHOLAR (Wildernesse Books, 1978) which received South Carolina's Winthrop College Excellence in Writing Award for 1978.

The other distinguished poets who contributed to the Regional Poetry session were Thomas Rain Crowe and Don Johnson. Samples of their poetry follow.

## LOOKING FOR LAND

Fast as the fool's trace
whispers
over high hills,
I try to buy land.

O, what a clown would
come into this place
so long
looking for blood!

How can any man Own a piece of the earth!

A week too late,
the silver goes back
into the pockets of our ancient lives.
And the land
our children would love
thickens
as we walk away.
Empty.
Feet tired.
Our hearts as heavy and as brittle as rust,
in leaving behind
this special place to die.

       Thomas Rain Crowe


## THE PERFECT WORK

Love is the perfect work.
A music which rings all the bells in the temple.
A special wind in the trees—

Listen to the way the drummer hits
lovingly his drum.
The way the dancer moves
over the warm earth.
And watch as children
leave their bodies behind on the old logs
around the fire and sing!

The world is aglow in the shadows of the
children singing. Of the sticks against
wood. Of the heavy silent breathing of the old ones
who sit off to the sides of the circle and pray.

When I am at work in my garden
I take off my shoes. I let
my other hands embrace dirt.

I plant myself in this place.
And knowing what love is, I
awake. In this place in my body.
Full of dream music.
Full of light!

       Thomas Rain Crowe

## SNAKE DOCTORS
*In the hills they call dragonflies "snake doctors."*

I knew
snake doctors kiss bitten moccasins
curing the sickness of snake fights.
Peewee Worley, who was eight,
had seen it, down behind Carruthers' barn:
two snakes, fanged together
poison-locked, until, as if by signal,
they untied and lay there side
by side unmoving, like two friends
grown tired of wrestling.

But when the dragonfly appeared,
hovered green above their heads,
then touched each one in turn just once
and left, the life rolled slowly
back along the slackened skins, building
coils, allowing each to slip away—
toward the chicken house,
toward the trough,
where Peewee found them both
and hoed their heads off.

       Don Johnson

COMMUNITIES: PARTICIPATION OR RETREAT
Progress Is Our Most Important Product
    Tom Boyd; Berea College
Getting Organized: Appalachian Participation in Urban
Community Councils
    Phillip Obermiller; Northern Kentucky University
Attributes of Rural Families
    John Photiadis and Lucille Bryant; Morgantown, WV
    Convenor: Esther Lefever; Director; The Patch, Inc.; Atlanta, GA

# Progress Is Our Most Important Product: Decline in Citizen Participation and the Professionalization of Schooling in an Appalachian Rural County*

by
Tom Boyd

Of the 52 states and territories of the Union, on the basis of the number of illiterate white voters of native white parentage, Kentucky is 49, leaving whites in North Carolina, Louisiana, and New Mexico alone lower. (*Biennial Report of Superintendent of Public Instruction 1907-1909*)

*Fact:* The least-educated adult population in the nation. In 1980 only 56 percent of those 18 and over had a high school diploma. Only 11 percent had a college education. *Fact:* One of the highest high school dropout rates in the nation. In 1981 Kentucky's rate was 33 percent; only eight states did worse. (*Louisville Courier-Journal*, Oct. 30, 1983)

These comments, separated by seventy-five years of change in public education, give evidence of interest in the results of formal education; but their tone also indicates the way lack of educational attainments are managed as major stigmata in an urban, industrial society. The Commonwealth of Kentucky receives these signs as Saint Francis and others did—light marks symbolic of pain—Appalachian Kentucky carries the very wounds evidencing deep penetration.

Efforts for improved public education in this century carry all the attributes of 'progress': increasing specialization of effort, increasing efficiency in management and administration, even greater expenditures for new plant and equipment. They have also been associated with the decline in citizen participation that has accompanied the strengthening of external ties binding local communities to a wider society goverened by professionals and urban middle class interests.[1] This paper traces the history of change in formal education in Jackson County, Kentucky, a part of central Appalachia.

A number of recent empirical researches carry on the documentation of educational deficiency in the mountains that has long been a part of the national definition of the region as a problem area. These contemporary efforts are noteworthy in that they strive to spread the blame to others than the victim; nonetheless they continue to provide evidence (now in the social science idiom of scales and tests) of the stigma of deficiency when students are examined or measured. DeYoung, Vaught, and Porter have demonstrated that on the Comprehensive Tests of Basic Skills in Kentucky, "... the school districts having the higher percentages of below average readers tend to come from Appalachia".[2] In another study developing measures of school inputs, processes, finances, and outcomes DeYoung has concluded:

> Appalachian county school districts in Kentucky have poorer input, process, outcome, and financial characteristics than do non-Appalachian county districts or independent districts.[3]

Rech and Rech in a study of pupils in the Appalachian mountains of Western North Carolina and urban North Carolina used the Piers-Harris Children's Self Concept Scale along with interviews with many children.

> The scores obtained from the application of the self concept scale indicate significant differences between the two populations. The rural Appalachian children possessed a significantly more negative general self concept than did the urban non-Appalachian children.[4]

All of these studies conclude that the source of these problems lies, at least in part, in the separation between schools and the majority of the citizens of the rural areas of Appalachia.

Jackson County in Eastern Kentucky is a very rural county; the 1980 census lists the population as 100 percent rural. One major newspaper in the state marked it in front page detail recently in the following terms:

> Only 28.6 percent of the county's adults have completed high school—the third-lowest ranking among the nation's 3,137 counties.
>
> Fewer than 40 percent have gone beyond the eighth grade. In last year's statewide testing, Jackson County ranked 167th out of the state's 183 school systems. *Many people, including*

> *educators, seem to have grown tired of even hoping for better.*[5](emphasis mine)

This fatigue on the part of educators and other observers—if an accurate assessment—is of very recent vintage. Jackson County, as the rest of rural America, has in the past been the object of many "hopes for the better". These efforts from outside the county and from the profession of education may explain many of the present conditions; they are rarely cited with such figures are given.

The series of Biennial Reports of the Superintendents of Public Instruction in Kentucky from the turn of the century onward give evidence of aspirations for Jackson County schools. From 1899-1919 the section titled "Epistolary Reports of County and City Superintendents" also gives some of the thinking of the county superintendents on this subject. These aspirations and thoughts are all in the direction of centralization of power, consolidation of schools, and the adoption of management techniques as being progress for the county's schools.

In the 1899-1901 report the State Superintendent praises the work of the teachers in the Commonwealth and goes on to say, "next to the work of the teacher in importance is the work of the (county) superintendent".[6] Words of criticism are used when the subject of the management of school affairs is tackled.

> To say the present common school trustee system is an absolute failure would be probably too severe a criticism, but to say the least, it is unsatisfactory.[7A]

The system of local trustee control was under attack for many years. At this time the duties of the local trustees were vast—a list of 16 activities covered everything fom school records, maintenance, and teacher employment to a pupil census and the duty "to urge upon parents the necessity of prompt and regular attendance of their children".[7B] The county superintendent received the trustees' reports every year but at this time he had little control over these locally selected citizens.

The 1899-1901 report suggests a better form of management,

> The plan in brief is this: Place all the schools of the entire county ... under the management of a county board of education, to be composed of the county superintendent, and one member elected from each magisterial district of the county by the voters thereof ... [8]

The press for centralization of control and management was strong from the turn of the century onward. The Jackson County Superintendent, R. M. Bradshaw, in his report agreed with this direction of change and added further comments as to why it was obviously desirable.

> The present trustee system should be abolished and in its place

a county board of education created, consisting of a member from each magisterial district having *an educational qualification,* elected by the people and *exercising the same powers as the boards of education in our cities.*[9](emphasis mine)

Here we first find the juxtaposition of educational qualifications and urban educational practices defined as progressive activity for this entirely rural area.

In 1908 the County Administration Law brought this form of organization to all of Kentucky; it made the county the unit of administration and set up county boards. From 1909 onward Jackson County has had such a school board with six, and now five, citizens elected from the magisterial districts. However, at this time the sub-district trustee still existed. The 1914-15 *Kentucky Educational Directory* said the county had no graded schools and it listed 71 of these citizen-trustees who were to be found residing all over the county. In spite of the existence of county boards the sub-district trustees dominated affairs making it difficult for the county boards to bring about what some observers saw as progress— the consolidation of schools.[10]

In the 1907-1909 Biennial Report the state superintendent explained in detail his concern that the trustee system had an unfortunate tendency to allow "political influence" in school affairs as opposed to what would now be called "professional management" of these activities. His justification for embarrassment is telling:

> The old school district system which has prevailed in Kentucky until recently, *was discarded in the Northern States nearly 75 years ago,* and has been discarded in every Southern State excepting Arkansas.[11](emphasis mine)

The "politics" that derived from citizen involvement, as well as the knowledge that the practice of trustee management was abandoned elsewhere, were major arguments to justify the centralization of power in education and the removal of supervision from the hands of citizens. The issue of educational attainment as a qualification for the exercise of power was evident early on and the final stroke on the bill of indictment of trustees was the matter of cost and the efficiency of popular election.

During the period of trustee control it was pointed out that much of the population of any area, and especially a rural area, was illiterate and it was from such a population that school officials were elected. One observer stated it succinctly.

> These men were good, honest, upright men but they had little or no education, and *therefore they possessed a very limited vision of the possibilities of education.*[12](emphasis mine)

The 1909-1911 Biennial Report records Superintendent Davis of Jackson

County giving clear justification and need to reduce citizen participation in the name of economy and efficiency.

> I believe all vacancies in the office of subdistrict-trustee should be filled by appointment by the County Board of Education. I also favor the election of trustees "viva voce" compensating the trustees so elected with the money annually expended for holding school elections.[13]

The argument against trustees was clearly based on the believed superiority of central control; it was also linked with the fact that many citizens were unable, or unwilling, to make the necessary effort to provide a major modern structure for education—the consolidated school.

Early on the Jackson County superintendent praised the idea of consolidation linking it with the graded instruction found in urban areas.

> I ... believe that we could consolidate several of our districts into one large district ... and have a school building sufficient for four or five teachers; that is, a room for each grade, and then we might hope to have our schools graded as well as any college or normal school.[14]

The wishes of professional teachers were also used as a justification for consolidation in this period.

> It is my opinion that, with longer terms of schools, we would have more professional teachers, and with our little local schools consolidated, we would have better graded schools.[15]

The State Supervisor for Rural Schools in 1916 chided the citizens of the Commonwealth in terms of being once again behind the rest of the nation—now the new issue was this one of consolidation. He said the only hope for improvement (ie consolidation) was, "the enactment of laws standardizing public school buildings and making the State Department of Education responsible".[16] Consolidation accompanied the transfer of power that had recently replaced the district with the county; but, the way to attain this newest goal for progress in education was to further transfer power from the county to the state level. Superintendent Chapman also invoked the newly popular idea of efficiency as a justification. "Consolidation in its best form [creates] a larger school where more efficient work may be done, or equivalent work at less expense."[17]

During the period 1899-1919 Jackson County attempted to meet these desires to conform to urban America but it was a difficult task and some cases of skepticism as well as despair are notable. Superintendent Davis in 1913 wrote:

> As to consolidation and transportation, it is impractable (sic) because the roads are so poor and there are so many mountains

to be crossed by the pupils. The county being one of the poorest in the State, makes consolidation almost impossible. Where possible, it is, in my opinion, the one step needed in our schools.[18]

In 1919 Superintendent Minter echoed this assessment:

> We have no consolidated schools in this county. In most parts of the county the roads are so bad and the population so sparse that consolidated schools are impractical. About half the school population would be unable to attend for at least half the term.[19]

Nonetheless he ended his report on a note of hope lest deviant local conditions be seen as defeating progress. "A sentiment for better roads seems to be growing and this is the first step toward consolidated schools."[20]

Scrutiny of these documents and reports produces one area of stated pride in progress made during this time. A new form of equipment gave the county superintendent a noteworthy event for the 1914-1915 report.

> Since my last report we have built three new school houses and *purchased and installed patent desks and seats* in seventy of the schools in my county. [Our goal is] . . . to have comfortable school houses, with patent seats and desks, in every district of the county.[21](emphasis mine)

In the 1916-1917 report the spread of formal education and this new equipment go hand in hand.

> We have either built or repaired almost every school house in the county, have established nine new districts, and have *furnished every school house in the county with patent desks during my incumbency.*[22] (emphasis mine)

The purchase of manufactured desks and seats was, in this rural timber-producing county, an important symbol of the successful quest for progress on the part of this Superintendent. At least in this effort he could comply with the urban industrial standards sought by the profession of education. The historian Thomas Clark has described how 'patent' goods as symbols of real or imagined modernity spread across the rural South in an earlier period. Drummers and stores were agents of the new industrial age—in this respect so was the increasingly powerful school superintendent.[23]

From 1921 onward statistical tables dominate the Biennial Reports in a new format representing the theme of numerical accounting as an adjunct to efficient management. Statements of events, plans, and achievements—the epistolary reports of county superintendents themselves—disappear. The replacement is prepared by the State Department of Education that is growing in power.

In his 1921 report the state superintendent writes of the county school administration law as the most important school legislation enacted by the General Assembly of 1920. Through this mandate the sub-district trustees are at last removed. Attention is now directed at the qualifications of the rural superintendent as being the major problem of management. The mirror for reflection remains an urban one.

> The county school administration law of 1920 was designed primarily and specifically to give to each county in the state... better leadership. The superiority of the city schools to the county schools is primarily due to the better ability, the better preparation, and the better leadership of city superintendents as compared with county superintendents. [This law]... makes it possible to secure for the administration of county schools, the same sort of leadership that cities have enjoyed for years.[24]

When problems were described in detail the blame was clearly shifted to a person not having the requisite, new professional skills. "Too many county superintendents were not properly prepared, and did not have the administrative ability and educational leadership the position demanded."[25]

By 1940 the Jackson County School system still had many small schools. County-wide consolidation had proved to be difficult but there were some district level mergers to provide multi-grade and multi-teacher schools. The seventy-three schools in the county were still dominated by the one-teacher school; there were fifty-nine of these with the rest being eleven two-teacher schools, one three-teacher school, and two twelve-grade schools.[26] The report of a teacher working on improvement of instruction illustrates transportation problems.

> The difficulties of transporation enter into teacher reports frequently. Jackson County has no railroad and few improved highways. Many of the rural schools are situated far from the main highways on dirt roads that become impassable in bad weather. The supervisors reached a number of these schools on horseback.[27]

For forty years comments of state, county, and other observers reflect awareness that consolidation is dependent upon road conditions; other aspects of the new structure received more sanguine attention.

The State Superintendent of Rural Schools produced a fourteen page report extolling the virtues of consolidated schools.

> First. The consolidated rural school secures better buildings, better equipment, better teachers, better attendance, more sanitary conditions, greater school spirit and greater efficiency along all lines.
>
> Second. This type of school may become, and almost invariably does become, a community center and a rallying point for all

the educational, moral and industrial forces of the community.

Third. While the difference in cost between the one-room school system and the consolidated system is very little, if any, the advantages of the larger school are so much greater that they more than compensate for the difference in cost, should there be any.

After all else has been said, the best argument for consolidation and transportation is that they *get more children into school, keep them there better and for a longer time, and give them opportunity for more rapid progress.*[28](emphasis mine)

It was believed that as roads were built consolidation would follow swiftly behind. Just to make sure readers would be aware this was the wave of the future the report concludes on a strong note. "As no successfully consolidated school, so far as is known, has ever returned to the old way . . . consolidation is surely beyond the experimental stage." (Chapman, 1917)

The author of another study of the consolidation process in Kentucky in the 1920's got caught up in the mood of the times. "The history of consolidation in business, in manufacturing, in education has shown the key note of success."[29] It was believed that such a process would attract and hold better teachers, give better instruction to the children, produce better buildings and equipment, and allow the teaching of new subjects.[30] The growth of the consolidation movement could only be hindered by transportation problems, conservatisism of people, financial conditions, and inadequate leadership.[31] From the 1920's onward consolidation was seen to be a natural extension of a process that produced efficiency in the growing urban, industrial economy. Outside the lack of physical resources the only things that could prevent it were deficient or inadequate people.

A 1969 history of Kentucky small schools produced by the State Department of Education argued that the larger schools offered,

> . . . better trained teachers, greater variety of curricular and extra-curricular activities, *better adaptation on the part of graduates to the present social order,* and better leadership in business, industry and government, resulting from a broader and better education.[32](emphasis mine)

During a fifty-year period the state abolished 98 percent of the one-teacher schools, most of the remaining ones were found in Eastern Kentucky. Three factors were cited as making this consolidation possible. First there was the obvious growth in the possibility of pupil transportation as school buses were developed. Second, "growth of population in small villages and towns . . . made it necessary to abolish small schools and construct larger ones". And third, "from 1955 to the present, emphasis on accreditation and evaluation has been a large factor in the decline".[33] The population shift away from rural areas aided consolidation, perhaps doing away with the personal inadequacies that led to opposition to the process as well. After 1955 the principle factor was the control of the State Department of Education with professional evaluation and standards being advanced as links with state financing of county educational programs.

In 1961 Jackson County still had 31 schools—a reduction of 41 from the 1940 figure. Sixteen one-teacher schools remained in existence; the rest of the county's schools were five two-teacher, two three-teacher, five general elementary and three twelve-grade schools. The county had been loosing population over the years. From 1940-50 there was a 19.8% loss, from 1950-1960 a 18.5% loss, and from 1960-1970 there would be a 6.3% loss. Efforts to consolidate the Jackson County school system could finally be completed during the decade of the 1960's, roads in the county had been improved somewhat, there was some loss of population in the outlying areas, and federal and state dollars were available for educational expenditure to bring change. This decade brought a further change at the state level; the yearly publication, *Profiles of Kentucky Public Schools* began to publish data that allowed comparison of schools in the rough terms of inputs to educational programs and the results of schooling. Such data collected for one county system over time allows us to compare time periods using these same variables.

Table 1 gives data on the performance of the county system for the period 1966-67 (the first year such statistics were complete) to the present. Appendix 1 gives the method the State Department of Education uses to develop these educational indicators. Comparison with data for the entire state during the same time period allows us to view any changes relative to a wider norm for performance that is not solely urban. Looking at the change in these figures an assessment of the claims for consolidation can be made in its own terms of better buildings, greater efficiency, getting more children into school, keeping them for a longer time, and giving them opportunity for more rapid progress. Scrutiny of the fourteen-year period from 1966 to 1980 gives a picture of changes in the system as consolidation was completed and as the first group of pupils left schooling having had a full 12 years of the transformed, transportation-oriented rather than neighborhood-oriented, county school system.

In 1980 the county has only five elementary schools and one high school. The elementary schools consist of three major multigraded schools in the larger population concentrations near the most important highway and two smaller more remote schools the State Department of Education has recommended the county close. The single consolidated high school, according to Department of Education figures, is thirty-five miles away from the more distant pupils; many children are on busses at 6 a.m. in order to reach high school by 8:15 a.m. By the 1981-82 school year transportation was 15.4% of total current expenses, and the county was derided by weathermen on television newscasts for being closed so often when ice was on these mountain roads.[34] Figures 1-7 compare county and state figures and chart changes in teh educational indicators as the county system has begun to have an educational effort that includes approximately 3,000 miles of total bus travel on any given day.

Facilities for schooling have changed dramatically since 1940, the three newest buildings are recognizable as schools found anywhere in the nation and the high school has had the most recent status benefit of modern construction—expensive removal of asbestos used in the construction of the library. All three have gyms for indoor physical education and the ubiquitous pursuit of prowess in basketball—patent desks and chairs abound.

In 1966-67 the county pupil/teacher ratio was 27.7 to 1 and that was only one more pupil more than the state ratio of 26.6. By 1979-80 the Jackson County ratio declined to 20.7 and the state ratio was reduced to 21.0. In 1966-67 the percentage of students enrolled who were in attendance was 90.8%, the state average was 94%. By 1979-80 the county figure was 89.7% and the state 93%. During this period of culmination for the process of consolidation, the county did not improve its performance relative to the state averages for pupil/teacher ratio and percent attendance.

Throughout the United States the 1960's and 1970's were a period of inflation as well as increasing amounts of money spent on public education. In 1966-67 Jackson County spent $346 per pupil when the annual current expenses were divided by the average daily attendance; by 1979-80 the figure was $1,184. The state change during the same period was from $357 to $1,452. In the initial period, expenditure in Jackson County was 97% of the state average, by 1979-80 it had dropped to 82% of the state figure. When the cost per pupil for instruction alone is considered the figure for Jackson County in 1966-67 was $253; by 1979-80 the amount spent was $772. The state change during the same period was from $280 to $970. The culmination of the consolidation effort led to the county declining from 90% to 80% of the state average of dollars being spent per pupil for instruction. From this view consolidation has not led to an increase in the county expenditure relative to the state average expenditure per pupil. This might be viewed as supporting the claims of greater "efficiency" that were promised by the proponents of the process.

In the 1966-67 school year 57.5% of the Jackson County students entering ninth-grade in 1962 graduated from high school. These young people had come out of any one of twenty-six elementary schools. In 1979-80 the percentage had dropped to 46.2%. The dramatic drop this year may be due to the closing of the small private high school, but in years before this the figure had dropped below 50% five separate times and climbed above 57% only three times. The state figures for this period were 69% and 65%. Jackson County had a percentage point decrease of 11 and the state a decrease of 4 points. The early county figure was eight-tenths of the state percentage and the new figure was a decline to about seven-tenths of the state percentage.

The 1966-67 school year saw 28.7% of the high school graduates entering college and by 1979-80 the figure was 23.9%. Ten times during this time period the percentage was below the initial figure and only three times was it above the figure for the students with the more neighborhood-based elementary education experience. During this same period the state percentage fluctuated much less; the initial figure was 42.4% and ending figure was 42.8%. For Jackson County the early figure was 68% of the state percentage and the later figure was 56% of the state percentage. Such figures do not demonstrate that the process of school consolidation improved the ability of the schools to "hold pupils" or to "motivate and prepare" them for higher education.

The claims of educational improvement through school consolidation have not been supported in this Appalachian county. Things have stayed the same or declined further. More modern buildings have been built, the pupil/teacher ratio and expense per pupil have shifted. But there has been no increase in "getting more children into school", "keeping them for a longer time", and the "opportunity for more rapid progress"—if anything things have gotten worse and these figures don't necessarily show the entire picture. In Kentucky pupils may stop attending school at age 16; many of these dropouts never reached the ninth grade to be counted in the figures for percentage of ninth grade graduating from high school. Nonetheless, as the figures show, the new system did not greatly increase retention of the pupils that did reach the ninth level of state graded educational attainment.

What social processes have gone on during the period from 1961 to the present? There has been increasing centralization in the distribution of educational facilities in this reduction from 31 to six schools. Schooling is, with two exceptions that are condemned to be closed soon, found in the population concentrations. There has also been a centralization of power and participation as the reduction in schools means a longer bus ride for pupils and greater distance for parents to travel to participate in school meetings, events and the like. This 'de-ruralization' of education has taken place in a county where more than two-thirds of the pupils are considered "economically deprived children". The state figure is 32%. These events have been organized, directed and managed by the profession of education from outside the county with some citizens accepting the process as progress.

Opposition has not been totally absent. Some members of the Hisel community have recently thwarted attempts to close their two-teacher elementary school and the school board has supported them by going against the wishes of the Kentucky Department of Education, keeping this school open on a year-by-year basis. However, in some cases this has been used by newspapers, teachers, and educational administrators as further evidence of the backwardness of education in Jackson County rather than a wise decision in the face of a wrong policy.[35]

Evaluations of the effects of consolidation on school systems are not frequent in the social science literature of today. The conventional wisdom seems to be that it has been successful so there is no need for analysis; any problems are the result of incomplete or thwarted consolidation. Another view holds that it is a "natural" process not worthy of scrutiny. As Rosenfild and Sher point out in an article entitled "The Urbanization of Rural Schools, 1940-1970",

> By the 1960's consolidation, as a political issue, had ceased to be a legitimate subject of debate or policy analysis. Consolidation and other urbanizing practices were no longer perceived as *reforms* championed solely by the progressive elements of society. Rather, they had become accepted educational *standards* supported not only by the full range of the education profession, but also by the mainstream of American society.[36]

Claims of cost effectiveness abound in terms of "economies of scale" and greater efficiencies in larger schools. But at least one study has shown how after a certain size is reached new diseconomies of scale emerge in more busses, higher fuel costs, faster depreciation and the cost of new administrative specializations.[37]

Studies of the effect of consolidation on participation of citizens and students alike show results similiar to the ones found in Jackson County, but such studies are rarely, if ever, cited in state analyses. A study of high school size and student participation published in 1964 found that when students were transferred to a larger county high school they had a *decrease* in their participation in extracurricular activities and the amount of satisfaction associated with, "acquiring knowledge and developing intellectual interests".[38] A case study of a school consolidation struggle in rural West Virginia showed how sides taken are often in terms of "experts versus amatures", "professional educators versus parents" etc.

> For members of the middle class (including professional educators) consolidation is an effective way to strengthen influence and control within the community, while furthering their aspirations for their children. Yet, to the rural poor and working class, consolidation represents an attempt to destroy what is often their only sphere of public influence and their last

vestige of control over their childrens' education and socialization.[39]

Decline in participation is impossible to refute. It is often a result of consolidation that is admitted not as a cost but as something desirable in a "complex" world. When, it is admitted as a cost it is frequently justified as being necessary for the educational benefit of improved pupil performance—this study shows that such a benefit is a false assumption.

The early consolidation studies took place in urbanized areas; they did not control for family economic conditions as an effect upon learning and thus showed some positive correlation between school size and student achievement. Recent studies demonstrate that when researchers control for I.Q. and socio-economic status the result is, "a complete reversal of the traditional conclusions about the correlation between size and achievement".[40] A review of the literature, one author claims, shows that not one of the controlled studies demonstrates a positive correlation between size and achievement independent of social class.[41] Jackson County has two-thirds of its pupils in the status the state measures and terms "economically deprived".

We have seen that the impetus for consolidation in rural Kentucky came from comparison with urban areas. This is not unique to Kentucky or Appalachia; the process and the results in terms of participation are similiar in areas of the nation having a better reputation.[42] In urban America community control of schools gave way to a "corporate-bureaucratic model" as part of a drive "taking the schools out of politics".[43] A similiar theme was sounded in the complaints about Jackson County and other rural areas. In American urban education this happened in a much earlier period, as state and county Superintendents often proclaimed in their early reports, and it was a major transfer of power from parents (many of them recent immigrants and most working class) to professionals.

The professionals were not immune to forces for change themselves. From the turn of the century onward there has been considerable adoption of business values and practices in educational administration. At this time professional administrators in urban areas began to be perceived as business managers rather than educational philosophers.[44] The demise of county "epistolary reports", and the State Superintendent replacing this with statistical reporting methods, in the 1920's, demonstrates this well as do all the surveys and cost accounting material that begins to appear at this time.

In urban America at the turn of the century school boards were being reduced in size and their composition was changing, in that they were increasingly dominated by businessmen.[45] Administrators responded to this pressure on their work in a positive way. A 1916 text book *Public School Administration* explained that businessmen, manufacturers, and bankers made the best school board members and those who would not be adequate were politicians, saloonkeepers, and uneducated or relatively ignorant men.[46] The pressures for change in school board composition in Jackson County was largely from the profession of education not local businessmen! Even today, perhaps due most to the nature of the population in the county, the school board is not dominated by manufacturers, businessmen and bankers. Also, as we have seen, this school board is not pushing as hard as the state and the profession for the remaining consolidation effort.

What does the future hold for Jackson County and the rest of Appalachian Kentucky? The commonwealth has seventy-three elementary schools with less than eight teachers. All of these small schools, having at least one instance of a teacher assigned to more than one grade, are slated to be consolidated into larger graded schools.[47] As part of this the Moore's Creek and Hisel schools in the county will be closed.

For Jackson County the State facilities survey recommends the construction of a new upper elementary school for all 7th and 8th grade pupils.[48] It will be built next to the existing high school and means that two more complete grades will be bussed to the central education facility each day.

Legislation pending in the 1984 Kentucky General Assembly will raise the minimum educational level for new school board members from an eighth-grade to a high school education. Jackson County has 2,313 citizens 18 years old and over who meet this educational qualification. In the future only 28.6% of the population will be eligible for participation as a school board member.

In the 1981-1983 *Biennial Report* the Superintendent of Public Instruction has recommended the following,

> Election of county school district boards of education should be at large rather than by subdistricts so that the boards represent and advocate for *a sound county-wide public education* and not a regional or sub-district one.[49](emphasis mine)

When implemented this change will at last lay to rest the "problem" of the local interest and sub-district trustee, they have gone from 71 to five in number. With the adoption of this recommendation from the professionals there is no longer any assurance that peripheral areas will be represented and a county-seat population might produce all five school board members.

The educational lights have gone out all over this central Appalachian county. During the past forty years the processes of centralization of power and consolidation have brought urbanization in the provision of schooling, the decline in local participation, and the alienation of citizens that occurs when the universal and whole, in this case socialization, is transferred into the hands of professionals alone. This has not totally due to professionals. In every Appalachian county some citizens have seen it in their interest to promote this cause. They have accepted the ideology of individual advancement and social mobility and believed that the urban school—"The one best system"—was the way to attain it.[50] They overlooked the fact that in such a distribution someone has to be on the bottom. In terms of stigmata Kentucky carries light marks symbolic of pain, but many Appalachian counties have had profound penetration leaving deep wounds.

## APPENDIX 1
Definition of Indicators used in *Profiles of Kentucky Public Schools*

1. *Pupil/Teacher Ratio:* This was calculated by dividing the enrollment obtained from the Superintendents' Annual Statistical Report by the total number of classroom teachers as reported on the federal and state salary schedules.

2. *Percent of Attendance:* Data on the Annual Statistical Report was used to calculate this by dividing the aggregate days attendance by aggregate days membership.

3. *Annual Current Expenses Per Pupil in Average Daily Attendance:* Data obtained from Annual Financial Reports collected by the Division of Finance from the local districts and the Superintendents' Annual Statistical Reports collected by the Division of Pupil Personnel. The total current expenses were divided by the ADA to arrive at the figure. Current expenses include administration, instruction, attendance services, health services, pupil transportation, operation of plant, and fixed charges.

4. *Cost Per Pupil for Instruction:* Instruction costs were calculated by dividing the total spent for Instruction by the average daily attendance. The total for instruction excluded money spent in this area from Title I and IV of ESA. (This exclusion is due to accounting requirements for federal reporting.)

5. *Percent of Ninth Graders Graduating:* The Superintendents' Annual Statistical Report submitted by the local districts to the Division of Pupil Personnel is the basis for this calculation. It lists the total graduates by age and enrollment by grades. The number of graduates was divided by the number of ninth graders enrolled three years ago. \*\*In districts which have merged or experienced a significant enrollment increase or decrease the figures can be misleading.

6. *Percentage of High School Graduates Entering College:* The School Data Form is the source of graduates entering college. High School

graduates are reported on the Superintendents' Annual Statistical Report and divided into the number entering college.

7. *Percent of Economically Deprived Children:* This was taken from records of the Office of School Food Services indicating the percentage of children eligible for free school lunch benefits in proportion to total children of school age in the district.

## NOTES

1. For a consideration of this process in a single Appalachian rural community see Tom Boyd, "Floating Down The Stream Of Time: An Appalachian Rural Community Confronting Mass Society", unpublished paper presented at the 1982 Appalachian Studies Conference.
2. Alan DeYoung, et.al., "Evaluating Educational Performance in Appalachian Kentucky", *Appalachian Journal*, vol. 9, nr. 1, (Fall 1980) p. 54.
3. Alan DeYoung, "The Status of Formal Education in Central Appalachia", *Appalachian Journal*, vol. 10, nr. 4 (Summer 1983) p. 323.
4. Una Mae Lange Rech and Gregory G. Rech, "Living is More Important than Schooling: Schools and self concept in Appalachia", *Appalachian Journal*, vol. 8, nr. 1, (Fall 1980) p. 20.
5. *The Louisville Courier Journal*, "In Jackson County the schools are failing to end the poverty cycle", p. 1, October 30, 1983.
6. *1899-1901 Biennial Report*, p. 11.
7A. *1899 Biennial Report*, p. 14.
7B. Moses E. Ligon, *A History of Public Education in Kentucky* (Lexington: Univ. of Kentucky Press, 1942) p. 118.
8. *1899-1901 Biennial Report*, p. 17.
9. *1899-1901 Biennial Report*, p. 238.
10. Ligon, *Op, cit.*, p. 214.
11. *1907-1909 Biennial Report*, p. 15.
12. Ligon, *op. cit.*, p. 119.
13. *1909-1911 Biennial Report*, p. 68.
14. *1901-1903 Biennial Report*, p. 160.
15. *1901-1903 Biennial Report*, p. 160.
16. *1916-1917 Biennial Report*, p. 273.
17. *1916-1917 Biennial Report*, p. 277.
18. *1911-1913 Biennial Report*, p. 101.
19. *1917-1919 Biennial Report*, p. 27.
20. *1917-1919 Biennial Report*, p. 27.

21. *1914-1915 Biennial Report,* p. 280.
22. *1916-1917 Biennial Report,* p. 34.
23. Thomas D. Clark, *Pills Petticoats and Plows: The Southern Country Store,* (Bobbs-Merrill, 1944) p. 21.
24. *1920-1921 Biennial Report,* p. 6.
25. Ibid, p. 7.
26. Mary J. Patterson, "A Demonstration in In-Service Education of Teachers", unpublished M.A. Thesis, University of Kentucky (1943).
27. Ibid, p. 66.
28. *Kentucky School Report, 1916-1917,* "Supplementary Report of J. Virgil Chapman, State Supervisor of Rural Schools", pp. 281-282.
29. Hattie C. Warner, "Consolidation of Rural Schools In Kentucky", unpublished M.A. Thesis, University of Kentucky, (1925) p. 21.
30. Ibid, p. 40.
31. Ibid, p. 29.
32. *The Little Red School House in Kentucky,* Division of Pupil Personnel Attendance and Accounting; State Department of Education; (June 1969) p. 2.
33. Ibid, p. 2.
34. Figures calculated from *1981-1983 Biennial Report.*
35. *Jackson County Sun,* August 5, 1982, "Hisel School to remain open" p. 1.
    *Jackson County Sun,* May 12, 1983, "Hisel gets one-year reprieve" p. 1.
    *Lexington Herald-Leader,* May 13, 1983, "Tiny School in Jackson gets 1-year reprieve", p. 1.
36. Stuart A. Rosenfeld and Jonathan P. Sher, "The Urbanization of Rural Schools, 1940-1970", pp. 11-42, in Jonathan P. Sher (ed) *Education in Rural America: A Reassessment of Conventional Wisdom,* (Boulder Colorado: The Westvies Press, 1977) p. 40.
37. Jonathan Sher and Rachel B. Tompkins, "Economy, Efficiency, and Equality: The myths of Rural School and District Consolidation", pp. 43-75 in Sher, *op. cit.,* p. 46.
38. Roger G. Barker and Paul V. Gump, *Big School, Small School: High School Size and Student Behavior,* (Stanford University Press, 1964) p. 153.
39. Timothy Weaver, "Class Conflict in Rural Education: A Case Study of Preston County West Virginia", pp. 159-204 in Sher, *op. cit.,* p. 161.
40. Sher and Tompkins, *op. cit.,* p. 63.
41. Ibid, p. 64.
42. Wayne E. Fuller, *The Old Country School: The Story of Rural Education in the Middle West,* (Univ. of Chicago Press, 1982).
43. David B. Tyack, *The One Best System: A History of American Urban Education,* (Harvard Univ. Press, 1974) p. 7.
44. Raymond E. Callahan, *Education and The Cult of Efficiency,* (Univ. of Chicago Press, 1962) p. 120.
45. Ibid, p. 150.
46. Ibid, p. 151.

47. Shirley Williams, "Jabez Elementary School: One for all, all for one", *The Louisville Courier Journal*, Jan. 9, 1983. Mr. Harmand Bisconti of the State Bureau of Instruction discusses these plans here.
48. *Comparative Facilities Survey of Jankson County Kentucky School District*, June 1973, Department of Education.
49. *1981-1983 Biennial Report*, p. 81.
50. For a discussion of the rise of this vertical view of life as opposed to the horizontal view see: Berton Bledstein, *The Culture of Professionalism*, (Norton, 1978).


*Funding for some of this research was provided by a James Still Fellowship administered through the Faculty Development Project of the Appalachian Center, University of Kentucky. Write to author for tables.

ECONOMICS I: MACRO
Appraising the Diversity of the Appalachian Economy
   Millicent M. Taylor; Tusculum College; Greenville, TN
Surviving the 1990s: Inter-Regional Variation in
Economic Problems
   Thomas R. Shannon; Radford University; Radford, VA
Historical Perspectives on Energy and Industrialization
in Appalachia
   Ted Couillard; Georgia Southwestern College; Americus, GA

# Surviving the 1990s: Inter-Regional Variation in Economic Problems

by
*Thomas R. Shannon*

   The national economy appears to be undergoing a major transformation with far-reaching social and political ramifications, Appalachia is participating in that transformation. However, because of its particular place in the traditional national economic division of labor and its particular heritage of economic, social, and political conditions, it is likely that the consequences of national trends on Appalachia are going to differ significantly from the consequences encountered in other regions.
   Moreover, the consequences of national economic trends are not likely to be completely uniform across the region. It is possible to identify certain common tendencies in the likely future economic development of the region[1]. Yet, it is also true that the region is characterized by considerable economic diversity. Traditionally, that diversity has been twofold in nature. First, many different types of economic activity have characterized the region. Second, many of those activities have been geographically concentrated in certain subregions of Appalachia, creating a geographical basis for diversity. More recently, to that traditional diversity have been added new economic activities of the sort formerly concentrated in the urban, industrial regions of the north. While less industry-specific and less geographically concentrated in specific subregions, there still has been some tendency for certain subregions to attract a larger share of this kind of new industry than others. Hence, a full understanding of the likely direction of economic change in Appalachia requires an

understanding of the differential impacts of national trends on its different economic activities subregions.

The present discussion represents a preliminary attempt to examine the differential impacts of national economic trends on the various economic activities and subregions of the southern two-thirds of Appalachia (West Virginia and the Appalachia counties south of it). Much (though not all) of the factual presentation will parallel a recent report of the ARC on near-term economic prospects of the region.[2] However, this discussion will go beyond the ARC effort by more critically assessing the problems economic trends will create and by looking at the implications of those trends for developing strategies to improve regional economic conditions in the future.

## National Trends

American industries are confronting increasingly intense competition from foreign procedures in both foreign and domestic markets. That competition is intensifying and spreading to more and more product markets. At the same time, the increasing size and conglomerate structure of American corporations has made them less dependent on continued success in one product line and better able to shift the location of their operations to different domestic locations or overseas. Hence, in response to increased competition (or simply to maximize profits) the large comporations have been shifting their production plants to low-cost areas. They have also been shifting their resources out of highly competitive, low-profit activities into such high-return activities as "high tech" products, resource extraction, financial speculation and the delivery of managerial, technical and financial services. The result has been the "de-industrialization" of many older industrial regions, the rapid growth of other regions in the United States and certain Third World countries, and the steady decline of whole industries (e.g. steel and autos). In addition, competitive pressures, the ability to relocate, and the willingness to disinvest in low-profit product lines has led to corporate pressures on workers to make wage and other concessions. It has also resulted in pressures on government at all levels to provide subsidies and regulatory relief in return for either not moving plants or staying in business at all.[3]

## Impact on Specific Appalachian Economic Activities and Subregions

These general national trends, combined with the specific problems of particular types of economic activities which characterize various subregions, seem likely to create a number of problems as Appalachia moves into the 1990's. These problems are lilely to be compounded by the fact that the labor force in Appalachia is projected to grow substantially between 1980 and 1990. As a consequence, a ten percent increase in the number of jobs available will be necessary just to maintain unemployment at the levels which characterized the late 1970's.[4]

## Coal:

The coal industry is the most geographically concentrated economic activity in the region: almost 90 percent of all the coal produced regionally is produced in a small number of counties in West Virginia, Virginia, and Kentucky. For Appalachia as a whole (ARC definition) coal mining provides about 300,000 jobs, either for miners or for workers in mine-related industries. The "coal counties" also remain among the most distinctive of Appalachia's subregions in terms of such things as: degree of absentee landownership, low quality of public services, poor physical infrastruture, employment instability, low educational levels, and environmental deterioration.[5] Overall, despite the partial recovery of the coal industry in the 1970's, the "coal counties" thus remain relatively socially and economically depressed.

Moreover, the impact of national trends and problems specific to the coal industry are likely to mean that continued reliance on the coal industry will not provide these counties with adequate employment opportunities over the near-term future—even if the current economic recovery continues on the national level. Energy conservation and the stagnation of the North Central industrial region—the area most severely affected by de-industrialization—will mean slow growth for the utilities which have been the largest customers for Appalachian coal in the recent past. The rapid decline of the steel industry and the rapid conversion of its production technology wil depress coal demand even further. In recent years, about one-fourth of Appalachian production has been exported.[6]. However, intense price competition from foreign mines with low wage costs (e.g. South Africa) limits potential export demand. Growing concern about the sulphur content of much of Appalachia's coal because of acid rain also will be likely to depress demand. In addition, it is likely that Appalachian coal will continue to lose national market share to strip-mined coal in the West. Western coal has been gaining not only because of topography advantages, sulphur content, and the cost advantages of strip versus shaft mining, but also because increasing concentration and outside ownership of the coal companies has made them more able and willing to shift to the West to avoid unionized shaft mines in Appalachia. Overall, the result is the official estimates, which may be too optimistic, project only modest growth in the demand for Appalachian coal through the mid-1990's. The resulting growth in employment would be 63,000 additional jobs, and even that modest increase is premised on the dubious assumption that there will be no further increases in labor productivity because of mine mechanization or the shift to strip-mining.[7]

Thus, the challenge to residents of the coal-producing area is formidable. The coal industry is likely to remain a major source of employment, and the coal counties will continue to have to contend with the familiar and severe problems of coal mining. At the same time, these counties will need major new sources of employment, but the very conditions created by coal mining will create problems for attempts to attract new employers.

### Textiles/Apparel

Textiles mills represent another traditional source of Appalachian employment which are both heavily concentrated in the region (about one-third of all employees in the industry)[8] and certain areas of the region (nationally, 60 percent of all employees are located in the states of North Carolina, South Carolina, Georgia).[9] Overall, about 200,000 workers are employed in textiles in the region.[10]

Textiles also represent one of the major industries in the United States particularly threatened by low-wage plants located in Third World countries. However, actual production of yarns, fibers, and fabrics is expected to remain high in the domestic industry. That is because basic textile production has a high potential for intensive automation. On the other hand, automation will involve the rapid closure of old plants, the bankruptcy or forced consolidation of smaller companies which lack capital to modernize, and the steady decline in employment opportunities in the industry.[11] (Employment has been declining since 1976.) Given the nature of employment patterns in the industry, declining employment will have a particular impact on some kinds of workers. Most textile workers are unskilled, 51 percent of the workers are women, and 19 percent are black (nation-wide figures). The percentage of women and blacks in the industry has been increasing in recent years.[12] Continued competition from foreign producers (who are also automating) is also likely to maintain pressures to keep wages low (currently, wages are 32 percent below the national average for all manufacturing),[13] working conditions substandard, and work discipline harsh.

The apparel industry is closely associated with textiles in terms of its location in the region and employs about the same number of workers. Nationally, employment in the apparel industry has been in decline since 1973, and the prospects for the industry are poor. It is the most labor-intensive industry in the country (85 percent of all workers are production workers). Small firms, the fragmented nature of the market, intense price competition, and the nature of the work all mean that the industry is not in a position to automate. As a consequence, the industry has been extremely vulnerable to foreign competition from extremely low-wage producers overseas—despite some of the lowest wage rates in U.S. industry.[14] Low wages, production speed-ups, the rapid development of urban "sweat shops" using illegal immigrants, and some federal limitations on imports have only served to slow the domestic industry's decline. Hence, major reductions in the region's employment opportunities in the apparel industry seem likely. This decline will especially impact on women workers who constitute 81 percent of the labor force.[15]

Employment declines in textiles and the apparel industry are serious problems for the region as a whole: about 10 percent of the labor force of the entire region (ARC definition) is employed in these industries.[16] The concentration of workers in the Carolina's and Georgia and the frequent location of plants in small communities make the likely subregional and local employment impact especially ominous. Hence, the challenge in textile and apparel dependent areas is to find alternative employment opportunities for workers who are generally unskilled and predominantly women. Efforts of the recent past by particular communities to attract new textile and apparel plants is a "beggar thyself to beggar thy neighbor" game. These efforts rely on local government subsidies, opposition to labor unions, and the acceptance of low wages and end up attracting a limited number of low quality jobs of uncertain stability, continuing low living standards, and straining local government budgets only to (often temporarily) move employment from some other community in the region.

## Furniture

Another traditional source of employment in the region has been the furniture industry, which is concentrated in a narrow north-south band centering in western North Carolina. It is also another labor-intensive industry and one which is just beginning to feel the impact of low-wage, foreign competition. Substantial foreign in-roads have occurred in the markets for low-priced furniture and furniture components, and imports now account for about 10 percent of total domestic sales. Prior to the recession of 1981-83, employment nationally was stagnant and larger producers were gaining market share.[17]

Hence, furniture dependent areas are likely to face stagnant or declining employment opportunities if they continue to rely on this traditional industry. Communities which rely upon smaller furniture companies as primary employers may face plant closings. Employees can be expected to face continued pressures in regard to wages and working conditions.

## Other Wood Products

Another traditional source of employment in the region (about 200,000 workers region-wide) is actually expected to experience some employment growth: timber and wood-related products. Declining timber reserves in the Northwest and projected long-term world shortages are likely to increase the demand for timber from the Southeast, including Appalachia. Assuming sustained economic recovery, the ARC expects short-term employment growth of about 20,000 (compared to 1980) as early as 1987.[18]

Growth in timber cutting and processing (e.g. lumber and pulp) may provide some additional employment, but it will also raise other issues in areas where the industry expands: hillside erosion and attendant flooding problems, disputes over timber rights, worker safety (logging is one of the most dangerous occupations), road deterioration, unstable employment patterns, the continuing problems associated with outside land ownership, the appropriate taxation of large tracts of timber lands, and disputes over the use of federal forest land. The last period of large-scale lumbering in the region brought with it massive problems which still linger, and the challenge is to avoid those problems this time around.

## Chemical and Related Products

A significant concentration of chemical and related products plants providing over 100,000 jobs exist in Appalachian Tennessee and South Carolina. Although official projections for the chemical industry as a whole are for continued but slower growth,[19] Appalachian plants tend to specialize in products destined for such industries as steel, textiles, and pulp and paper where demand is not expected to increase very much.[20] In addition, the chemical industry may be faced with significant foreign competition which will have to be met by plant modernization. (Worldwide there is excess capacity in many sectors of the industry.)[21] Such modernization would allow increased production but would not increase employment since chemical plants are highly automated and capital intensive. At the same time, locational factors work against the movement of the growing sectors of the industry into Appalachia.[22]

## "Newer" Manufacturing Industries

During the 1970's Appalachia did acquire a substantial number of new industrial jobs. These jobs frequently were in industries which were new to the region and represented branch plants of more traditionally Northern industries. Especially significant were plants for industrial electrical equipment, instruments, industrial machinery, consumer electronics, appliances, and transportation equipment. Overall, these industries provide about 450,000 jobs region-wide (ARC definition).[23] While less geographically concentrated than other, traditional industries, the greatest concentration of these plants is in the most southern part of the region -especially in a wide, low-density band west of Atlanta (which is now the most heavily industrialized area in the region).[24]

Nation-wide, industries such as machinery, electronics, and instruments are expected to grow and provide substantial increases in employment opportunities.[25] However, to maintain its current share (7 percent) of this projected increase (of about 3 million new workers nationwide), Appalachia will have to continue to offer conditions which attracted these industries in the 1970's: wages below the national average, low rates of unionization, and a "congenial" business climate (e.g. low taxes). In addition, labor intensive sectors of even these industries (which were often the first "runaways" from the North to Appalachia) are likely to be attracted to overseas locations and much of the industry has a high potential for automation.[26] Hence, particular plants and communities may be vulnerable to some employment loss, even if the region experiences a net gain.

### "High-Technology" Potential

"Hi-Tech" industry (e.g. computers, aircrafts, drugs, scientific instruments) is the popular panacea for national economic problems. Actually the promise of high-tech is largely illusory both because the number of jobs which will be created will be very modest (about 1.5 million by 1990) and the kinds of jobs available in the industry are not what people think. Employment in the industry is sharply divided between small numbers of designers, technicians, and other professionals and a majority of relatively low-wage, low-skill assemblers. (About 60 percent of Silicon Valley's labor force is composed of low-wage production workers or clerical workers.)[27] Pressures from foreign competition is already leading to the transfer of production operations overseas (e.g. Atari's plant closure in California).

Hence, the potential number of jobs the region could attract in hi-tech is limited, and production workers would be in direct competition with Third World wage and working conditions. Headquarters operations are not likely to be attracted to a region which lacks amenities for "upscale" professionals and an established network of scientific centers.[28]

### Military Production

Clearly one of the growth industries of the decade has been military procurement. Military procurement has been a source of modest but significant employment in the region. Appalachia's role in the military production system has traditionally been concentrated in a few types of activities: production of non-weapons supplies by traditional industries (e.g. apparel), power production for nuclear processing by the TVA, and the production of nuclear and non-nuclear (e.g. gun powder and rocket propellants) ordinance on a limited number of government-owned, privately operated facilities. As a recent Highlander Center report demonstrates, while some jobs (usually low-wage) have been created and some communities are very dependent on those jobs, the region has paid a high price in terms of environmental abuse, union-busting by military contractors, violation of worker health and safety, tax avoidance by government facilities, and the like. Generally speaking, military production has consequently reinforced Appalachia's traditional role in the national economy rather than functioning as a "modernizing" force in the region. The "good" (high-pay, high-skill) jobs for weapons production have been located elsewhere.[29]

Hence, while military procurement activities may continue to provide employment opportunities and provide some modest additional employment, those localities in which such activities are located seem likely to be confronted with a host of problems which will offset those limited employment gains.

## Services

Growth in the service sector was the most important source of employment gains in the nation and in Appalachia between 1970 and 1980. However, the regional growth did not parallel the national pattern in terms of the specific kinds of jobs created, the rate of increase in service jobs, or the resulting proportion of workers in the regional service sector by 1980. The type of jobs created region-wide (ARC definition) were concentrated (two-thirds of the total) in health services, retail trade, and educational services. Hence, two of the three major job categories which experienced rapid growth were in those service areas in which most jobs were both low-skill and low-pay. While that is true for most of the service sector, other areas in the service sector offer at least some additional employment in managerial and professional categories and major employment in clerical and related white collar categories (e.g. finance, marketing, wholesale trade, etc.). Related to this pattern was the fact that the gap in service levels (as measured by employment) between Appalachia and the rest of the country grew between 1970 and 1980 because service sector growth in Appalachia was below the national average. The end result is that Appalachia continues to have a much lower level of services, public and private, than the nation as a whole and relies much more on outside services -especially in the areas of finance, business, and technical services.[30]

That pattern seems likely to continue for a number of reasons. High quality business and professional services are oriented toward urban areas in general and corporate "headquarters cities" in particular. High service levels are also dependent on high average income levels and strong tax bases. Clearly, these are not conditions which exist in the region. Moreover, the major role of health services in the region is dependent upon federal policies and funding levels -both of which may change in the near future. Education is similarly vulnerable to funding cuts at the state level and the limitations imposed by local tax bases. Demographic changes almost assure limited growth or decline in educational employment. Hence, the disproportionate concentration of Appalachian service workers in retail trade seems likely to continue and will probable provide most of the projected growth in the service sector. Service sector growth is also likely to continue to be concentrated in the more urbanized counties of the region.

## SUMMARY

It is hard not to be pessimistic about the economic prospects for most areas of the southern part of Appalachia. Traditional industries in the region are extremely vulnerable to the effects of national de-industrialization and foreign competition—in addition to a number of industry-specific problems. Some parts of the region are likely to continue to be dependent on resource extraction, with only modest prospects for employment growth and all the attendant problems associated with the coal and timber industries. There *is* some potential for growth in the newer industries which are concentrated in the southern-most part of the region, but overall manufacturing employment may decline, and pressures on wages and working conditions may intensify. Service sector growth will concentrate on a limited range of jobs which are disproportionately low-wage.

## IMPLICATIONS

If this view of current economic trends and prospects is correct, it has some important implications for those who are seeking appropriate strategies for economic growth and "development" in the region.

First, the diversity of problems and economic characteristics of the different subregions will require that any general strategy be flexible enough to be adapted to the specific needs of each particular area. No single, rigid and specific approach can work for all the different areas in the region. For example, communities facing the collapse of employment in apparel factories face significantly different problems from coal mining communities faced with stagnant average employment and rapid cyclical swings in employment. That is not to say that certain commonalities do not exist. They do. The issues of land ownership, exploitative labor relationships, weak public services, poor infrastructure, lower than average living standards, and the like are common threads which must run through any discussion of the region. On the other hand, the various subregions and different communities of the region will have to deal with very different specific problems and will have very different resources to deal with their problems. All of which suggests that developing strategies to create jobs and improve economic conditions at least must *start* at the subregional or local level.

Second, regional diversity and the likely specific impacts of national trends on various subregions and industries provide additional reasons why the "economic development" or "modernization" model (i.e. the ARC approach of the 1970's) has such limited utility in the region. Simply trying to attract private investment (mostly in manufacturing) to "growth centers" or transportation corridors by building highways, training workers, subsidizing infrastructure, and planning industrial parks is a losing proposition. First, it oversimplifies the complex nature of the problems and needs of a diverse region—a problem which is not overcome by local planning commissions when those commissions are wedded to this general strategy. Second, and most fundamentally, such a strategy ignores national trends toward de-industrialization which: (a) limit the total potential for increases in industrial employment and (b)increasingly force Appalachian communities into competition with Third World countries in terms of wages, working conditions, and corporate subsidies. Appalachia is competing for a declining pool of jobs under conditions in which it can obtain additional manufacturing jobs only by attracting employers interested in docile, low-wage labor and a "friendly" regulatory and tax environment. Even the ARC staff seems to have finally acknowledged these problems and recent ARC projections are for a decline in total manufacturing employment in the region.[31] That leaves those hoping to attract private investment in conventional ways essentially "whistling in the dark," hoping for growth in the service sector by pointing out that the region is currently "underserviced" and therefore has the "potential" for service sector growth. As we have seen, those hopes are probably not well-founded. In short, trying to generate conventional investment in the region probably will not be enough in most areas.

Third, if diversity precludes a single approach and attempts to attract corporation investments will not be enough, some alternative approach seems to be needed. At least some tentative directions in which such an approach might head can be suggested here. The need for subregional and often community-specific solutions implies the creation of organizations at those levels to plan and mobilize people and resources. The likely inadequacy of outside corporate investment to create enough of the right kinds of jobs implies seeking new kinds of economic activities, organized in new ways (e.g. local entrepeneurs, community organizations, etc.). For instance, to draw on the experiences of other places and other times, one recalls the very extensive producers' cooperative movement in the Midwest in the early part of this century and the much more recent development of large numbers of "mini-hydro" plants in New England (which have restored the abandoned mill ponds along the fall line). Movement in this direction is, ultimately, a political act and a political problem in that it involves such things as: generating community support for onconventional solutions, mobilizing community participation, getting cooperation or involvement from local or state government, and fighting the likely legal and political opposition of entrenched interests at all levels of government. It also will require regional cooperation in creating an organizational framework for such things as dealing with common problems (e.g. legal and legislative), sharing expertise, and obtaining and channeling outside assistance.

To those who point the massive obstacles to such an effort and the past frustrations of such efforts there are several replies. First, there does not seem to be any alternative. Current economic trends are moving against the needs of the people of the region. While the traditional private sector will remain the dominant economic force and source of employment for the foreseeable future, it will not be enough by itself. Second, there *are* models, partial or flawed though they may be, of things that can and have been done within the context of the American system of political economy—especially in times of economic distress. Third, the beginnings of a cooperative framework and specific local organizations already exist and could provide a foundation on which to build.[32]

## CONCLUSION

Whatever the short-term effects of the current economic recovery may be, there are long-term structural changes occurring in the American economy which will have substantial and very often threatening impacts on the regional economy. The problems will vary substantially from community to community and industry to industry. However, it seems clear that waiting for outside corporate involvement to "solve" the problems of the region may entail a very long wait indeed. (Moreover, if the past is any guide, we would not like those "solutions" in any event.) Hence, communities and subregions in Appalachia need to begin to think in terms of how to tailor their resources to meet the particular problems they are likely to face. In doing so, they will have to rethink what constitutes acceptable solutions to their problems and create new organizational structures to implement their new strategies.

## REFERENCES

[1] See Thomas R. Shannon, "Appalachia as an Enterprise Zone: Some Speculations on the Future of Federal Policy Toward the Region," *Proceedings of the Appalachian Studies Conference: March, 1983* (Boone, N.C.: Appalachian Consortium Press, 1984).

[2] "Appalachia: The Economic Outlook Through the Eighties," *Appalachia*, vol. 17, no. 2 (November-December, 1983), pp. 1-14.

[3] Shannon, *op. cit.*

[4] "Appalachia: The Economic Outlook Through the Eighties," p. 1.

[5] William E. Hrezo and Thomas R. Shannon, *Appalachian Atlas: A Portrait of the Southern Mountains* (Radford University, 1984).

[6] "Appalachia: The Economic Outlook Through the Eighties," p. 8.

[7] *Ibid.*

[8] U. S. Department of Commerce, *1983 U.S. Industrial Outlook* (Washington, D.C.: U. S. Printing Office, 1983), p. 39-2; "Appalachia: The Economic Outlook Through the Eighties," p. 10.

[9] *1983 U. S. Industrial Outlook*, p. 39-1.

[10] "Appalachia: The Economic Outlook Through the Eighties," p. 10.

[11] *Ibid.*

[12] *1983 U. S. Industrial Outlook*, p. 39-2.

[13] *Ibid.* p. 39-3.

[14] *Ibid,* pp. 40-2—40-5.

[15] *Ibid,* p. 40-4.

[16] "Appalachia: The Economic Outlook Through the Eighties," p. 10.

[17] *1983 U. S. Industrial Outlook*, pp. 42-8—42-9.

[18] "Appalachia: The Economic Outlook Through the Eighties," p. 14.

[19] *1983 U. S. Industrial Outlook*, pp. 9-1—9-15.

[20] "Appalachia: The Economic Outlook Through the Eighties," pp. 11-12.

[21] *1983 U. S. Industrial Outlook*, pp. 9-1—9-15

[22] "Appalachia: The Economic Outlook Through the Eighties," p. 12.

[23] *Ibid.*

[24] Hrezo and Shannon, *op. cit.*

[25] "Appalachia: The Economic Outlook Through the Eighties," p. 12.

[26] *Ibid.*

[27] "Down in Silcon Valley," *Multinational Monitor*, vol. 14, no. 4 (April, 1983), p. 15.

[28]"Appalachia: The Economic Outlook Through the Eighties," p. 13.

[29]*Our Own Worst Enemy: The Impact of Military Production on the Upper South* (New Market, Tenn.: Highlander Research Center, 1983).

[30]"Appalachia: The Economic Outlook Through the Eighties," pp. 13-14 and 7.

[31]*Ibid.* p. 4.

[32]Steve Fisher and Jim Foster: "Models for Furthering Revolutionary Praxis," *Appalachian Journal*, 6 (Spring, 1979).

# Historical Perspectives on Energy, Industrialization and the Shaping of Appalachia

by
*Ted Couillard*

Among the scholar-researchers the competent historian will be best able to discern those forces that have operated to produce the tragedy of Appalachia. This paper is an effort to point up my belief.

From 1820 when the first "14 tons of coal" was mined America began its ascendancy among industrial nations. By 1850, only 10 million tons per year was produced. In 1890, 160 million tons was mined. In twenty years, from 1890-1910, however, the annual production of coal in the United States skyrocketed to 500 million tons per year.[1]

The growth of the American economy has been inseparably linked to the growth of the energy industry. That a cheap supply of energy could be guaranteed was an overriding concern of those who managed America's industrial affairs. These managers performed ably. Cheap coal was king until an even cheaper fuel, petroleum, replaced it just after World War II. Then began a period of almost thirty years when America showed the rest of the world what energy consumption levels in a high technology society could be. Suddenly in the winter of 1973-74 all Americans learned that if we were to continue our overprivileged ways we had to find a new source since we were wholly dependent upon a reliable supply of energy.

Few, perhaps, have fully understood the indispensable role of energy in a modern industrial nation. For example, after the Civil War, the production of iron and steel for American industry required efficient fuels. Coal met this demand. It was abundant in America and such men as Henry Frick with his coke ovens in Connelsville, Pennsylvania, enabled Carnegie, the steel king, to meet the new demands for Bessemer steel for railroad building, or the enormous demands for structural steel.

Generating of electricity was an essential step to industrialization also. Today our need for electricity is so great that coal is being replaced by nuclear plants for electrical production. Edison began producing electricity in the first electric generating plant in New York City in 1882. America was to be lighted by electric lights rather than the older kerosene lamps and gaslight from this time on. Electricity was cheap, convenient and efficient. After a supply of electricity was available, electric motors could revolutionize automation in almost all spheres of human activity.

Today, the three fossil fuels, petroleum, coal, and natural gas supply about 95% of our energy needs. Hydropower accounts for a mere 4% and nuclear energy supplies less than 1% at this time. This picture will change by the year 2000 when 26% of the total energy needs will come from the fledgling nuclear industry. Percentages do not mean much when one considers that the rate of consumption of energy of all kinds will continue to skyrocket as we pass from decade to decade. Coal's demand to generate electricity will be greater than it has been in the past and the nuclear demands will be truly astronomical.

In recent history Appalachia's character has been molded because of the production of coal from the region. No other single factor, or factors, has comparable impact upon the people and their present day culture.

In *Notes on the State of Virginia,* Thomas Jefferson expressed his hope that America would remain a virtuous agrarian society. He advised that manufacturing should be avoided by Americans and that we should buy our goods from Europe. In European nations he told us

> Manufacture must therefore be resorted to of necessity not of choice, to support the surplus of their people. But we have an immensity of land courting the industry of the husbandman ... Those who labor in the earth are the chosen of God, if ever he had a chosen people, whose breasts he had made his peculiar deposit for substantial and genuine virtue ... generally speaking, the proportion which the aggregate of the other classes of citizens bears in any state to that of its husbandmen, is the proportion of its unsound to its healthy parts, and is a good enough barometer whereby to measure its degree of corruption ... for the general operations of manufacture, let our workshops remain in Europe ... The loss will be made up in happiness and permanence of government.[2]

In his own time, Thomas Jefferson was criticized for this view, but today that such a view could be held by an American of such intellectual stature is incredible. Jefferson's hope for an agrarian society was far afield. The U. S. is an industrial nation today surpassing all others.

The poet, Walt Whitman, did not lament the fact that America's course was clear even before those giant strides toward industrialization had been taken. Whitman, like Jefferson, shared the view that the humble, virtuous man would comprise the polity and that all would be well.

The story of Appalachia is the story of coal and industrialization. Many people—perhaps tens of millions over the past 100 years—are involved. Today the economic picture for Appalachia continues to be very gloomy. Coal rich West Virginia leads the nation in unemployment, while the ten poorest counties in Kentucky persist in unrelieved economic depression. If one disregards Reagonomics which has produced the current depression, and examines the relative national economic prosperity of about a decade ago, the pattern of economic life in Appalachia can be discerned.

The per capita income of central Appalachians as late as 1970 was $2,306. The reality of what this means does not easily come home to us. The per capita income of nearly twenty million people in Appalachia is sharply less than for Americans elsewhere plunging large numbers well below the poverty line. Many impoverished Appalachians die from inadequate medical attention in the most remote and poorest areas. Hunger, disease, poverty, and illiteracy are never pleasant for anyone to contemplate for very long.

America's need for coal has produced Appalachia. This story really begins somewhere around 1880 although coal mining was accelerating even earlier especially in Pennsylvania. Today America still needs coal. Into the foreseeable future this need will continue[3], but changes have occurred that alter significantly the conditions of the past. Automation in the mines and technological advances in strip mining have reversed the need for a large work force to produce coal.[4] Industrial America has needed coal to fuel factories which enabled people to have jobs. Thus the coal was centrally important to a healthy economy for the nation, and the economy of the nation, in turn, had to be an overriding concern of government. Moreover, government's responsibility has always been to insure that the military strength of America be sufficient for the nation's defense. Military strength depends upon the industrial efficiency of America.

The simple law in economics that explains what happened to the Appalachians is the law of supply and demand. Everyone knows that the price of anything to be bartered, including human labor, depends upon how dearly it is wanted. If the supply of any commodity is greater than the demand, the price falls. If the demand is greater than the supply, the price rises. Such knowledge is dangerous in the hands of the wrong people. In a democratic society, when something is done to control the laws of supply and demand, extremely favorable results can accrue. This is, of course, wrong.

Many would argue that government was less than vigilant about the rapidly developing energy industry in this country. The cheap supply of coal was needed for the new industries that were expanding so rapidly just before and just after the turn of the century. If the cost of this all important fuel for steel production, fuel for the factories, the railroads, the steamships and for the generation of electricity, was to rise, the reverberations throughout the whole economy could be disastrous. Millions of industrial workers were involved, and efficient regulation of industrial production depended upon a predictable, reliable, and continuous supply of cheap energy. The highly monopolistic coal industry was certainly able to deliver on this score. There was plenty of much needed bituminous coal in Central Appalachia. There was also a large native population there from which to recruit the needed miners. The energy industry was able to produce and deliver cheap coal only because it was able to control the laws of supply and demand of labor needed for coal production. Such choices—the tampering with these laws—are, however, not so easy for right-thinking people and government to condone.

A monopolistic cartel such as that presided over by J. Pierpont Morgan and the railroad magnates under his control had enormous capital with which to achieve its objectives. It not only had this great economic power to make things happen, but it was also able to control large numbers of people who were part of its organization who also added to this enormous power to make things happen. The capital was supplied by Morgan and other financiers under his control. The government was interested in industrial expansion, a healthy economy, and an efficient fuel industry. Through manipulation of supply and demand laws as they regulate the barter of labor, the energy industry was able to guarantee that the workers would not rebel. Indeed they could not rebel. It appears that a slavery was imposed upon Appalachian miners that exceeded any contentions about demeaning slavery that the white masters of the antebellum south were supposed to have imposed upon the negroes for well over 100 years.

To begin with, mining coal is probably one of the least desirable jobs that a human can have. Jefferson did not approve of the much better jobs that could be had in factories. What, for Virginians, would Jefferson's view be of the dangerous job of mining coal? Great risk of injury, and loss of life, accompanies the miner's job. In short, history proves that mining coal is just about the least desirable work a man can perform. This means that not many will willingly do it. And since not many will do it, theoretically the price of labor in coal mining should be expensive. If the labor costs go up, the higher price of coal production means higher prices to the factories and industries that use it. If the factories must pay more for coal, the products produced cost far more when they are marketed. With some items, it is not of national concern, but in the steel industry for example, it is extremely unfavorable to the American economy when rolled steel can be produced in Japan far less expensively than in the United States. Industry must compete. It is clear that coal production must be kept inexpensive.

On this score—cheap production of coal—the energy industry has a remarkable record. They delivered coal in such abundance and so cheaply that American industry was never in doubt about the continued supply. They were able to do this because they attended to the necessary planning that had to be done. Here the story of Appalachia becomes quite disturbing. It was necessary for the cartel to control a whole region. It was necessary to control the population of the whole region. Ten million people or more; Impossible! you say. Not at all.

Proceeding with a clear knowledge of the law of supply and demand, the energy industry was able to manipulate the supply of labor to insure that there would always be a greater supply of labor than was actually needed. This, of course, required careful planning. It must be remembered, too, that the energy industry in 1910 was a cartel that had the power, both economic and political, to accomplish what it was about. No branch of government, no church, no labor union, no normal political group or faction, could accomplish what this cartel was able to accomplish. It is the nature of a cartel to build an organization involving a large number of people who depend upon their association with the cartel. They, too, are part of the cartel, but not as policy makers nor significant democratic voices to exercise influence in any way. The first concern was to build the organization of dependent workers. When this was accomplished, the power of the cartel was greatly enhanced. Very tight control of the coal miners in Appalachia was easily achieved.[5] The company housing, the company stores, the closely supervised communities of workers was all part of the organization building of the cartel. A labor union also organizes large numbers of people and wields great power, but its objectives are entirely different, and the democratic dialogue attending labor union activity distinguishes it from the industrial cartel immediately.

Such was the power and tight organization of the energy industry cartel in Appalachia as early as the eve of W.W.I. After building the cartel organization, the surrounding region had to be controlled if the cartel was to protect its existence. Careful planning prevented competing industry from luring members of the cartel organization to other jobs which would gain for the workers independence from the cartel. It is true that a worker and his family was free to return (if he could pay his bill to the company store and surely some of them could) to the hollow where he was born. But what could he do there? Perhaps he could fish or hunt squirrels. And no doubt many workers chose to return to their beloved mountains after a stint in the mining camps. Eventually, however, the mountaineer had to come back to his senses and agree to employment with the energy people, if he wished to enjoy industrial society's commodities. How could the mountaineer ever hope to buy an automobile to ride in, or a radio to tune into, that would bring him that wonderful music broadcast all the way from Wheeling, West Virginia, if he did not have a job? The radio station flooding with lovely music the moon-blanched mountains on any given night in North Carolina or Tennessee appealed powerfully to the mountaineer and worked magically calling the mountaineer back to his senses and to the mines. Clearly the cartel, even if it didn't own the station could exert its will. The power of a cartel is both economic and political. Its influence in the social sphere is, therefore, enormous. I have argued that after the turn of the century the existence of an energy cartel in this country that was bigger than government itself is something that a few reasonable men will doubt. Matthew Josephson is convincing about who owned the coal fields and how they acquired them. He writes:

> In the great Pennsylvania coal fields those resplendent magnates, the Vanderbilts, J. Pierpont Morgan and Cassatt of the Pennsylvania Railroad had after a process of "squeezing" smaller capitalists added most of the anthracite mines to their railroad domains.[6]

The real power was in the hands of a single man, J. Pierpont Morgan. "The hard-coal mines were nearly all indirectly owned by eastern railroads over whom Morgan held influence or a decisive voice..."[7] The much richer prize than Pennsylvania's coal was the Central Appalachian coalfields. When General Imboden bought so much of West Virginia for the "gentlemen of means" it was Morgan's empire again that controlled the Baltimore and Ohio roads.

> Similarly in the soft-coal regions, the Hocking Valley Railroad, the Baltimore and Ohio and Chesapeake and Ohio were soon swept into the unified control of the unified system which held through the "purchase or interchange of stock," at once the coal mines, the roads that carried their coal to market and the banks which financed them all.[8]

The best American historians will examine Appalachia carefully when the best 20th century American history is written. The story of coal, the energy cartel and American industrialization will be the dominant concerns of these scholars when they attempt to tell the story of modern America.

## NOTES

[1] Richard C. Dorf, *Energy Resources and Policy,* (Menlo Park, 1978) p. 90.

[2] Thomas Jefferson, *Notes on the State of Virginia,* Edited with an introduction by William Peden (Chapel Hill, 1955), pp. 164-5.

[3] Donald Whitehead reported to Congress that 600 million tons of coal are expected to be produced in Appalachia by the year 1985. Richard C. Dorf says U. S. coal production will top 1,000 million tons by 1985. See Richard C. Dorf, *Energy Resources, and Policy* (Menlo Park, 1978). p. 91.

⁴In 1932 there were 705,000 miners in Appalachia. In 1940 there were 439,000. The number has continued to decrease. See Helen Lewis "Fatalism or the Coal Industry?," in *Appalachia: Social Context.* p. 157.

⁵The dependency of large numbers of workers and their families upon the cartel was carefully planned and accomplished. Again the debt to Henry Frick is clear. Samuel Gompers complained the miners' children were "brought into the world by the company doctor, lived in a company house or hut, were nurtured by the company store . . . laid away in a company graveyard." Matthew Josephson, *The Robber Barons,* (New York, 1934) p. 373.

⁶Matthew Josephson, *Robber Barons* . . . p. 373.

⁷Josephson, *Robber Barons* . . . p. 373.

⁸Josephson, *Robber Barons* . . . p. 413.

NORTH GEORGIA MUSIC
Folk Visions and Voices
  Art Rosenbaum; University of Georgia
North Georgia Musicians and Groups in the 1920s and 1930s
  Gene Wiggins; N. Georgia College; Dahlonega, GA
  Eller Brothers and Ross Brown: Workshop/Performance
  Convenor: Zell Miller; Lieutenant Governor of Georgia

# North Georgia Musicians and Groups in the 1920s and 1930s
by
*Gene Wiggins*

## COMMERCIALLY RECORDED GEORGIA FOLK MUSICIANS OF THE 1920's

There is a special interest for the folklorist and social historian in the commercial recordings made by folk musicians in the 1920's. It is our first chance to either hear or see all the sorts of things rural southerners had been singing to each other. Folklorists had collected from the folk only a certain sort of thing. Toward the rest of what their informants were singing and playing, the folklorists sometimes had been hostile. Sometimes they had been just busy and forced to specialize. They did a good job. They did what most needed to be done. But now we have a broader definition of folk music, along with an interest in biography of folk musicians, in musical styles, and in total repertoire. The oldest material serving these interests was recorded in Atlanta beginning in 1923.

    Fiddlin' John Carson, who had put rural music on Atlanta radio in 1922, was recorded in 1923 at the suggestion of Atlanta record man Polk Brockman. Brockman had no personal liking for Carson or for his music. He wanted Carson recorded because he knew many people did like him. This 1923 recording in Atlanta was almost the first commercial recording made anywhere in the South. It was the first issued and successful recording of what came to be called country music, though we should remember that country music means one thing when we are talking historically and another thing when we are trying to distinguish types of music prevailing today. For a few years the recording of this type of music—or these *types* of music, for there was considerable variety—was mainly in the hands of northern, urban people who understood the music so little that they left nearly everything to the performers. For a few years there was no hard search for new performers. The companies either had the performers go to New York or recorded them in Atlanta. A large fraction of the people recorded in those early years lived in or near Atlanta, had known each other before recording, and continued to play shows together. At the first Atlanta Country Music Hall of Fame awards in 1982 Clyde Carson, Fiddlin' John's son and driver, stated, "Most of the people you have heard about tonight I have hauled in a 1914 T-Model." There was a local quality about much of the music, though people who knew each other well sometimes recorded widely different versions of the same song.

There was also an amateur quality. Many performers had been professionals of a sort, but pass-the-hat standards had not been high. It was a sort of music many people could approximate. It didn't have to be rehearsed to any fine point. There exists an issued record by Fiddlin' John's band in which John's fiddle switches from "Peter Went A-Fishin'" to "Little More Sugar in the Coffee." One of the band does not notice and continues to sing "Peter Went A-Fishing."

Radio and records produced a rapid change in this sort of music. It soon lost its local, spontaneous, amateur quality. It was corrupted or improved, depending on your point of view, by hardcore professionalism. The depression almost suspended the making of country records except those by such prime non-Georgia favorites as Jimmie Rodgers and the Carter family. In 1934 when things were looking a little better there were sessions by Georgia's Fiddlin' John Carson and Georgia's Skillet Lickers. The records made at these were not all flops. In fact the Skillet Licker pairing of "Down Yonder" and "Back Up and Push" was a considerable hit. Still, it was clear in 1934 that the heyday of the real old timers in the recording business was over.

Let us have a little closer look at these musicians, beginning with the first recorded, John Carson. Carson is usually said to have been born in Fannin County in 1868. However, there is some reason to think he may not have been quite that old and may have been born in Cobb County. Fannin County was the famous *mountain* county. A fictional and journalistic notion of the old mountain fiddler had developed in the nineteenth century, and when we first see newspaper publicity about Carson in 1913, he is already pretending to be a little more of a hick than he really was— at least by pretending to be a visitor from Blue Ridge, Fannin County, when he had lived in Atlanta since 1900. Country music had its ballyhoo years before it had any recordings, and Carson was something of a professional from the time he was a boy. He played and passed the hat, and he was hired to work political campaigns. Two of his nineteenth century political patrons were Bob Taylor of Tennessee and Tom Watson of Georgia. Carson moved to Atlanta in 1900 to work in the cotton mills. Three events of 1913 turned him away from cotton-mill work and made him more of a professional musician. One was the beginning of a well-publicized series of fiddlers contests in Atlanta. He got a lot of publicity in the reporting of these, and became better known. Second was a textile strike which caused him to quit his job in the mill. Third was the murder of Mary Phagan. Carson composed songs about Mary—apparently four of them eventually, though only three have survived—and peddled song sheets. He had become well-known in Atlanta and was doing shows in other towns when Polk Brockman, in 1923, decided to see how he would sell on records. His records sold quite well for a number of years. On the first sessions he fiddled and sang alone. Then he added a band—the Virginia Reelers—which included his daughter Rosa Lee, who was given the name Moonshine Kate. Carson recorded some 123 distinct pieces plus a good deal of redoing of things he had already done, sometimes with important changes, sometimes not. I classify 42% of his output as pre-twentieth century folk material. The oldest specimen we have of several songs now well-known is on the recordings of John Carson.

The first time Carson recorded with a band he employed a little banjoist named Land Norris, who went on to record on his own several songs with banjo accompaniment. Norris was born in Gilmer County in 1877 and was a fur trader. He wandered through the mountains buying furs, and he learned a lot of comic songs from the people he traded with. He was notable for changing the name of nearly everything he recorded. For instance "Cripple Creek" became "Red Creek" and "Sourwood Mountain" became "Dogwood Mountain." A notable theme in Norris' recordings is satire on the clergy. Preachers were apt to regard banjo pickers as sinful, and banjo pickers were apt to frame anti-clerical stanzas in retaliation.

There were two Earl Johnsons in Fiddlin' John's early retinue—Freckled-faced Earl, a comedian and one-string fiddler, and Fiddlin' Earl, a four-string fiddler. Fiddlin' Earl, born in 1886, was a Gwinnett County piano tuner who could read music and allegedly could play citified stuff. He continued to be heard on some of Carson's sessions, but he also formed his own band, which is named on some records Earl Johnson's Entertainers and on others Earl Johnson's Clodhoppers. The later name is more typical. Most of the old Georgia bands sought ultra-bucolic names. In addition to Earl Johnson and his Clodhoppers we had Arthur Tanner and his Corn Shuckers, Gid Tanner and his Skillet Lickers, Fate Norris and his Plow Boys, Lowe Stokes and his Swamp Rooters, etc. Johnson recorded about 60 sides, singing on many and on others playing the wildest and fastest fiddle of the time.

Fiddlin' John Carson was not the oldest of the rural Georgia musicians we can hear on the old records. His friend Rob Stanley, born in 1858, was at least a decade older. It was Uncle Rob Stanley who encouraged the more famous Gid Tanner to move to the Lawrenceville-Dacula area. Rob's daughter Roba was only 14 when she, her father and a Bill Patterson cut a record in 1924, Rob singing "Nellie Gray" on one side and he and Roba singing "Whoa Mule" on the other. Roba recorded other records with her father and Patterson, as well as with a Virginian named Henry Whitter, who had recorded before Fiddlin' John but did not have his records issued until after the success of John's. Roba, who is still living, was found by Charles Wolfe and me in 1977 and has received some notice under the epithet "First Sweetheart of Country Music." A couple of her songs do have the coquettish derision of males we sometimes associate with hillbilly gals, but several of her songs have a male persona. In one case he seems to be a moonshiner and in another a black chicken thief. However, in 1924 there was no competition for the title "Sweetheart of Country Music," and one didn't have to sound very seductive. A little over a year after her first recording, Roba married, moved to Florida, and gave up music.

Andy Jenkins was born a little south of Atlanta in 1885. From the age of three weeks he was blind. By 1918 he was preaching in Atlanta and selling newspapers on the streets. In 1922, he and his second wife and his stepdaughters were doing programs on WSB. Later, in addition to the family recording as the Jenkins Family, Jenkins recorded solo as Blind Andy and Gooby Jenkins. As far as any modern taste for his singing is concerned, Jenkins comes in behind even Land Norris, who does have one number on reissue longplay. As far as I know, Jenkins has none; but he was a phenomenal songwriter. Some of his songs, thought to be mountain or western folksongs actually were composed on the busiest streets of Atlanta. Like Wordsworth, Andy composed aloud and he liked to be where there was a lot of street noise so people wouldn't think he was crazy. Some of his songs were great hits as recorded by other people. The best known probably are "Death of Floyd Collins," "Billy the Kid," and "God Put a Rainbow in the Cloud."

The Cofer Brothers, Leon and Paul, born in 1899 and 1901, also recorded with a Ben Evans as The Georgia Crackers. They sounded more black than Appalachian. Once some old-time music buffs conjectured that they were black, but I eventually found their younger brother and sister and found that they came from a relatively cultured white family. Their father was a Methodist minister and song writer, P. A. Cofer, who published a pair of books of religious songs. All the Cofers were trained in sacred music, but Rev. Cofer also employed blacks on his farm and at his three sawmills. It was the songs and the style of their black friends that Leon and Paul drew on most when they recorded. The formative years of the Cofer brothers were spent in middle Georgia, many of Leon's early years at the Macon academy for the blind. However, they were born in North Georgia and had moved to Atlanta by 1923. I think there is a discernable Appalachian element in their music.

The Skillet Lickers get considerable attention in Art Rosenbaum's last book, because they were a big influence and because the book deals directly with Gordon Tanner, lead fiddler of the 1934 session and son of the most famous Skillet Licker, Gid Tanner. Gordon and his son Phil continued Skillet Licker music until Gordon's death in 1982. Phil and his son continue it yet. James Gideon Tanner, generally known as Gid, was born near Monroe in 1885. At Uncle Rob Stanley's instigation, he later moved to Dacula. He became well-known as a fiddler and comic singer at the fiddlers' conventions in Atlanta before World War I, and when the ground was too wet for farming he would go to Atlanta and play on the streets, accompanied by Gordon when Gordon was very young. When the Okeh record company scored a hit with John Carson, the Columbia record company naturally sought the services of the other of the two fiddlers best known in Atlanta. Gid agreed to go to New York and record if he could take with him a blind singer and guitarist named Riley Puckett. Puckett was a decade younger than Tanner, and the initial duo was augmented later by still younger men—Clayton McMichen, Lowe Stokes, and Bert Layne. It was given the name Skillet Lickers. There are at least six places in Georgia officially or unofficially named Lickskillet. In the old days people didn't talk about living in depressed areas or being disadvantaged. They talked about licking skillets. There had been a Lickskillet Band at the fiddlers' conventions years before. With the possible exception of the band of North Carolinian Charlie Poole, the Skillet Lickers are the 1920's band most listened to today. There is one reissue longplay of John Carson, one of Earl Johnson, one the the Georgia Yellow Hammers, but at least six of the Skillet Lickers, as well as three of Riley Puckett, who remained their star singer as well as cutting many records apart from the Skillet Lickers.

With the Georgia Yellow Hammers, of Calhoun, as with the Skillet Lickers, two older men recorded first and then the band was enlarged with younger fellows. The old timers were Bud Landress and Bill Chitwood and the major additions were Phil Reeve and Ernest Moody. All the Yellow Hammers had been involved in religious singing convention music as well as instrumental music. Actually they were a good vocal quartet that could play instruments adequately, and they had two talented song writers—Bud Landress, who wrote "Picture on the Wall"—done in recent times by Ross Brown and the Eller Brothers—and Ernest Moody, who wrote "Kneel at the Cross"—done in recent times by Lester Maddox. Moody lived until 1977. When I interviewed him, I found him to be a well-read ex-school teacher who had what I think of as the pre-1950's-school-marm conception of folk music. According to that conception folk music is found only way back in the mountains, it has definite British elements, its pretty and sweet, and it isn't played for money. He was too nice to say so, but it was evident he thought I had goofed in regarding him as having been a purveyor of folk music. I don't know to what extent I changed his thinking as to the value of what the Yellow Hammers had done, but shortly before he died his daughter wrote me that she had caught him singing,

> Oh the bell cow—grab her by the tail;
> Oh the bell cow—milk her in the pail.

Only people close to my age know how much anti-hillbillyism once existed. In the thirties and forties people almost had me thinking that the people I have been talking about were not so precious as they seemed to me. Their music is not as smooth as the music you hear in the dentist's office, but if it ever really gets in one ear it won't go out the other. If you haven't yet tried it, do so.

HISTORICAL DIVERSITY IN APPALACHIAN COMMUNITIES
Diversity in Ante-Bellum Mountain Life: The Towns of Western North Carolina
  John Inscoe; Univ. of North Carolina; Chapel Hill, NC
The Vinland Settlement
  Roy G. Lillard; Cleveland State Community College; Cleveland, TN
Demography of Western North Carolina Blacks
  Wilburn Hayden; Western Carolina University; Cullowhee, NC
"Ripshin"
  Roberta Roy; East Tenn. State Univ.; Johnson City, TN
  Convenor: Ed Cabbel; John Henry Memorial Foundation; Princeton, WV

# Diversity in Antebellum Mountain Life: The Towns of Western North Carolina

by
*John C. Inscoe\**

In the first issue of *Mountain Life and Work* in 1925, the journal's co-founder, Olive Dame Campbell, wrote, "There is no fundamental reason for separating mountain people from lowland people, nor are mountain problems so different from those of other rural areas in the United States."[1] This was an extraordinary statement, particularly at a time when social consciousness of the poverty, ignorance, and isolation of the people of the Southern Appalachians was at its peak. In the midst of the stereotypes of backward mountaineers that were rapidly establishing themselves in American minds, such a perspective was refreshing, though its accuracy to mountain life in the early twentieth century is debatable. But when applied to the same area in an earlier era, the decades just before the Civil War, the statement takes on new significance and becomes a far more applicable assessment of mountain society at that time.

Historians have only slowly and reluctantly come to recognize the fact that antebellum society in the Southern Appalachians had much in common with that of the rest of the South.[2] By the 1840s and 1850s, as advances in trade and transportation elsewhere in the South accelerated, the topographical disadvantages of the highlands and the delays in getting railroads and other internal improvements into their region had begun to be recognized by some mountain residents as possible hindrances to their full participation in the economic development around them. At the same time, settlers were beginning to push back into the more secluded coves and hollows that would sooner or later cut off much of their contact with the outer world. But to most, these trends were seen as little more than temporary setbacks which, as in other frontier situations, would soon give way to the inevitable march of progress. They did not view themselves as part of a separate region with special problems which should set them apart from the rest of the South. Any distinctions in their geographic or demographic situation were seen as minor aberrations which would soon be overcome and allow their eventual integration into the broader economic network around them.

Southern Appalachia was of course a predominantly rural area, even more so than the antebellum South as a whole. It was populated largely by small farmers and its economy was based on a system of diversified and primarily subsistence agriculture. But to leave such a description of antebellum mountain life at that, as is so often done, is to overlook what was, by the mid-nineteenth century, a far more varied, complex, and vigorous society. Nowhere was this more true than for the western counties of North Carolina, and nowhere was it reflected more than in the development of the towns and villages there. Though often overlooked by those seeking to characterize the Southern Appalachian experience, it was those communities that formed the vital centers of mountain society and, as such, they exerted an influence on the social and economic character of the region far greater than their size alone would have warranted.

This paper is an attempt to demonstrate the significance of these non-rural factors on an essentially rural society by examining the origins, functions, and influence of its towns on the mountain region of North Carolina in the years before the Civil War. Whether they developed as county seats, as commercial centers, or as tourist resorts, they generated much of the area's progress, diversity, and entrepreneurial spirit. These characteristics not only gave them much in common with their counterparts throughout the South, and thus make Mrs. Campbell's observation so apt, but they also served as a link to communities elsewhere. Thus, though many remained quite small and crude, even by the standards of the rural South, these mountain towns became their region's strongest force against any tendencies toward isolation or alienation from the outside world. Very few mountaineers were so secluded that they did not have access to, or make use of, some such community.

There seems to have been no pressing need for towns or the services they offered among the earliest settlers in western North Carolina. Their primary goals were simply to acquire land and make it as productive as possible. In most parts of the region, it was only the formation of new counties and the need for a seat for their newly organized local governments that led to any efforts at establishing a concentrated non-rural community. Morganton, the earliest town in the western part of the state, was established only when the legislative act creating Burke County in 1777 also stipulated that a commission fix the location for a courthouse, a prison, and stocks. Even then, it was seven years later, when the creation of the Morgan Judicial District gave some urgency for the need for a courthouse, that a site was selected and a town plan drawn up.[3]

Between 1835 and 1860, nine new western counties were created. Despite the fact that several had had substantial and well-established populations for several decades, they often had no community or commerical center to designate as a county seat. Thus Marion in McDowell County, Webster in Jackson County, Sparta in Alleghany, Waynesville in Haywood, and Wilkesboro in Wilkes were all established in locations chosen strictly for their accessibility and topographic suitability and their central location within the new county boundaries.[4]

In other instances, the presence of a store or trading post was the determining factor in the selection of a site. James Harper had operated a large store, tannery, blacksmith shop and harness shop for a full decade before the site of his enterprises was chosen for Lenoir, the county seat of newly-formed Caldwell County in 1841.[5] Likewise, Jordan Councill's mercantile operation became such a focal point for trade and communication in his area that it, with the new name of Boone, was designated as Watauga County's seat in 1850.[6] Cherokee County was created from Indian territory soon after the 1838 removal of the tribe, and its county seat, Huntersville (later called Murphy), was established on the site of an earlier trading post from which Colonel Archibald Hunter had maintained a brisk business with the Indians.[7] Macon County too was part of former Indian territory and its county seat, Franklin, grew from the foundations of what had once been a sacred Cherokee village.[8]

The potential economic and political significance of these seats of local government were fully recognized by county residents, and bitter disputes sometimes broke out between communities or sections of a county as to which would reap those benefits. In several cases, the more obvious choices were passed over in favor of smaller communities or even relatively unsettled locations as the result of hard-fought contests between rival factions. Buncombe Courthouse, later called Morristown and finally Asheville, was built on a plateau where a wagon road forded "the big branch between the Indian graves." Such an obscure locale was a compromise choice between the county's most concentrated settlements at Reems Creek and Swannanoa, though even that so-called mid-point was considered a victory for the northern section of Buncombe and a loss for those to the south, whose selection committee refused to sign the final report.[9]

The location of Yancey County's seat was a source of rivalry between two individuals. In 1833, Thomas Ray and John Bailey, both among the area's earliest settlers and most prominent citizens, sought to establish the town near their own homes by offering the county generous allotments of their own land for that purpose. The decision seems to have been based merely on the size of the donations, as Ray's fifty-acre offer on the Cane River was passed over in favor of Bailey's hundred-acre gift on the Toe River, where the town of Burnsville soon emerged.[10]

With Madison County's formation in 1851, the small but lively village of Jewell Hill, the site of the area's militia muster and court sessions, was assumed to be the logical choice for county seat except by the few, but influential, citizens of Lapland, a smaller settlement farther up the French Broad River. Zebulon Vance, who had grown up there, donated fifty acres for the new town, and was so confident that his action would settle the matter that he wrote his fiancee, Harriett Espy: "You may expect to see, next time you pass this place, a flourishing and romantic little village."[11] His influence, along with that of his uncle Adolphus E. Baird, who had long operated a tavern and inn there, and Samuel Chunn, whose stockstand was equally well established, finally won the day for the Lapland site in 1855, though by only a single vote of the selection committee.[12] Its name was promptly changed to Marshall, but it was still another four years before the court began to meet there instead of at Jewell Hill.

The most heated contest was that in Henderson County. After it was created in 1838, a three year controversy raged over the location of its county seat of Hendersonville, whose name at least had already been determined. Advocates for a site on the French Broad River were opposed by those favoring one along the Buncombe Turnpike. "River" and "Road" factions, as they came to be called, remained so adamant that it took three appeals to the state Supreme Court and a referendum election throwing the decision to the county's voters before the "road" location was finally agreed upon.[13] In this, as in other disputes, commercial interests were at least as decisive as political factors in the choices made. Both the French Broad and the turnpike offered potential for substantial trade between North Carolina's mountains and South Carolina and Georgia. The final decision was based largely on the judgment of county residents that the latter held the greater promise as a trade route and was thus the one they wanted their new seat of local government most accessible to.

Not all mountain towns owed their origins to demands for commercial centers or county government bases. Tourism contributed to the early growth of several communities. Natural mineral springs and their reputed healing powers began attracting visitors to western North Carolina early in the nineteenth century. These sites, along with others whose attraction lay merely in their cool climates, healthy air, and mountain scenery, often began with hotels, inns, or seasonal private residences that formed the cores of what grew into fully operational and multifunctional towns and villages. Though many of western North Carolina's most successful and well-known resorts did not emerge until late in the nineteenth century, Warm Springs in Madison County, Flat Rock in

Henderson County, and White Sulphur Springs and others in Haywood County were all fully established and thriving by the 1830s and 1840s.[14]

Once established, all of these mountain communities attracted enterprising men of various training and background whose skills and services did much to move most parts of the region beyond the frontier stage of development and added diversification and complexity to an otherwise agricultural economy and farming populace. The governmental function of the county seats, along with the judicial function of their county and circuit courts made lawyers, judges, clerks, and other office holders prominent among their earliest residents and most frequent visitors. Merchants, artisans, tavern and inn keepers, and land speculators recognized the business opportunities offered by these newly emerging towns, and their early moves to them often enabled them to engage in several types of commercial ventures simultaneously with profitable results.[15]

These professional and business men were among the few mountain residents with enough capital to acquire slaves, so that the region's largest slaveholders were, more often than not, town rather than rural residents. Many put their black property to work in their stores, hotels, or "factories" so that much of the black labor force in the western part of the state was concentrated in its towns and villages rather than scattered on its farms. This, along with the influx of slaves brought along by slaveholding tourists, led a British visitor to Asheville in 1842 to express dismay at the large proportion of black residents there. Though his estimate is somewhat exaggerated, he wrote that the town had "a population of 200 persons, of whom not more than 120 are whites."[16]

Churches, and soon after schools, became integral parts of most mountain communities. Many of them, particularly in the smaller villages, relied on circuit ministers and teachers who provided local residents with regular and influential contacts with the outside world and served to bind them more closely to other mountain towns as well. The larger and more prosperous communities were able to support at least one, and often several, ministers and teachers. As permanent residents, they added to the diversity of the population and encouraged more widespread social contacts by drawing into town residents from surrounding areas and giving them a sense of community participation and belonging. Both schools and churches, which often shared a single building, not only provided a social center for community life but served as a focal point for local civic pride. In 1855 a woman in Macon County's Oak Hill Community described the festivities surrounding the opening of a new school there. "There seems to be quite a spirit of improvement astir among the good people in our quiet little village," she wrote. "We are making roads, building bridges, rearing dwelling houses and churches at a rate that would astonish you."[17] Her enthusiasm reflected a spirit that was typical of many late antebellum mountain towns and villages, whose citizens actively promoted the development of their communities and were optimistic about their future progress.

But despite similarities in their origins and certain integral features shared by all these communities, variables in their geographic locations, their dates of origin, their rates of development, their appeal to outsiders, and the abilities and ambitions of their citizens led to sharp contrasts in the character of western North Carolina's towns during the antebellum period. The older, more established towns, such as Asheville and Morganton, and to a lesser degree Lenoir and Wilkesboro, developed a thriving commerce, which along with their functions as county seats, gave them as diverse and as affluent a populace and economy as any small town in the antebellum South. The latter three, situated in broad fertile valleys on the east side of the Blue Ridge, served the market needs of western farmers by providing an accessible outlet to the piedmont. At the same time, they served as gateways for traffic moving up into the mountains from the rest of the state. The mere appearance of these towns reflected their relative prosperity and earlier roots. Of Morganton, "the oldest village in the mountain district," one visitor noted "its pleasing avenues and inviting residences," and concluded that "from a society point of view, the town sustains its ancient reputation for polish and cleverness."[18]

Asheville though had already established its preeminence as the social and commercial center for the western part of the state. In 1795, soon after the selection of Bumcombe Courthouse's site, two enterprising brothers, Bedent and Zebulon Baird, recognized its profitable real estate potential and bought all of the designated land. After donating a central lot as the site of the courthouse, they laid out streets and lots which they sold to families and businesses as they moved into the area. From this promising start, the town prospered and grew, thanks to its scenic and accessible location at the intersection of the wide valleys of the French Broad and Swannanoa rivers which made it a natural crossroads for most trade and travel west of the Blue Ridge. By the late antebellum period, its residents included many of the region's most able and ambitious citizens and it consisted of over twenty stores or businesses, a courthouse, a jail, three churches, three large hotels, several schools and a female college. In 1856, British journalist Charles Lanman described it as "a very busy and pleasant village, filled with intelligent and hospitable inhabitants, and is the center of a mountain land where Nature has been extremely liberal and tasteful in piling up her mighty bulwarks for the admiration of man."[19]

Due to the scenic settings and cool, pure air of Asheville and other mountain communities, summer tourism played a major role in their economic and social vitality. In 1827, Charles Baring, a prominent Charleston rice planter, sought relief from the ill effects of the swampy coastal climate on his wife's health and built a lavish estate at Flat Rock. Others from South Carolina and Georgia soon followed him and Flat Rock,

Hendersonville, Asheville, Warm Springs, and other communities soon gained reputations throughout the South as "charming refuges from the hot plains of the lowlands."[20] Local residents quickly sought to capitalize on the various needs of the influx of visitors from May to October every year. Among the most successful and influential citizens of Asheville were its hotel owners. James Patton's Eagle Hotel and James M. Smith's Buck Hotel were among the town's largest buildings and were so often filled to capacity that nearby homes profited by accommodating their overflow.[21] Like the Walton House in Morganton, which advertised that it was "supplied regularly with Fresh Fish from Norfolk and Newburn, in fact with every delicacy usually found at First Class Hotels," these establishments prided themselves on the quality of their accommodations and service.[22] Among their most basic services were the various forms of transportation they provided. The Eagle Hotel, for instance, declared that it was "in readiness at all times to convey passengers to any part of our beautiful Mountain Country." In addition to daily or every-other-daily stagecoach service to Greenville and Spartanburg, S. C., Greenville, Tenn. and Morganton, Salisbury, and Charlotte, N. C., its livery stable offered "superior saddle and harness horses and a lot of entirely NEW Vehicles: consisting of Hacks, Carriages, Buggies etc., which are safe and comfortable."[23]

In addition to the commercial boom brought about by the "summer people," as they were referred to by mountain residents, those tourists themselves did much to shape the characters of those communities to which they flocked. An Asheville native boasted that the town was "adorned with many beautiful residences, the result of cultivated taste among its inhabitants, or the summer residences of citizens of South Carolina." He went on to praise his fellow residents "who, in a spirit of improvement, a love for the beautiful, and a taste for the refined, make gardens of waste places, and turn the barren hillsides into blooming undulations."[24] A young female visitor wrote of a ride she took on the outskirts of Asheville along the Swannanoa River. "It was," she exclaimed, "quite a merry drive indeed; [I] saw a great many fine farms and residences and a good many people riding out—some in buggies and some on horseback in riding costumes, looking quite like city folks and city life."[25]

Even more impressive to travelers were the Hendersonville and Flat Rock communities, where the affluence and taste of its transplanted South Carolinians and Georgians was apparent in the fashionable clientele of their hotels and even more so in the "baronial style" of their estates. To a New York traveler, they "rivaled in elegance and taste any villa or mansion on the Hudson," and an aristocratic British visitor said that they reminded him "more of English than anything we had seen in America."[26] Just as Baring had led many of his fellow Charlestonians into the area, his plantation, with its magnificent columned home, beautifully landscaped lawns and gardens, private chapel and rectory, complex of stables and servants' quarters, and vast private park for deer hunting, served as a model that inspired others to imitate or even outdo it.[27]

The social activities in these communities were fully in keeping with the lavish settings in which they took place. As summarized by a Hendersonville woman, they included "quadrilles danced under candled chandeliers, gracious conversations over three o'clock dinners in silver laden banquet rooms, morning gatherings on latticed porches, Carriage drivers over Little River Road . . . and picnics on the mountain ridges."[28] The participants in this leisurely and sophisticated lifestyle were equally as impressive to another British observer. He described those at a ball he attended as being "good-looking with good figures and good dancers and manners easy and polite."[29]

The mineral springs resorts catered to an equally affluent clientele in much the same manner, if on a smaller scale. In addition to its healthful waters, Warm Springs, the most well-known and well-attended of these, "presented more attractions to the seeker of pleasure than probably any watering-place in the South." Elaborating on those attractions, Charles Lanman wrote that "Music, dancing, flirting, wine-drinking, riding, bathing, fishing, scenery-hunting, bowling, and reading are all practiced here to an unlimited extent."[30]

In sharp contrast, many of the more western county seats, most of which were formed later, remained small, crude, frontier-like communities. While most visitors describing these towns tactfully chose to extol their magnificent and "romantic" physical settings, Augustus S. Merrimon, a young Asheville attorney who practiced in various circuit courts throughout western North Carolina in the early 1850s, was more openly contemptuous of them and their residents. Of the state's western-most town, Murphy, he wrote in his diary that it "is a small place and poorly improved. There are several small stores here that seem to do a small business. All of them together would not make one good one." Waynesville, despite the presence of several fashionable resorts in the vicinity, was no more appealing to Merrimon, who found it "a dirty small village and there is no place of entertainment in it fit to stay at. One would suppose it to be a large negro quarter to see it from a distance."[31] Its buildings, he wrote, were already delapidated and decayed, including their courthouse which had been built only a few years earlier.[32]

But it was Jewell Hill (where Madison County's court still met despite the selection of Marshall as its county seat) that Merrimon found most offensive. Its men were generally drunk, as were its women, whom he described as "dirty, filthy strumpets." He wrote with disgust: "I do not know any rival for this place in regard to drunkenness, ignorance, superstition and the most brutal debauchery."[33] British geologist George Featherstonaugh echoed these sentiments in recording his impressions of Franklin. "What a dreadful state of things!" he wrote. "Here was a village most beautifully situated . . . that might become an earthly Paradise, if education, religion, and manners prevailed . . . But I could not learn that there was a man of education in the place disposed to set an example of the value of sobriety to the community." He revealed his own national bias by concluding that the town served as a "perfect specimen of that kind of equality which democratic institutions often lead to."[34]

Somewhat more objectively, the celebrated writer and journalist Porte Crayon described the relative lack of physical or economic development of Bakersville, then in Yancey County in 1857:

> Its principal streets is built up on one side with a rail-fence, and on the other with two cabins, set back from the street. The back streets and alleys, which are laid off *ad libitum*, contain the stables, cowshed, and hen-houses. The only public buildings worthy of note are an applejack distillery . . . and a springhouse, which has no commercial value. During the dark of the moon the town is lighted with pine-knots; and its police force, consisting of six big dogs, is at all times uncommonly vigilant and active.[35]

Swiss geologist, Arnold Guyot, made extensive tours throughout the Carolina highlands in the late 1850s and found few of the communities he visited worthy of even that much attention. Of Watauga's county seat, he wrote: "There is not so much as a village in the whole County, for Boon (sic), the county-seat . . . contains but a few dwellings clustered around the Court-house."[36]

But regardless of their rate of growth or the degree of sophistication of their citizens, all of these mountain towns exerted an influence far in excess of their size. The "backwardness" of these western-most communities described by contemporary observers often failed to acknowledge their commercial and social vitality. In 1860, Boone, whose very existence Guyot all but denied, actually consisted of six stores, two tanneries, two hotels and several boarding houses, at least one saloon and the blacksmith shop. The demand for lumber to keep up with the pace of construction in the community was great enough to make three sawmills among the town's most successful enterprises in the 1850s.[37]

Community studies have provided a number of models by which these towns may be categorized in terms of function and relationship to the dispersed populace of the region. In several such studies of twentieth-century Appalachian communities, Art Gallaher, Jr., has distinguished five types of community in terms of their contact with and access to the "outside world." These range from the most extreme cases of social and geographic isolation through progressively more complex and sophisticated communities to the region's few urban centers. The fourth level of community development along his scale is that of county seat community, in which its political and trade-centered functions provide "systematic links to the greater society which exist in more variety and in more institutional areas" than in the three preceding levels.[38] Pushing this scheme back to the antebellum period, and applying it to western North Carolina's towns and villages, most, if not all, met the criteria for Gallaher's county-seat model, whether they were indeed county seats or only tourist resorts or commercial centers.

The government and judicial functions of the actual county seats entailed regular contacts by its residents with agencies and individuals outside the region and meant frequent visits from various officials and other professionals. The impact of tourists and seasonal residents on those in and around the resort communities was even greater. But to the majority of mountain residents, those farmers and their families beyond the bounds of these communities, contacts with these particular outside influences were minimal. Travelers only occasionally veered from their well-beaten paths and their encounters with more remote local residents, when they did so, were only sporadic and superficial. Likewise the contacts between county officials and their county's more rural citizens came only when they bought or sold land or paid their taxes.

It was as commercial centers that almost all of these towns, from Asheville and Morganton to Franklin and Murphy, exerted their most pervasive influence on their region, and it was through their real functional cores, the commercial establishments, that rural mountaineers maintained their most substantial and immediate link with the world beyond their own. Just as stores and trading posts were often the nuclei around which communities grew, so they remained vital to the further prosperity of both town and county residents. Many businessmen provided various services as well as merchandise, so that a "store" was often only one of several operations conducted by a single owner. Jordan Councill of Boone, William McKesson of Morganton, Jesse Siler of Franklin, and James Harper of Lenoir are only four examples of merchants who operated tanneries, blacksmith shops, and mills in addition to their mercantile businesses, and each of them was among the most prominent and influential leaders in their communities. By meeting multiple needs for their areas, they and their counterparts in other mountain towns served as the primary, and often the only, contacts many western Carolinians had with the outside world. Their dependence on these men, based on personal contact as well as economic need, made their influence considerable. A Buncombe County resident recalled that "old settlers in the country each had his merchant in Asheville, not only to supply his wants, but in whom he confided as a trusted friend."[39]

In addition to supplying local residents with a wide variety of manufactured goods and imported food staples, these store owners provided equally as vital a service as an outlet for those surplus goods that those same customers wished to sell. The scarcity of cash often necessitated a barter system, the flexibility and localized nature of which allowed for a readily available means by which most mountain farmers could, and often did, move beyond mere subsistence farming and enter the market economy, if only in a limited way. While farm produce and meat from slaughtered livestock were the most basic of local goods bartered, the inventory of several mountain stores indicates that a wide variety of distinctively mountain products were also common in these transactions. A British woman visiting Asheville seemed somewhat offended by the diversity of goods carried in shops there. Merely to buy "a bit of ribbon," she had to face "horrible raw hides . . . masses of mica . . . and every imaginable thing for sale."[40] Leander Gash owned a large store on the present site of Brevard, where he stocked "hams, venison, hides, and feathers, chestnuts, chestnut bark, apples, cabbages, wild honey and mountain herbs."[41]

Several merchants specialized as dealers in ginseng, the root of a small plant native to the North Carolina mountains, which was sold to China, where its medicinal qualities were in great demand. Calvin Cowles of Wilkesboro bought it, along with other roots and herbs, from mountain residents who gathered it in the forests of the state's northwest corner and brought it down to his store.[42] Bacchus Smith and Nimrod Jarrett of Yancey County found the ginseng, or "sang," business so profitable in the 1830s that they ran three factories at which over 86,000 pounds of the freshly-dug green root were steamed, dried, and prepared for the Chinese market.[43]

These various products in turn provided merchants with the means by which they engaged in expanded versions of such transactions elsewhere. As early as 1802, Francois Andre Michaux described the trade pattern he observed in passing through Morganton:

> One warehouse only, supported by a commercial house at Charleston, is established in this little town, where the inhabitants, for twenty miles round, come and purchase mercery and jewellery goods from England, or give in exchange a part of their produce which consists chiefly of dried hams, butter, tallow, bear and stag skins, and ginseng, which they bring from the mountains.[44]

This pattern was typical and continued to be practiced in most mountain communities throughout the antebellum period. In Ashe County alone, residents were said to have sent to market goods worth "upwards of Thirty Thousand Dollars yearly."[45]

Some merchants, particularly those in the northern section of North Carolina's mountain region, looked to the north for their primary business contacts. Calvin Cowles made annual trips to Washington, Philadelphia, New York and Boston, where he found ready markets for his ginseng and other roots and herbs. These he sold for cash which he then used to purchase the merchandise with which he would stock his Wilkesboro store for the coming year.[46] James Harper of Lenoir sold deer and other animal skins and furs to markets in Baltimore and Philadelphia and obtained much of his merchandise from mercantile suppliers there.[47]

But these men also participated, along with the majority of western North Carolina merchants, in the far more well-established trade network to the southeast. Charleston and Columbia in South Carolina and Augusta, Athens, and Savannah in Georgia were regular trade centers for mountain businessmen, and trips to one or more of these towns at least once a year, along with regular correspondence and shipment of goods throughout the year, were routine for most of them. Joseph Cathey was the postmaster and storeowner at Forks of the Pigeon in Haywood County. He planned his trips after consultation with South Carolina and Georgia as to the prices on "the bacon, lard, and feather markets." He then headed south, usually in February, with wagon loads of smoked meat, tanned hides, feathers (in demand for beds), and apples. He was accompanied by varying sized herds of livestock, moving on foot, all of which he had bought from or traded with farmers from all over the county. In 1854 he sold "40 cattle and sheep" for $1386 in Augusta. He then used the cash to purchase saddles, bridles, and tools from a "hardware importer," and various supplies from a druggist before moving on to Charleston where he bought coffee, sugar, candy, salt, and rifle powder from a wholesale grocer, and paint, oil, and glass from a "staple and fancy dry good" establishment.[48]

With considerable variations in the type of goods sold and bought and in the cities visited, annual trips like Cathey's were made by at least two or three store owners in every mountain town. Through such business practices they served as middle men who enabled almost any mountain farmer to participate in the broader southern market economy. But even more important, their experiences and contacts in the deeper South combined with their pervasive influence among their fellow mountain residents to make them the region's predominant "culture carriers," providing links with the rest of the South that were not merely economic, but social and political as well.

Mountain towns of course did much to facilitate and promote this lively interstate commerce. But several of them were the beneficiaries of an even more extensive trade network that ran through the Carolina highlands. This was the phenomenal movement of livestock from the upper South, particularly Kentucky and Tennessee, to the plantation markets of the southeast. Beginning as a trickle about 1800, the annual flow of hogs, cattle, sheep, horses, and even turkeys, and ducks grew steadily through the 1820s and 1830s to become a virtual flood with the opening of the Buncombe Turnpike. This major thoroughfare in the western part of the state not only increased the capacity for moving larger herds on hoof but enabled wagon traffic as well to utilize the same route. An 1849 traveler on the turnpike noted that:

> an immense number of cattle, horses, and hogs are annually driven over it to the seaboard markets. Over this road also quite a large amount of merchandise is constantly transported for the merchants of the interior, so that mammoth wagons with their eight and ten horses, are as plenty as blackberries and afford a romantic variety to the stranger.[49]

Running along the already well-travelled French Broad valley from Tennessee directly south through three mountain counties to South Carolina, the turnpike brought a commercial boom to the towns of Marshall, Warm Springs, Asheville, and Hendersonville. Local merchants, inn and tavern keepers eagerly sought to accommodate the demands of the drovers and their herds. They also benefitted greatly from the business generated by the many farmers in the vicinity attracted by the ready outlets for their own livestock and grain crops. As a major juncture with other routes, Asheville was from the beginning the center of the livestock trade and served as a point of convergence at which animals from all over North Carolina mountains joined those from other states already midway on their journey. By the late antebellum years, 140,000 to 160,000 hogs alone were estimated to have passed through the town every year, with an estimated value of between two and three million dollars.[50] Some butchering was done in Asheville, with cured meat, bacon, and lard either sold locally or held for later trips south. But the vast majority of animals merely continued on hoof to their southern destinations.

Thus, antebellum mountain residents by no means made up the poverty-stricken, stagnant, and backward society which came to characterize much of Southern Appalachia in later years. Far from being physically or psychologically isolated from the world around them, western North Carolinians maintained strong profitable ties with their lowland neighbors. On the eve of the Civil War, they anticipated even greater prospects for economic and social intergration as their long-awaited plans for railroads through the mountains were on the verge of becoming a reality. Among the primary causes and the primary effects of this vitality were the towns and villages of the region, and particularly their citizens. The leadership, contacts, ambitions and diversity of interests and talents of mountain town residents had much to do with making their region not merely like other rural areas, as Mrs. Campbell suggests. Because of the special elements of its tourist trade and livestock traffic, western North Carolina may well have been even more lively and diversified than most.

## NOTES

[1] Mrs. John C. Campbell, "Flame of a New Future for the Highlands," *Mountain Life and Work* I (April 1925), 9.

[2] Among the most perceptive works on this theme are Gene Wilhelm, Jr., "Appalachian Isolation: Fact or Fiction?" and Wilma Dykeman, "Appalachia in Context," both in J. W. Williamson, ed., *An Appalachian Symposium* (Boone, N. C.: Appalachian State University Press, 1977); and Gene Wilhelm, Jr., "Folk Settlements in the Blue Ridge Mountains," *Appalachian Journal* 5 (Winter 1978).

[3] Edward W. Phifer, Jr., *Burke: The History of a North Carolina County* (Morganton, NC: 1977), 66-67.

[4] Mildred B. Fossett, *History of McDowell County* (Marion, NC: 1976), 85, Ora Blackmun, *Western North Carolina and Its People to 1880* (Boone, NC: 1977), 266; John P. Arthur, *Western North Carolina: A History from 1730 to 1913* (Raleigh, 1914), 169, 174. See also David L. Corbitt, *The Formation of the North Carolina Counties, 1663-1943)* (Raleigh, 1950), 3-4, 117-118, 129, 142, 227-228.

[5] Nancy Alexander, *Here Will I Dwell: The Story of Caldwell County* (Salisbury, NC: 1956), 93-95.

[6] Betty McFarland, *Sketches of Early Watauga* (Boone, 1973)

[7] Blackmun, *Western North Carolina*, 274.

[8] Arthur, *Western North Carolina*, 174.

[9] Foster A. Sondley, *Asheville and Buncombe County* (Asheville, 1922), 72-73.

[10] Jody Higgins, ed., *Common Times: Written and Pictorial History of Yancey County* (Burnsville, NC: 1981), 42.

[11] Zebulon B. Vance to Harriett N. Espy, February 19, 1853, in Elizabeth R. Cannon, ed., *My Beloved Zebulon: The Correspondence of Zebulon Baird Vance and Harriett Newell Espy* (Chapel Hill, 1971), 184. See also George W. McCoy, "Madison County Marks Its Centennial," Asheville *Citizen-Times*, January 14, 1951; Manly Wade Wellman, *The Kingdom of Madison* (Chapel Hill, 1973), 66.

[12] Wellman, *Kingdom of Madison*, 70.

[13] James T. Fain, Jr., *A Partial History of Henderson County* (New York, 1980), 15-18.

[14] Lawrence F. Brewster, *Summer Migrations and Resorts of South Carolina Low-Country Planters* (Durham, 1947), 64-68.

[15] Wilhelm, "Appalachian Isolation," 78, 85.

[16] James S. Buckingham, *The Slave States of America* (London, 1842), Vol. II 202. For a discussion of slaves in the mountains, see John C. Inscoe, "Mountain Masters: Slaveholding in Western North Carolina," *North Carolina Historical Review* LXI (April 1984), 143-173.

[17] Mollie Carrie to Leander Gash, March 1855, Gash Family Papers, North Carolina Department of Archives and History.

[18]W. G. Zeigler and Ben S. Grossup, *In the Heart of the Alleghanies of Western North Carolina* (Raleigh, 1883), 342.

[19]Charles Lanman, *Letters from the Alleghany Mountains* (New York, 1849), 427.

[20]William W. Malet, *An Errand to the South in the Summer of 1862* (London, 1863), 215. See also Brewster, *Summer Migrations and Resorts*, and Blanche Marsh, *Historic Flat Rock*, (Asheville, 1961).

[21]Sondley, *Asheville and Buncombe County*, 84.

[22]Advertisement, *North Carolina Standard*, Raleigh, July 16, 1859.

[23]H. E. Coulton, *Guidebook to the Scenery of Western North Carolina* (Asheville, 1860), 14-15.

[24]Coulton, *Guidebook*, 17-18.

[25]Mollie Carrie to Leander Gash, August 3, 1855, Gash Family Papers, NCDAH.

[26]"Picturesque America: On the French Broad River, North Carolina," *Appleton's Journal*, December 17, 1870; Buckingham, *The Slave States of America*, 197.

[27]Malet, *Errand to the South*, 235-237; Marsh, *Historic Flat Rock*, 3.

[28]Marsh, *Historic Flat Rock*, 3.

[29]Malet, *Errand to the South*, 234.

[30]Lanman, *Letters from the Alleghany Mountains*, 125. For brief descriptions of Warm Springs and other antebellum resorts in western North Carolina see John Disturnell, *Springs, Waterfalls, Sea-bathing Resorts and Mountain Scenery of the United States and Canada* (New York; J. Disturnell, 1855), 137-138.

[31]A. R. Newsome, ed., A. S. Merrimon Journal, 1853-54," *North Carolina Historical Review* (July 1931), 315.

[32]Newsome, "Merrimon Journal," 310.

[34]George W. Featherstonhaugh, *A Canoe Voyage Up the Minnay Sotor*, Volume 2 (London, 1847; Reprint, St. Paul, 1970), 281.

[35]Porte Crayon, *The Old South Illustrated*, 230,231.

[36]Myron H. Avery and Kenneth S. Boardman, eds., "Arnold Guyot's Notes on the Geography of the Mountain District of Western North Carolina," *N. C. Historical Review* (July 1938), 27.

[37]John P. Arthur, *A History of Watauga County, North Carolina* (Richmond, 1915), 147-153.

[38]Art Gallaher, Jr., "The Community As a Setting for Change in Southern Appalachia," in Lloyd Davis, *The Public University in its Second Century* (West Virginia Center for Appalachian Studies and Development, 1967), 26.

[39]Wilma Dykeman, *The French Broad* (New York, 1955), 59.

[40]Dykeman, *The French Broad*, 59.

[41]Otto H. Olsen and Ellen Z. McGrew, eds., "Prelude to Reconstruction: The Correspondence of State Senator Leander Sams Gash, 1866-67," *North Carolina Historical Review* LX (January 1983), 40.

[42]See the survey for the various entries in Calvin J. Cowles Papers, Southern Historical Collection, UNC Library, Chapel Hill.

[43]"The Late Bacchus J. Smith," Asheville *Citizen*, August 6, 1886.

⁴⁴Francois Andre Michaux, *Travels to the West of the Alleghanies*, reprinted in Reuben G. Thwaite, ed., *Early Western Travels, 1748-1846* (Cleveland, Ohio, 1904), 290.

⁴⁵A. R. Newsome, ed., "Twelve North Carolina Counties in 1810-1811," *North Carolina Historical Review* V (October 1928), 420.

⁴⁶Various entries, Calvin J. Cowles Papers, Southern Historical Collection and NCDAH.

⁴⁷Alexander, *Here Will I Dwell*, 93-95.

⁴⁸See various bills, receipts, and correspndence, 1850-1854, in Joseph Cathey Papers, NCDAH. The community of Forks of the Pigeon later changed its name to Canton.

⁴⁹Lanman, *Letters from the Alleghany Mountains*, 123.

⁵⁰Thomas L. Clingman to J. S. Skinner, February 3, 1844 in *Selections from the Speeches and Writings of Hon. Thomas L. Clingman of North Carolina* (Raleigh, 1877), 116.

*This paper is the winner of the Appalachian Studies Conference Student Paper competition.

THE THREE R'S: RESEARCH, RESOURCES, RECORDS
**The Great Smokies: Diverse Perceptions of the Park as a Resource**
   David Carpenter; Western Carolina University; Cullowhee, NC
**Regional Research in Federal Archives**
   Charles Reeves; Gen. Serv. Admin., Regional Archives; Atlanta, GA
**Portraying Diversity: An Appalachian Atlas**
   William Hrezo; Radford University; Radford, VA
   Convenor: Helen Kimsey; Mountain Regional Library;
   Young Harris, GA

# The Great Smokies: Diverse Perceptions of the Park as a Resource

by
*David Carpenter*

The 50th anniversary of the Great Smoky Mountains National Park is being celebrated this year. This park, the most heavily visited national park in the country, provides many types of recreational experiences for its visitors. People visit the park for a number of different reasons, with many kinds of expectations. They see the park as a place to take the family camping, and pitch their tent or park their recreational vehicle in one of the park's campgrounds; they go to the park for a backpacking trip, to hike many miles into the wilderness-like interior of the park; people also use the park as a drive-through scenic area, often between their stops in Cherokee and Gatlinburg, and see the park through the windshield of their car or other vehicle. Some individuals think of the park as a wildlife refuge, and visit it with hopes of seeing bears or other animals. The park serves as a museum to yet other people, who take tours of the pioneer homestead at Oconaluftee, or who might visit other preserved cabins, gristmills, or other exhibits and reminders of the lifestyles of the early settlers in the region. A survey of park visitors, conducted in 1975, found that most visitors believed that the purpose of a national park was two-fold; "To preserve wildlife" and "to provide a place where people can come to enjoy nature." The survey also found that three out of four people (73%) agreed that in the park and its region that "you can find just about everything you want."[1] An individual's perception and resulting attitudes toward the park, or for that matter anything else, is largely a function of the person's past history and present situation. Two people can look at, or think about the same thing and have two very different perceptions of it, or ideas as to what it represents.

In its 50th year, as in the preceding 49 years, there is a wide range of opinions as to what represents the essence of the Great Smoky Mountains National Park or its greatest value. If we look back to the years just preceding the park's establishment, or even many, many years earlier, we find a wide diversity of opinions as to what kind of resource was thought to be represented by the lands of the Great Smokies.

As early as 15,000 years ago, nomadic hunters called the Paleo-Indians moved eastward from the Great Plains region and probably used the park area for big-game hunting. Sometime around 7000 B.C., the descendants of these nomadic people gradually changed into a larger, more sedentary population. Gathering activities became more important, and over the following centuries, agricultural activities gained dominance over hunting and gathering activities as a way of life for the Indians. The first European contact with these resident Indians, the Cherokees, occurred around 1566 or 1567.[2]

Around the year 1760, white settlement in the region gained momentum. By the early 1800s, the centuries-old villages, culture, and homeland of the Cherokees had been swept over by the incoming flood of white settlers and their need for more land. By the time of the Civil War, virtually all of the land suitable for farming was occupied by white settlers.[3] The region in some ways became a preserve of sorts for a traditional way of life for many years. Industrial development, modernization, and various social and cultural developments did not come as swiftly to the mountain region as to other areas.

The mid-nineteenth century saw a few wealthy "flatlanders" begin coming up from Charleston, South Carolina and other lowland areas to escape the oppressive summer heat in the much cooler mountain climate. Some of these people also built summer homes. Thus was started the summer home/tourism industry which in later years was to have such a significant impact on the mountain region—its land, its people, and its culture.

In the 1880s lumber companies had begun to mount large-scale commercial logging operations in the region.[4] The face of the region began to change. It was in the 1880s, also, that the idea of a national park in the region was first proposed. Rev. C. D. Smith of Franklin, North Carolina may have been the first person to write a proposal for a park in the southern highlands,[5] but this is not known for sure. It is recorded, however, that Dr. Henry O. Marcy of Boston, Massachusetts read a paper before the American Academy of Medicine in New York on October 29, 1885 entitled: "Climatic Treatment of Diseases: Western North Carolina as a Health Resort."[6] In the closing paragraph of his paper, published in The Journal of the American Medical Association, Dr. Marcy said that: "The wise legislator, seeking far-reaching results, would do well to consider the advisability of securing under state control a large reservation of the higher ranges as a park.'"[7]

Another physician, Dr. Chase P. Ambler of Ohio, received a reprint of Dr. Marcy's paper and was impressed by his idea for a park. When Dr. Ambler moved to Asheville, North Carolina in 1889, and became aware of the beauty of the area first-hand, he became a strong advocate for the establishment of a park. On a fishing trip up to the Sapphire region of western North Carolina, Dr. Ambler asked the advice of his companion Judge William R. Day, also from Ohio, as to how a park could be promoted. Judge Day, who had just returned from the Paris Peace Commission Conference, suggested the formation of an organization in Asheville to push the national park proposal.[8]

In November of that same year, a convention was held in Asheville and the Appalachian National Park Association was established.[9] An active campaign was launched to garner support for a national park in the Southern Appalachian mountains and, in 1900, the Association presented a memorial to Congress. This document listed numerous reasons for establishing a park, and also supplied maps with proposed locations for the park.[10] Soon after this, however, the Association found out that the federal government had already gone on record as opposing the purchase of lands at any future time for national park purchases. The Association then changed its name to the Appalachian National Forest Reserve Association, and changed its goal accordingly.[11]

In December 1905, the Association, after its years of promoting the establishment of first a national park and then later national forest reserves, asked the American Forestry Association to take over its campaign. An agreement was reached and the Appalachian National Forest Reserve Association was dissolved. Its efforts, however, had helped contribute to a compaign which was later to result in the passage of the Weeks Act in 1911. The Weeks Act authorized the establishment of national forests, and stimulated interest in the idea of national parks.[12]

By the early years of the nineteenth century, the lumber companies had moved their operations into the Smokies. The furious pace of large-scale logging operations had far-reaching effects on the region, its economy, and its people in the early years of the century. Around 1909 the logging reached its peak in the Smokies and the region.[13] Mountain sides had been stripped of large tracts of virgin timber, prized for its size and quality. Destructive timber-cutting practices sometimes described as "git, slash, & go"[14] were reported to have been widespread. But the demand for lumber remained high, and the timber industry remained a very strong force in the mountain region. Another force, however, was building strength. Horace Kephart, author of *Our Southern Highlanders*, was only one of a number of people who were to contribute to a second, ultimately successful, national park movement. This second major movement to establish a national park in the Southern Appalachians began around 1923, and it was begun on the other side of the Smokies, in Knoxville, Tennessee.

In the summer of 1923, Mr. and Mrs. W. D. Davis of Knoxville had made a western vacation trip and had visited some of the national parks. Mrs. Davis admitted that the scenery in the western parks was very pretty, but she insisted that the Great Smoky mountains contained scenery just as beautiful. "Why can't we have a national park in the Great Smokies?" she asked her husband. Mr. Davis, who was then manager of Knoxville Iron Company, liked the idea and as soon as they had returned to Knoxville began enthusiastically telling his friends about "this wonderful national park we are going to get in the Great Smokies."[15]

Mr. Davis submitted his idea for a Great Smokies national park to Dr. Hubert Work, Secretary of the Interior, in the Fall of 1923. Around thirty other claims for national park sites in other areas of the East had also been received by Secretary Work, though, and he decided to appoint a committee to investigate the proposed park sites.[16] In December of the same year, a dinner meeting at the Cosmos Club in Washington, D.C. helped to begin an active campaign for a national park in the Appalachians. Stephen Mather, Hubert Work, and Zebulon Weaver, a Congressman from Asheville, N. C., were present at the dinner.[17] The following week Congressman Weaver made a public statement in support of a park's establishment. The momentum was gaining for a new national park in the Southeast, but there was some amount of disagreement as to where it should be located.

The Southern Appalachian National Park Committee, appointed by Secretary Work to study the proposed locations for a park began its study in 1924. Ironically, the committee would not schedule a visit to Knoxville to hear about the Great Smokies area, but were due to stop in Asheville to study the Grandfather Mountain/Linville Gorge area as a possible site for a park. Despite efforts by the Great Smoky Mountains Conservation Association to get the committee to visit Knoxville and study the Great Smokies park proposal, the committee refused to change their schedule. They did, however, finally and reluctantly agree to give a hearing to representatives of the Tennessee association during their stop in Asheville. A delegation from Tennessee, well-armed with enlargements of numerous pictures taken in the Great Smokies area by the association's official photographer, Jim Thompson, met with the Southern Appalachian National Park Committee in Asheville. After a three-hour meeting with this delegation, and after the pictures of the Great Smokies had captured their interest, two of the five members of the committee agreed to take a personal look at the area. They were to be greatly impressed with their tour of the Smokies and sights such as the flame azaleas in bloom on Gregory Bald. Other members of the committee later visited the area and also had high praise for the Great Smokies.[18]

A recommendation from the committee was made in December 1924 for the establishment of both the Shenandoah and the Great Smoky Mountains National Park. In their official report the committee said: "The Great Smokies easily stand first because of the height of mountains, depth of valleys, ruggedness of the area, and the *unexpected variety* of trees, shrubs, and plants."[19]

In the following months bills were passed in the Senate and the House to approve land acquisition for the park. In April 1926 President Coolidge signed a law allowing purchase of lands for the park.[20]

The legal stage had been prepared for the establishment of the Great Smoky Mountains National Park. But a very large obstacle remained. The creation of the seventeen national parks prior to this time had been accomplished by the setting aside of lands already belonging to the federal government. But the minimum 300,000 contiguous acres needed for the Great Smoky Mountains National Park would have to be purchased from the private owners of some 6,600 separate tracts of land[21] and then later offered by the states of North Carolina and Tennessee for acceptance by the Secretary of the Interior. The Great Smoky Mountains Conservation Association in Tennessee and its sister organization in North Carolina, called the Great Smoky Mountains, Inc., had already begun campaigns to raise money and gain public support for the purchase of the land. Over a span of years, roughly 12 million dollars was to be needed for the purchase of the park lands.[22] The money came from North Carolina and Tennessee state expenditures and from private donations. Five million dollars in matching funds were donated by John D. Rockefeller, Jr. from the Laura Spellman Rockefeller Memorial Fund. And finally, federal money, allotted by President Roosevelt, completed the park land purchase fund.[23] But although the money to purchase park lands was eventually found, and the long campaign to establish the park was ultimately successful—it is important to understand the reasons why people spoke out, sometimes eloquently, both in support of the park, and also in opposition to it.

The local western North Carolina newspapers were some of the strongest supporters of the park movement. The timber and pulpwood companies, who owned approximately 85 percent of the land in the proposed park area, were some of the strongest foes of the park movement.

The *Asheville Citizen* in December of 1925 had this to say about the lumber industry:

> When the life of the forest is turned into death in the wake of the juggernauts of the lumber industry, there appear the naked skeletons of former sylvan monarchs, sacrificed to feed industry that eats without thought for the moment.[24]

Four days earlier the paper had printed a full page advertisement paid for by the Champion Fibre Company, which owned over 92,000 acres of the choicest land in the Great Smokies area.[25] The Champion ad had stated, in part, that:

> The proposed area once established as a National Park withdraws for all time and regardless of changed economic conditions one of the very large national resources of Western North Carolina from all industrial use.
>
> The acquisition for Park purposes of the virgin timber area of the Smoky Mountains involves problems that are extremely difficult of solution because of the fact that these lands were purchased for specific industrial uses.[26]

The Jackson County Journal, in an article on February 9, 1927, portrayed the battle between park proponents and the lumbermen as:

> A fight between nearsightedness and farsightedness; a battle between those who love their state, and are anxious that she shall continue in her glory and those who believe that the natural resources of the country are the property of a few men of this generation, and that the coming generations are not to be considered.[27]

The conflict seemed finally to be between conservation and industrial consumption—and a decision as to whether tourism or manufacturing would be most characteristic of the region's economic future. In the mountain region in the 1920s and 1930s there was an increasing emphasis on the economic benefits of tourism, and the establishment of a national park was seen as having extremely beneficial consequences for tourism and the regional economy. An article in the Asheville Citizen in 1931 included a quote by Ray Lyman Wilbur, at that time Secretary of the Interior, who pointed out that: "The crop of visitors is easy to harvest—recreation gives them health, happiness and satisfaction and they in turn give prosperity to park neighborhoods."[28]

A pamphlet published by the Great Smoky Mountains Conservation Association of Tennessee speculated that:

> Not only will multitudes of vacationists be attracted by the splendors of the Great Smokies; the same multitudes will at the same time be attracted by the enjoyments promised enroute.
>
> Those multitudes will spend freely, just as similar multitudes do in Montana and California.
>
> But it is not only money that will be turned loose, it is tourists—with eyes and ears open. Returning home, they will advertise both states by word of mouth. Americans of the best type will find much to tempt them to settle down and stay—

among other things, the survival of old-time standards of morals and manners and the absence of aliens.[29]

The conservation and preservation of the proposed park's vegetation cover was also seen as providing another type of economic bonus for the region. A publication by the Wachovia Bank and Trust Co., in 1931, noted that: "The Great Smoky Mountains act as a watershed for many streams having enormous possibilities for water power development . . ."[30] *The Outlook* weekly in 1925 had previously stated, in support of the establishment of eastern national parks, that:

> One reason China is a decadent, famine-stricken country is because *individual interest* has gradually consumed the trees and left the surface barren. One reason that India has hundreds of abandoned dams and water reservoirs is because the mud has washed down from deforested areas and filled them full of earth. The brightest prospect of modern business and social life lies in the expected development of electricity by water power. How can we keep the water clear? By keeping a plant-life cover on all unused land.[31]

A Tennessee pamphlet predicted that: "The Tennessee Valley is destined to become an American Ruhr, the industrial zone of America. [And that] the Tennessee [river] possesses even greater energy than the stream which turns the wheels of German manufacturing."[32]

A recognition grew that the new national park in the Smokies would likely greatly increase and firmly establish tourism as a dominant "industry" in the mountains, and would also serve as a huge sponge-like watershed for hydroelectric projects downstream from its headwaters. With the once-booming timber business already on a decline in the area, support for the new park increased. Condemnation privileges had been granted by the federal government and gave new leverage to land-purchasing activities. The lengthy land purchase negotiations with the timber and pulpwood companies appeared to be on their way toward resolution.

The large tracts of land critical to the park's formation were at last being acquired, but there were other parcels of land which also had to be purchased. Land which meant much more than just a raw industrial resource to the people who owned it.

There were around 1,000 families who lived within the boundaries of the Great Smokies before the National Park Service took over the area for park management. These residents owned about 400 log cabins, barns, and other buildings, and 700 frame structures.[33]

Many stereotypes existed of these people, who were often called "mountaineers," "highlanders," or "hillbillys." Some had called them "the purest Anglo-Saxon stock in America."[34] This mistaken belief or "fable" about the mountain residents was only one of many persistent images of these people.[35] They were sometimes described in a positive sense as hardy, self-sufficient people. Other more prevalent stereotypes pictured the mountain residents as lazy, uncivilized, poverty-stricken, criminal, ignorant, or backward.

Two assistant editors of the *National Geographic,* in 1930, thought that the Park Service should let the inhabitants of the Smokies area stay on the land, because "the mountaineers, not the scenery were the real tourist attraction." Arno Cammerer, then Assistant Director of the National Park Service, did not agree, and called these editors "all wet." He went on to say that "the worthy mountaineers . . . would leave; the only ones anxious to stay were those anxious to make money from the tourists. And that "there is no person so canny as certain types of mountaineers and none so disreputable."[36] It is interesting to note that one of the strongest motivations of many of the local businessmen and social leaders in promoting the park was also to "make money from the tourists."

Some of the inhabitants of the Smokies were glad to sell their land and move away, but other residents did not want to move. They had spent their lives in the area and to them the Smokies were *home.* The Walker sisters of the Little Greenbriar section of the Smokies belonged to the latter group. The Walker sisters, of whom there were originally seven, were self-reliant and preferred a traditional lifestyle which was closer to that of their preceding generations than to their contemporaries. The Walker sisters loved their farm and log house. Louisa Walker summed up their feelings about their home and the coming of the Park in a poem. Dr. Hans Huth, hired by the Park Service to compile a report on the preservation of mountain culture, noted that this poem was "ironically enough a satire on the Park Service. Whether this was purely naive, or a clever little speculation on the mind of the public, is difficult to tell."[37] I think that it is quite clear that Louisa Walker meant to communicate in her poem. Following are some excerpts from her poem, entitled "My Mountain Home":

> There is an old weather bettion house
> That stands near a wood
> With an orchard near by it
> For all most one hundred years it has stood.
>
> But now the park Commissioner
> Comes all dressed up so gay
> Saying this old house of yours
> We must now take away

> They coax they wheedle
> They fret they bark
> Saying we have to have this place
> For a National Park
>
> For us poor mountain people
> They don't have a care
> But must a home for
> The wolf the lion and the bear
>
> But many of us have a title
> That is sure and will hold
> To the City of peace
> Where the streets are pure gold
>
> And no park Commissioner
> Will ever dare
> To disturb or molest
> Or take our home from us there.[38]

The Walker sisters kept their house and farm through a concession by the federal government and the Park Service that allowed, in "meritorious cases," for individuals to be issued leases on their property. The leasees, called "stay-ons," were paid for their land, but then could live on it under certain restrictions for the rest of their lives, after which time the authority for the lease expired. Only people judged to have good character and unclouded reputations were to be granted leases. The leases were designed to lessen the resentment of the Smokies residents to the ultimate loss of their land, and allowed some of the older folks to finish out their lives in their long-time homes.[39] In 1941, there were approximately 200 families living within the park on leased property.[40]

As the park land was being acquired, many individuals expressed fears that the cultural history of the Smokies area might be lost. The Park Service also had a growing recognition, if somewhat limited, that aspects and examples of mountain culture should be preserved. A report, prepared for the Park Service, offered suggestions as to how the Service could preserve mountain culture. This report contained a proposal for the establishment of a "mountaineer museum"[41] which could show "types of mountaineers in photos."[42] The report also explored a suggestion that a "buffer area" could be created in some traditional community of "mountain culture" on the border of the park. This buffer area would be preserved by "making it inaccessible and by discouraging intercourse with the outside world." In looking at a proposed buffer area, though, it was determined that most of the inhabitants were "undersirable people, many having criminal records . . ."[43] The problem of finding good examples of virgin mountain culture with desirable people, was not the only objection to the plan. The Walker sisters were used as an example of what might likely happen to "protected 'old mountaineers' undergoing acculturation by unavoidable intercourse with tourists."[44] In addition it was noted that "progress . . . cannot be kept out of an area indefinitely with radio propaganda pouring in daily . . ." Lastly, the question was asked: "Is it legitimate to try to retard the development of an entire section of the country, even through it might be for a worthy purpose?"[45] The buffer area plan was scrapped.

A second proposal entailed the relocation of carefully selected settlers to live in the park and to do farming or crafts work. These people would work under supervision which "would correspond to the procedure employed by the Bureau of Indian Affairs in dealing with the Indians. Supervision must be even closer, so that only certified work can be put on the market."[46] But it was concluded that if mountain culture was dying and it could only "be found among old mountaineers whose character was shaped many years ago and who, by chance, might be available for transfer to the park, it would be very doubtful whether the undertaking of the complicated experiment would be worthwhile." However, it was decided that younger settlers could be utilized who "must be mountain people" but would not necessarily have to come from one of the border areas that were supposed to be in a "culturally primitive state." Especially since it was thought "highly doubtful" that there were any " 'naive' mountaineer who would go into the traditional way of life if he could avoid it." In order to find prospective, respectable people for "settlers," the president of Asheville College was interviewed and responded to a question that yes, "among his students there were quite a few girls who would probably be quite happy to live in the park . . ."[47]

Some of these proposals and the early attempts of the National Park Service to develop new programs and policies aimed at meeting the Service's additional responsibilities for cultural preservation may now seem humorous to us. But, the Park Service had previously been predominantly concerned with the preservation of natural resources and the plants and animals of the parks. It took time for the Service to begin to understand and encompass the responsibilities of cultural preservation and interpretation. The Park Service increasingly recognized the value of the human/cultural history of the park, and established interpretive displays and exhibits in many locations in the Great Smokies. An archives collection was established. Efforts were made to stabilize a select few of the abandoned dwellings and other structures in the park. A former Assistant Superintendent of the park, David Condon, said in reference to the former residents of the area that: "Although their homes are now gone from within its boundaries, [they] have left behind them an aura of mystery and a lore and history of outstanding appeal."[48]

In the past, the Great Smokies area has been seen in many ways—as a hunting ground, as a raw industrial resource, as a proposed health resort, and as a home to many families. The Smokies came to be seen as an extremely valuable resource, worthy of protection and preservation. People's perceptions of the Great Smokies had changed over the years as their country and society had likewise changed. Representative Zebulon Weaver from Asheville, North Carolina gave a speech before the U. S. House of Representatives in 1926, and had this to say about the Smokies as a national park:

> We have had, it is true great stretches of wilderness in riotous abundance, but now they are disappearing. It is not only important but it is necessary to look to the future.
>
> The setting aside of this area is necessary because of the vast increase of population. People are beginning to crowd upon themselves. More and more they are turning to the outdoors for health and recreation and life itself, for nature is the mother of us all, and contact with nature and the out of doors is still the sovereign remedy for the ills of man, both physical and mental. For this purpose there is no place in eastern America that surpasses the Great Smokies.[49]

Today, the Great Smoky Mountains National Park has such a diverse recreational appeal that over eight million people visit it annually. It has been classified as an International Biosphere Reserve and serves as a living laboratory for scientific study. But, to a majority of its visitors, the park is an experience to eagerly look forward to on their vacations, to be savored during the visit, and to be remembered and talked about afterwards.

Robert Sterling Yard, an executive secretary of the National Parks Association who had come to visit the Smokies and determine if they really were worthy of park status, was asked by Horace Kephart what his verdict was about the Smokies. He replied: "They have one quality that is unique." Kephart asked what this quality was. Yard answered: "Charm." He continued: "The Smokies are natural wonders; but they are more than that. One can see a stupendous phenomenon of nature that awes one with its majesty; but when he has seen it once—well, he has seen it. But the Smoky Mountains have enduring charm. Having seen them once, they lure you back again and again."[50]

# NOTES

[1] Amusement/Recreation Marketing Service, Inc., *Visitor Sampling Survey, Great Smoky Mountains National Park: Final Analytic Report* (n.p.: n.p., 1975), p. 40.

[2] U.S. Department of the Interior, National Park Service, *Final Environmental Impact Statement for the General Management Plan, Great Smoky Mountains National Park, North Carolina—Tennessee* (Denver, Colo.: National Park Service, Denver Service Center, 1982), pp. 57-58.

[3] Ibid.

[4] U.S. Department of the Interior, National Park Service, *General Management Plan, Great Smoky Mountains National Park, North Carolina—Tennessee* (Denver, Colo.: National Park Service, Denver Service Center, n.d.), p. 12.

[5] Virginia T. Lathrop, "The Great Smokies Become a Park," *Greensboro News*, 13 May 1934.

[6] Charles Webb, "History of Park Traced," *Asheville Citizen*, 31 August 1939, p. 4, cols. 1-2.

[7] George W. McCoy, "Dedication of Park Climaxes Movement Launched Years Ago," *Asheville Citizen Times*, 1 September 1940, sec. B, p. 3, cols. 6-7.

[8] Lathrop, "The Great Smokies Become a Park."

[9] "Article in 1899 Citizen Tells Story of Origin of National Park Movement," *Asheville Citizen*, 17 June 1934, sec. B., p. 4, cols. 2-5.

[10] McCoy, "Dedication of Park Climaxes Movement Launched Years Ago."

[11] Ibid.

[12] Ibid.

[13] Wilma Dykeman and Jim Stokely, *Highland Homeland, the People of the Great Smokies* (Washington, D.C.: U.S. Department of the Interior, National Park Service, 1978), p. 123.

[14] Carlos Campbell, *Birth of a National Park in the Great Smoky Mountains* (Kingsport, Tenn.: The University of Tennessee Press and Kingsport Press, Inc., 1960), p. 94.

[15] Campbell, p. 13.

[16] Campbell, p. 22.

[17] Jesse R. Lankford, "The Campaign for a National Park in Western North Carolina, 1885-1940," Master's thesis, Western Carolina University, 1973, pp. 47-48.

[18] Campbell, pp. 22-28.

[19] Campbell, p. 29.

[20] Campbell, p. 138.

[21] Campbell, p. 68.

[22] Campbell, p. 135.

[23] McCoy, "Dedication of Park Climaxes Movement Launched Years Ago."

[24] "Bleak Skeletons, Monuments to Lumbering," *Asheville Citizen*, 29 November 1925, caption to photograph, p. 2, cols. 2-4.

[25] Campbell, p. 80.

[26] "The Champion Fibre Company and the Proposed Smoky Mountain National Park," *Asheville Citizen*, 25 November 1925, full-page advertisement, p. 3, cols. 1-8.

[27] "Now and Hereafter," Editorial, *Jackson County Journal*, 9 February 1927, p. 4.

[28] "Title to Vast Tract in Park is Transferred," *Asheville Citizen*, 3 November 1931, p. 1, col. 7.

[29] Great Smoky Mountains Conservation Association, *Great Smoky Mountains* (n.p.: n.p., n.d.), p. 18.

[30] "The Purpose of this Issue," *The Wachovia*, 24, No. 10 (1931), p. 15.

[31] William C. Gregg, "Two New National Parks?" *The Outlook*, 30 December 1925, p. 663.

[32] Great Smoky Mountains Conservation Association, p. 23.

[33] Hans Huth, *Report on the Preservation of Mountain Culture in Great Smoky Mountains National Park* (n.p.: U.S. Department of the Interior, National Park Service, 1941), p. 2.

[34]Maude Waddell, "South Gives Nation Its Most Beautiful Playground," *Charlotte Observer*, 18 January 1931, sec. 3.

[35]Charles L. Perdue, Jr. and Nancy J. Martin-Perdue, "Appalachian Fables and Facts: A Case Study of the Shenandoah National Park Removals," *Appalachian Journal*, 7, No. 1-2 (1980), pp. 85-86.

[36]Ibid.

[37]Huth, p. 12.

[38]Robert R. Madden and T. Russell Jones, *Mountain Home: The Walker Family Homestead* (Washington, D.C.: U.S. Department of the Interior, National Park Service, 1977), pp. 18-19.

[39]Leon M. Siler, "U.S. to Allow Deserving Folk to Live on Land," *Asheville Citizen*, 13 September 1931, p. 1, col. 1.

[40]Huth, p. 2.

[41]Huth, p. 4.

[42]Huth, p. 7.

[43]Huth, p. 11.

[44]Huth, p. 12.

[45]Huth, p. 13.

[46]Huth, p. 15.

[47]Huth, p. 17.

[48]Campbell, p. 57.

[49]Zebulon Weaver, *The Great Smoky Mountains National Park*, U.S. Congress, House, 14 May 1926 (Washington, D.C.: GPO, 1926), pp. 9-10.

[50]Horace Kephart, "The Last of the Eastern Wilderness: An Article on the Proposed Great Smoky National Park," *World's Work*, Apr. 1926, pp. 630-632.

TOURISM THEN AND NOW
A Change in Helen
   Helen, Georgia Chamber of Commerce
Appalachian Tourism: An Historical Overview
   Stuart Sprague; Morehead State University; Morehead, KY
A Plunge into the Past: Henry Ford and Friends Tour the Southern Appalalchians
   Charles Gunter; E. Tenn. State University; Johnson City, TN
   Convenor; Scoop Scruggs; Helen, GA

# A Plunge into the Past: Henry Ford and Friends Tour the Southern Appalachians

by
*Charles Gunter*

In the midst of World War I, four famous Americans—Thomas Edison, Henry Ford, Harvey Firestone, and John Burroughs—gathered in Pittsburgh, Pennsylvania, in August, 1918, to commence a two-week trip which would take them through portions of Pennsylvania, West Virginia, Virginia, Tennessee, North Carolina, and Maryland (see Figure 1).

This was not the first trip for a portion of the party, nor was it to be their last. The idea of their trips germinated at the time of the 1915 World's Fair in San Francisco, when Ford and Firestone journeyed there to celebrate Edison Day at the fair. With time to spare, the three of them decided to visit Luther Burbank at his home in Santa Rosa; and ran up there in their private rail cars.[1]

Enroute to San Diego, after visiting Burbank, Firestone suggested that the party proceed by automobile since crowds of people were threatening to make it impossible for them to keep moving. They had such a wonderful time together that Edison suggested that the three of them go camping the next year.[2]

The 1916 camping expedition, the first of the back-to-nature junkets, was a tour of New York and the New England states. John Burroughs, a friend of Edison, joined the group at his home in Roxbury, New York; but unfortunately, Henry Ford was unable to join the group due to business commitments. The 1916 trip set in motion the roles that the men followed for subsequent trips, including the 1918 camping trip. Firestone assumed the responsibilities of being general manager and commissary

FIGURE 1

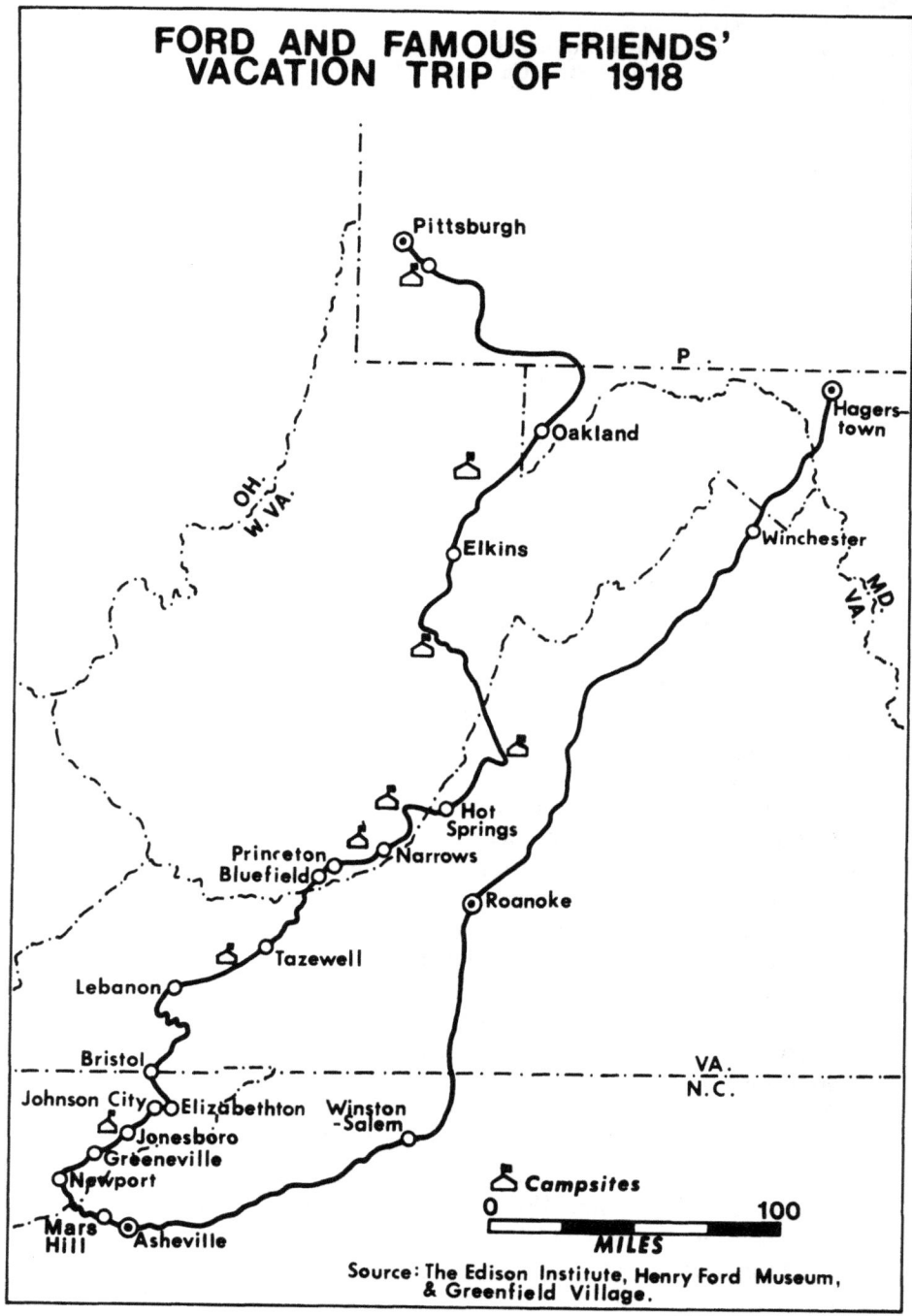

officer. When Henry Ford joined the group in 1918, he contributed his expertise in keeping the mechanical equipment in working order. John Burroughs, a seventy-nine year old naturalist, would be expected only to ply his craft of observing the landscape—both physical and cultural.[3]

Perhaps, the best explanation of what Edison was to do was written by Firestone, when he commented:

> Mr. Edison was to decide where we should go. He has always chosen the route. First, he writes to us giving the route. Then he writes again, giving another route, and when we actually start he commonly selects a third route. We never know where we are going, and I suspect that he does not, either. He rides in the front seat of the front car and directs the caravan by compass. He dislikes paved roads and never does he select a main highway if he can find a byway. And never does he take us into a large town if he can find another way around. When he thinks we have gone far enough, he decides to camp, and then we camp.[4]

A trip planned for 1917 was cancelled due to America's entry into World War I. However, by August, 1918, conditions in Europe had improved enough; and the party decided to break away from the war effort for several weeks. "Except for Mr. Burroughs," Firestone said, "we were all head over heels in our war work, but we had decided that a couple of weeks off would freshen us all a bit and make us better able to go on with our jobs."[5]

One may ponder how Thomas Edison, Henry Ford, John Burroughs, and Harvey Firestone—each a national figure in his own chosen profession and used to having his own way—could come together for annual camping trips and deepen their friendship for one another.[6] As Charles E. Sorensen pointed out, Ford always was grateful for Edison's enouragement when he initially was experimenting with his gasoline engine in 1895. Their friendship began at that time. However, aside from the camping trips they seldom saw one another. Although Ford and Burroughs shared a common interest in birds, the naturalist was primarily Edison's friend. Ford and Burroughs saw each other only during their camping trips. Ford's relationship with Firestone was mainly of business origin.[7]

One journalist has said that "if you want to probe beneath the surface and get at a man's real character, watch him when he is at play. When he plays he is like a horse out of harness."[8] David Lewis in *The Public Image of Henry Ford* mentions that many movie theaters throughout the United States in 1918 showed Ford, Edison, and Burroughs participating in "high-kicking, stair-jumping, sprinting, tree-chopping, and tree-climbing contests."[9]

Instead of lounging around on a verandah at a mountain lodge or journeying where roads were in excellent condition, these men—especially Edison—sought to travel to new country; the more untraveled and remote it was, the better the group liked it. They choose to sleep in tents and eat their meals in the open. When night came, they built their own camp fire and enjoyed talking, on some occasions, to almost midnight (see Figure 2).[10]

When the caravan started from Pittsburgh on August 18, 1918, it included "three touring cars and three trucks, laden as one writer described with 'genius and generalship and cooks and culinary contraptions'."[11] In addition to the famous four, there were also Harvey Firestone, Jr., two or three friends, a Japanese chef, and various assistants.[12]

They were ten days in making the journey from Pittsburgh to Asheville, North Carolina; and only once did some of these distinguished gentlemen sleep under a roof.[13] It is only the last three days of this journey to Asheville that this study seeks to investigate.

A previous study by Donald Rice has explored their travels in West Virginia;[14] and the purpose of this paper is to continue the route they followed through Virginia, Tennessee, and North Carolina (to Asheville), and to identify some of the party's interesting experiences while in this region.

Left to right are John Burroughs, Henry Ford, Harvey Firest, Jr., Harvey Firestone, Sr., Thomas Edison, and unidentified. Location unknown. Photo courtesy of Archives, The Firestone Tire and Rubber Company.

On Sunday, August 25, the party set out from their camp on Wolf Creek, which was between Narrows, Virginia, and Princeton, West Virginia; and proceeded through Princeton and Bluefield before making camp in Tazewell County, Virginia that night.[15]

"Coming into the South for someone from the North," wrote John Burroughs in *Under the Maples,* "is a plunge into the past."[16] Elaborating, he said, when you go into Virginia there is a change which is reflected in a more local or provincial attitude. One frequently encounters individuals who are unacquainted with the world beyond their door-steps. He remarked, "their unsophistication is shocking to see."[17]

In referring to the cultural landscape, Burroughs noted that the quality of the roads left much to be desired. Understandably, an eighty-two year old man might be concerned about the constant bouncing around of an automobile on a dirt and gravel road. He declared that occasionally one would pass from a fine stone road to a rather rough dirt road. Many times there were no bridges over small streams, but fording places were accessible. He recalled that in certain portions of Virginia, the county rather than the state constructed the roads.[18]

The first major stop in Southwest Virginia was Tazewell, a community of some 1,500 people in 1918, located about twenty miles from Bluefield. The party would have traveled on a rock paved road and would have had to ford streams on four occasions enroute from Bluefield. Mr. H. H. Thompson, a Tazewell native, was a young man when he saw the group on the main street of the community dressed in "duster coats" and wearing "goggles." He states:

> I was a young boy around nine years old when I came on four or five "T" model Fords parked on Main Street in front of L. A. Tynes' Ford Agency. Tynes, who also operated a garage, was standing on the sidewalk in front of his place shaking hands with Henry Ford. Thomas Edison was leaning against the car and, I think Firestone and Burroughs were still sitting in the back seat. It must have been around 4 p.m. as I was driving cows lower down the street to customers. In those days everybody had a cow and pastured them in rented pasture. I was very close to the company of men, but just looked them over and went on with my cows ... Later that afternoon, the party continued along on the old Fincastle Turnpike, went into the west end of the cove, and camped on Senator (State Senator) S. J. Thompson's farm which was located approximately fifteen miles from Tazewell ... S. J. Thompson talked to them for quite a while and gave them permission to camp any place they liked. The site chosen was near the top of a hill just beyond

the senator's home. This camping site was in the western end of the county about five miles east of Wardell.[19]

The trip was nearing its conclusion almost a week later when the weekly *Clinch Valleys News* (of Tazewell, Virginia) reported in its August 30th edition that distinguished visitors passed through last Sunday. "These gentlemen were on vacation," the writer said, "and slipped into town from the east and out again stopping a few minutes in front of the hotel."[20]

A piercing remark by the writer of the newspaper article perhaps expresses the sentiment of citizens of the community. He declares:

> The people of Tazewell regret exceedingly that they did not have the pleasure of shaking hands with the distinguished men, but wish it distinctly known, that these famous men would have been wiser and happier perhaps by a little personal contact with Tazewell people.[21]

On Monday, August 26, the party left their camp early, and proceeded on what was then the best road—mostly clay and rock—which routed them through Elk Garden, the home of the former governor of Virginia (Henry Carter Stuart of Russell County). Following a visit there, they drove approximately ten miles to Lebanon, the county seat; and spent several minutes there, before pressing on to Bristol, via Hansonville and Abingdon.[22]

In all likelihood, the headlines of the August 27th edition of the *Bristol* (Tennessee) *Herald Courier* could have read "Thomas Edison and Henry Ford Are Visitors Here," but war news pushed this article to page three.[23] When the visitors arrived in Bristol around noon on the twenty-sixth, they proceeded to the Hotel Bristol on Moore Street. Although no notice of their coming was given, scores of local citizens came to an informal reception hastily arranged after the visitors ate lunch.

After the reception, members of the party separated from one another to enjoy their individual pursuits. Mr. Burroughs retired to a hotel room for a brief rest and didn't rejoin the party until they were ready to leave. Ford, Firestone, and his son, Harvey, Jr., took a brief tour of the city. They visited the local Firestone agency of Charles J. Harkrader on Cumberland Street where they posed for pictures.

While Firestone talked about automobiles and tires with local dealers and manifested an interest in everything going on around him, the topic of conversation with Ford concerned the war and his own candidacy for U. S. Senate from the state of Michigan.

Asked how long he thought the war would last, Ford said, "Well, of course no one knows, but I would say about another year. I think it is safe to say that the Allies have retreated for the last time. The retreating hereafter will be done by the Germans. We want peace on the right terms and we'll get it."[24]

Referring to his candidacy for the U. S. Senate, Ford indicated that he was not seeking office, and furthermore, that his campaign had not cost a single penny.[25] Interestingly Ford was a candidate for both parties and won the Democratic nomination.[26]

Ford did tell local townspeople, during the visit, that "the country in this section is magnificent. I was greatly impressed with the mountain scenery through Southwest Virginia and am glad we took this route."[27]

Edison, in contrast to Ford and Firestone, "contented himself digesting the latest war news in the hotel lobby." Apparently unconcerned by the close scrutiny of the crowd, he intently read his newspaper and smoked his cigar.[28]

Leaving Bristol, the tourists traveled approximately eight miles to "Maplehurst", a 265 acre farm owned by W. H. Cox. Cox, a prominent businessman of Sullivan County, Tennessee, was a relative of John I. Cox, Governor of Tennessee in 1907, who previously resided at "Maplehurst." The visitors expressed their delight over the visit, after an inspection of the farm and a glass of cool buttermilk. Ford complimented Cox on owning one of the best tracts of land that he had observed on their trip.[29]

Although only seven years old at the time, Walter C. Smith vaguely remembers seeing the party. His family resided on the estate, while his father was farm manager. His only recollection of the visit pertains to a request for his older brother to run up to the house and get a glass so that the visitors could get a drink at the springhouse. Heretofore, a tin-cup had been used by everyone.[30]

Leaving "Maplehurst" early in the afternoon, the visitors traveled through Bluff City, Elizabethton, and Milligan College enroute to Johnson City, Tennessee. The presence of an old mill at Milligan College likely caught Ford's attention. One observer remarked about Ford:

> The old fashioned grist-mills along the road, with their huge overshot wheels, were of never-failing interest to him ... he is never tired of talking of how much power is going to waste everywhere.[31]

Later in the afternoon a crowd estimated from 500 to 1,000 people turned out in Johnson City to get a peep at four of America's most illustrious citizens. The *Johnson City Staff* newspaper office was overwhelmed by people seeking information after a brief notice appeared that the party was coming through the city.[32]

A chauffeur on the trip, whose account was later transcribed by Lester Hopper said:

Coming into a skyscraperless village, known as Johnson City, I led our caravan right up to the main street. In a few minutes the thoroughfare was crowded; folks came running from every direction... stores were forgotten; political arguments and whittling bees were disbanded; the town closed shop to pay its respects to the great visitors.[33]

As the party rolled to a stop in front of the Majestic Theater on Main Street, John Burroughs, looking very much like a Rip Van Winkle with his gray whiskers, stepped from a car and started walking down the street. Ed Brading and Munsey Slack, two prominent citizens of the town, immediately recognized Burroughs and introduced him to several directors of the Chamber of Commerce.[34]

Edison, who was seated in a car with Ford and Firestone, was, according to a newspaper account, one of the most modest men that had ever visited this part of Tennessee. One resident of the community told Edison that he wanted to shake hands with the "greatest man in the world." Due to his hearing difficulties, Edison blushed and modestly denied the accusation.[35]

Abe Slack, a *Staff* carrier, was most fortunate in having the opportunity to sell Thomas Edison a paper. When Edison's car stopped on Roan Street the inventor waved to him. Upon receiving a paper, Edison gave the youngster a dime. As the youngster fumbled in his pocket for change Edison grabbed another paper and told him to keep the change.[36]

Before their departure for Jonesborough, Ford and Firestone expressed that they liked the city and this section of the country. They were favorably impressed with the paved streets and the "general air of progressiveness."[37]

When the tourists arrived in Jonesborough, evidently the party stopped briefly along the main street before proceeding to the Will Lee farm located south of the community. Likely, the party inquired about a possible camp site and were told the the Lee farm located along the Bristol to Memphis "Highway" was considered a good location.[38]

Upon their arrival at the Lee farm around 4:30 p.m., a member of the party sought permission to camp, but he failed to identify who they were. With permission granted, a site was selected about a quarter mile from the road, and some six to eight tents were erected in close proximity to a spring and a wooded area. Burroughs, however, wished to be able to hear the birds when he awoke in the morning, and his tent was set up about an eighth of a mile away from the main camp. Edison even rigged electric lights for the camp, running wires to the battery of one of the automobiles (see Figure 3).

While setting up the camp, several of the Lee children took up with the campers. It was during this time that one of the most publicized

*View of Camp Robert E. Lee near Jonesborough, Tennessee. Photo courtesy of Archives, The Firestone Tire and Rubber Company.*

incidents of the entire trip was recorded. Henry Ford and one of the youngsters began cutting fire wood. While using a small cross-cut saw, Ford remarked,"Young man, do you know that you are sawing wood with Henry Ford." The youngster, eight years old at the time, quickly replied, "Do you know who you're sawing wood with?" And, when Ford answered, "No," the youngster said, "You're sawing wood with Robert E. Lee." Ford and the others laughed heartily. No doubt, the play on names was what amused the group.[39]

Around the camp fire that night some forty to fifty local citizens joined the famous party, although they tore down a portion of the Lee's fence in achieving their objective. Several stayed until almost midnight. Apparently, the tourists enjoyed the company and were not perturbed that people came and talked with them.[40]

One anecdote of the visit to the Jonesborough area told of a youngster, George DeVault, who, when he saw Edison, immediately greeted him as a well known friend. He had read about Edison's experiment of trying to incubate eggs. He said:

> Say, Mr. Edison, I've read about you. You have, smiled Edison, and what was it you read. Why I read about you settin' on those eggs to hatch 'em. Mr. Edison joined in the shout of laughter that followed. Don't ever try it son, he advised soberly, it won't work.[41]

When the party pulled out around 9:30 a.m. on Tuesday, August 27, they sent someone up to the door who gave the Lee family $5.00.[42] On the way to Asheville, North Carolina that morning they stopped briefly in Greeneville before driving on to Newport, Tennessee, where they had lunch at the Mims Hotel. Although the hotel had no advanced notice, a "scrumptious" dinner of fried chicken, country ham, steak, and a variety of fresh vegetables all for the grand charge of 50¢ each awaited the party.[43]

Further stops were made at Mars Hill and Weaverville, North Carolina before the campers arrived at the Grove Park Inn in Asheville around 8:30 p.m. Enthusiastic students and friends at both Mars Hill College and Weaver College insisted on greeting the visitors and calling for speeches. Firestone obliged by referring to Edison as the greatest man in the scientific world in a brief but well-worded speech at Weaver College.

Entering the outskirts of Asheville, the visitors were met by Secretary Buckner of the Asheville Board of Trade, who headed a welcoming delegation and was driving a Ford car. In his remarks, he graciously assured the party that "the Asheville atmosphere had been specially talcumed and perfumed for the occasion."

On Wednesday, August 28, the party inspected the Grove Park Inn, which had opened five years earlier as one of the nation's finest resort hotels; visited Overlook, an English Gothic style castle being built for Fred L. Seely, who designed the Grove Park Inn; and saw Chunn's Cove, which had tentatively been selected by Seely as a possible camp site had the party wished to camp out. Later in the morning, in what appears to be a spur-of-the-moment decision, the party decided to resume their journey.[44]

Thus, the camping portion of Ford and his famous friends' tour through a portion of the Southern Appalachians had ended. John Burroughs left the party at Asheville and went to Washington, D.C. by train. The others forsook camping as they made their way to Hagerstown, Maryland, where the 1918 trip ended.

NOTES

[1]H. S. Firestone (by Samuel Crowther), "My Vacations with Ford and Edison," *System the Magazine of Business*, vol. 49 (May, 1926), p. 644.

[2]Ibid.

[3]Dorothy B. Huyck, "Over Hill and Dale with Henry Ford and Famous Friends," *Smithsonian*, vol. 9 (June, 1978), pp. 88-89.

[4]Firestone, *loc. cit.*

[5]_____(by Samuel Crowther), "Was There Ever Another Vacation Like This?," *System, the Magazine of Business*, vol. 49 (June, 1926), p. 790.

[6]Mary B. Mullett, "Four Big Men Become Boys Again," *American Magazine*, vol. 87 (February, 1919), p. 34.

[7]Charles E. Sorensen (with Samuel T. Williamson), *My Forty Years with Ford.* New York: W. W. Norton and Company, 1956, p. 19; Keith Sward, *The Legend of Henry Ford.* New York: Rinehart and Company, Inc., 1948, p. 110.

[8]Mullett, *loc. cit.*

[9]David L. Lewis, *The Public Image of Henry Ford: An American Folk Hero and His Company.* Detroit: Wayne State University Press, 1976, p. 223.

[10]Mullett, *loc. cit.*

[11]Donald L. Rice, "Clearing Up a 'Hazy Proposition': Ford, Firestone, and Edison Explore West Virginia," *Goldenseal,* vol. 9 (Spring, 1983), p. 47.

[12]Mullett, *loc. cit.*

[13]*Ibid.*

[14]Rice, *op. cit.*, pp. 46-50.

[15]The map and itinerary of the 1918 camping trip is a part of "Our Vacation Days of 1918" written by John Burroughs (reprinted in *Men and Rubber*) and *Under the Maples* by Burroughs. Courtesy of The Edison Institute, Henry Ford Museum and Greenfield Village.

[16]John Burroughs, *Under the Maples.* Boston and New York: Houghton Miffin Company, 1921, p. 120.

[17]*Ibid.*, pp. 120-121.

[18]*Ibid.*, p. 121.

[19]Letters from H. H. Thompson, Tazewell, Virginia, March 1 and 6, 1984.

[20]"Distinguished Visitors Pass Through," *Clinch Valley News* (Tazewell, Virginia), August 30, 1918, p. 4.

[21]*Ibid.*

[22]*Ibid.*; Thompson, *op. cit.*, letter of March 6, 1984.

[23]"Thomas Edison and Henry Ford Are Visitors Here," *Bristol* (Tennessee) *Herald Courier,* August 27, 1918, p. 3.

[24]*Ibid.*

[25]*Ibid.*

[26]"Ford Is Behind in Election Returns," *Bristol* (Tennessee) *Herald Courier,* August 28, 1918, p. 2.

[27]"Thomas Edison and Henry Ford Are Visitors Here," *loc. cit.*

[28]*Ibid.*

[29]*Ibid.*; Muriel C. Spodon, *Historical Sites of Sullivan County.* Kingsport (Tennessee): Kingsport Press, 1976, p. 175.

[30]Interview with Walter C. Smith, Bristol, Tennessee, February 13, 1984.

[31]Firestone, "Was There Ever Another Vacation Life This?," *op. cit.*, p. 792.

[32]"Edison, Ford, Firestone and Burroughs Visit Johnson City," *Johnson City* (Tennessee) *Staff,* August 27, 1918, p. 3.

[33]Lester Hopper, "Five Wizards in the Wilds," Unpublished paper, courtesy of Archives, Firestone Tire and Rubber Company.

[34]"Edison, Ford, Firestone and Burroughs Visit Johnson City," *loc. cit.*

[35]*Ibid.*

[36]*Ibid.*: Interview with Mrs. Nat Copenhaver, Bristol, Tennessee, March 7, 1984. Mrs. Copenhaver, the daughter of Munsey Slack, the owner of the *Johnson City Staff* in 1918, has confirmed much of this account. She indicated that the dime given to her brother by Edison is still in the family's possession.

[37]"Edison, Ford, Firestone and Burroughs Visit Johnson City," *loc. cit.*

[38]"Ford and Edison Spend Night Here," *Jonesborough* (Tennessee) *Herald and Tribune*, August 29, 1918, p. 1; Interview with Robert E. Lee, Johnson City, Tennessee, January 10, 1984.

[39]George Kelly, "Robert E. Himself Describes Big Event," *Johnson City* (Tennessee) *Press-Chronicle*, May 23, 1956, p. 4; Interviews with Robert E. Lee, Johnson City, Tennessee, January 10 and February 2, 1984; "Ford Saws Wood With Robert E. Lee," *Bristol* (Tennessee) *Herald Courier*, August 30, 1918, p. 4.

[40]Interview with Robert E. Lee, Johnson City, Tennessee, January 10, 1984.

[41]"Mr. Edison Gives Advice to Jonesborough Boy," *Johnson City* (Tennessee) *Staff*, August 29, 1918, p. 8; conversation with George deVault, Bristol, Tennessee, March 14, 1984. Mr. DeVault, eight years old at the time of the visit, was brought to the Lee farm by his uncle, Sidney Murray, who was then major of Jonesborough. Although he saw the whole party, his visit was confined mostly to Thomas Edison. When brought to Edison, Edison put young George on his knee. The exchange between the two occurred but Edison's method of incubating eggs was changed from trying to hatch them using body heat to "settin' on them."

[42]Interview with Robert E. Lee, Johnson City, Tennessee, January 10, 1984.

[43]Letter from E. R. Walker, III, Newport, Tennessee, January 29, 1984. Mr. Walker quotes Mrs. James Murray, the daughter of Mr. and Mrs. Charlie Mims, the proprietors of the hotel.

[44]"Thomas A. Edison, Henry Ford and Party Now Here," *Asheville* (North Carolina) *Citizen*, August 28, 1918, p. 1; "Edison-Ford Party Left City Yesterday," *Asheville* (North Carolina) *Citizen*, August 29, 1918, p. 10.

MOONSHINE AND BEYOND
More Than Moonshine: Aspects of Mountain Cooking
   Sidney Farr; Berea College; Berea, KY
A Touch of Mountain Dew: Art and History of Whiskey-Making in North Georgia
   Ray Rensi and Leo Downing; N. Georgia College; Dahlonega, GA

# A Touch of Mountain Dew: Art and History of Whiskey-Making in North Georgia

by
*Ray Rensi and Leo Downing*

## INTRODUCTION

In order to understand the art of moonshining one must first examine the people involved. The two cannot be separated as the act of producing illicit whiskey is an extension of the values, beliefs and lifestyles of the moonshiner. Moonshiners are an individualistic people who believe they have the "right" to do whatever they choose with the product of their labor. Their cultural heritage is one of distrust and hatred of what they perceive as unwarranted government intrusion into their private affairs. However, in a mass society that demands conformity their days, and thus this occupation, seem to be ending.

This study examines the practice of moonshining in northern Georgia and attempts to explain some of the reasons for its decline in the region. The study is presented in three sections. The first gives a brief historical review of the practice of moonshining in America. Only by examining the actions of their ancestors and what moonshining meant to them is it possible to understand the current moonshiner. The second section will detail the more common manufacturing methods used in making corn "likker." The third section offers several explanations for the most recent decline of moonshining in northern Georgia. The information and explanations put forth in the second and third sections were gathered from interviews with revenue agents, local law enforcement personnel, ex-moonshiners and some individuals still engaged in moonshining. The explanations offered by them are impossible to empirically verify, but should be viewed as the opinions and experiences of the best experts in the field.

# MOONSHINE AND MOONSHINERS

Man's search for a good stiff drink seems to be as old as civilization itself. In fact, some historians refer to the manufacturing of alcohol as "the second oldest profession" (Carr: 1972). Until the discovery (or more probably the rediscovery) of the distillation process by mid-east alchemists professional technique was largely limited to the natural fermentation processes of various fruits and grains. Grapes and the art of winemaking were introduced to Europe by Phoenician traders through ancient Greece and Rome. A type of beer, produced from barley, was also introduced at approximately the same time. These drinks were well received by the populace and their method of manufacturing was spread throughout empires of both civilizations. While there remains considerable controversy over the exact discoverer of the distillation process, the knowledge seems to have been disseminated by mid-eastern alchemists. By the end of the eleventh century, most of Europe had some operating knowledge of the distillation process. (Kellner: 1971)

The roots of north Georgia moonshining can be found in early Ireland and Scotland. Both societies made widespread use of the distillation process in the manufacture of whiskey from barley. The skills of both groups had advanced to a very high degree when, through the actions of King James I, they began to combine their skills. In 1610, in an attempt to solidify his control over Ulster (Northern Ireland) James I, through land grants, enticed thousands of Scots to emigrate and settle there. The new residents, though at political odds with the older occupants, exchanged their collective knowledge on the art of distillation. For more than thirty years, the manufacturing of whiskey was unhindered by any government intrusion. In 1642, Parliament ended this respite and imposed an excise tax on liquor. This tax evoked a considerable amount of hostility throughout Ireland and Scotland and, in order to escape the tax, led to the first illicit manufacture and distribution of whiskey. Public sentiment was so strong against the tax that government employees in charge of collecting the tax were openly subject to harrassment and even death in trying to discharge their duties. (Trevelyan: 1952)

The Ulstermen (Scots-Irishmen) began to emigrate to America in large numbers beginning in 1717. This migration was largely motivated by the promises of freedom from government intrusion offered in the new land. Though there had been continuous resentment in Ulster against the government, several new restrictions on economic trade imposed on Ireland by England prompted the mass immigrations in the early eighteenth century. The migration continued until 1776 with an estimated 250,000-400,000 Ulstermen coming to America. Most settled in Pennsylvania and pushed down the Appalachian Mountain range.

These new citizens brought with them both a love for whiskey and a dislike for "unnecessary" government intrusions or restrictions. They found the new land fulfilled these desires and developed a fierce loyalty toward it. When the Revoluntary War broke out, they fought bravely for the patriot cause and distinguished themselves in many battles, particularly at the Battle of Kings Mountain. After the war these patriots returned to their homes (and their stills) intending to reap the full benefits of freedom for which they had fought an oppressive English government.

The rewards and benefits of the war were short lived as feelings of hostility and alienation from the new government began to emerge. The first problem involved a redrawing of the land possessions of Virginia and Pennsylvania. This shifting resulted in many backwoodsmen losing their homesteads or incumbering new heavy mortgages on their already "owned" property. The second, and the most significant development was the introduction of an excise tax on stills and distilled liquor. The tax was introduced by the Secretary of the Treasury, Alexander Hamilton, as a means of eliminating the twenty-one million dollar war debt. This was seen as a tremendous burden for the frontiersmen because they had found new uses for their whiskey that greatly increased its importance to them. The pioneering spirit of this group usually put them at the forefront of the early migratory waves in this country. As a result of this they settled in some of the more "wild" mountain areas of Tennessee, Kentucky, Virginia, Georgia, and the Carolinas. This isolation, though providing a bountiful food supply, cut them off from the trade centers of early America and created problems in transporting their crops to market for hard coin and necessities. They soon discovered that by first distilling their harvest into moonshine a pack mule (the only method of transporting goods available to them) could carry twenty-four bushels in liquid form compared to four to eight in raw form. Distilling thus became an economic necessity for many of them and the new excise tax was seen as a threat to their livelihood and survival.

The tax became law on March 3, 1791 and not only required a tax to be paid on liquor, but provided for the payment of bounties to snitches who turned in an unregistered still. The reaction to the new tax was similar to the earlier excise tax imposed in Ireland. Revenue agents across the country were threatened, beaten and even "tarred and feathered." Tension built up over the new tax and finally erupted in the first case of open insurrection in this young country's history, referred to as the Whiskey Rebellion. (Hofstadter and Walace: 1970). The rebellion was instigated by the enforcement of the tax against a group of western Pennsylvanians. It was finally put down by an army of over 10,000 state militiamen from four states under the personal leadership of George Washington and Alexander Hamilton at a cost to the country of $1,500,000.00.

In addition to creating a great deal of hostility, the excise tax and foreclosures in Pennsylvania resulted in a migration of the former Ulstermen and their descendants to more remote parts of the country. These pioneers pushed further south down the Appalachian Mountains and further west by way of the Cumberland Gap and Ohio River. These movements gave them some respite from government intrusion. However, it was not needed for very long as under the support of President Thomas Jefferson, Congress repealed the excise tax on June 30, 1802. Other than a short three year return to the tax to pay off the debt from the War of 1812, the mountainmen were free from all government intrusion into their whiskey making until 1862.

On July 1, 1862, Congress passed legislation that created what would become the Internal Revenue Department and improvised taxes on a large number of various items including moonshine. A short time later, they provided for various agents to enforce the new system and prosecute violators. Due to the isolation of the moonshiners, the small number of agents and the large number of tax evaders it was difficult for agents to enforce the law. They often had to resort to snitches or entrapment techniques. Both methods of law enforcement did little to endear them to the general populace and resulted in increased isolationism and mistrust among the moonshiners.

A type of respectful battle of wits continued for many years between the moonshiners and the revenuers until it finally escalated to a full blown war when National prohibition went into effect on October 28, 1919. While doing little to curb the nation's thirst for alcohol, Probation was a blessing for moonshiners as the value of their wares increased by ten-fold overnight. Due to the increased demand for illicit alcohol and the riches available for those who could produce it a major change took place in moonshining. The production of moonshining went from a craft to an occupation. Unscrupulous men from various urban areas, with promises of riches, recruited moonshiners to work for them in the mass production of illicit whiskey. Emphasis was now placed on producing as much liquor as possible in the shortest period of time. These goals contradicted the laborious care taken by the old time moonshiners and so new techniques and additives were found to speed up the entire process. These changes often produced a harmful or even deadly alcoholic drink that paralyzed more than 15,000 people nationwide. (Dabney: 1974: 108).

Various law enforcement agencies increased their enforcement efforts nationwide. However, because of the large amount of money at stake and the less than honorable men involved in the operation, it often resulted in a gun battle with casualties on both sides. The battle between the two forces was often glamorized in the accounts of the day with colorful stories of Al Capone and his battles with Eliot Ness. The glamorized battles were far removed from the rural moonshiners working under contracts for middlemen and go-betweens in organized crime. However, the effect on moonshining art was dramatic, as the moonshiner's greed quickly stripped him and his occupation of any honor.

The repeal of Prohibition in 1933 did not eliminate the market for illicit moonshine, but it did reduce its price considerably. Because of the availability of legal liquor on which excise taxes had been paid, the only way to meet the competition was to reduce the price of moonshine below legal liquor. This resulted in the end of the enormous profits and greatly reduced organized crimes' involvement in the moonshining industry. To fight this continual evasion of tax laws the Bureau of Internal Revenue created the Alcohol Tax Unit in 1934, which evolved into the Alcohol, Tobacco, and Firearms Division of the IRS (taken over in 1973 by the Treasury Department). After the prohibition era, and still today, most of the larger moonshining operations (what few are left) are designed to produce quantities of cheap "rotgut" to the urban ghetto areas of major cities. These 'shiners are in the same mold as their Prohibition predecessors with little care or attention paid toward the quality of the product. An old adage in the business is, "This whiskey is made for selling, not drinking." Smaller operators or individuals sometimes attempt to ensure drinkability (not quality), but because of time restraints, cannot produce the same liquor as their ancestors. Generally run-ins with the law for both the small and large operations were limited to the transportation aspects of the business. Delivery men, referred to as "trippers," often engaged in high-speed chases with federal, state and local authorities in making their deliveries to urban centers from the rural manufacturing sites. However improvements in communications and transportation, along with increased cooperation between law enforcement agencies, has made the life of a tripper extremely harrowing and short-lived at best. Few remain in the business for long without being caught and once caught they are watched carefully, thus ending their illegal careers.

## THE MANUFACTURE OF CORN "LIKKER"

The procedures used to produce moonshine can vary greatly from moonshiner to moonshiner depending upon the technology in use, the amount and type of spirits desired and the speed of manufacturing needed. The discussion that follows will detail the simple methods first employed as well as some of the more common variants of the trade.

The first step in the process was in choosing a proper site for the procedure. The moonshiner had two important points to consider in making his decision; secrecy and water. Secrecy was needed, not only to protect the operation from the legal authorities, but also pirating neighbors who might steal his mash or his tubing. Fresh water was needed for both the mixing and tempering of the moonshine as well as a coolant for the condensation part of the distillation procedure. Soft branch water being the most desirable, moonshiners can often judge the quality of the water by examining the flora surrounding the branch. Red horsemint or yellowroot generally indicate good whiskey water, while touch-me-nots grow around unsuitable hard water. Another testing method is to fill a jar with water and shake well, then tilt it on its side. If air bubbles rise when it is tilted, then it's good water.

The second step in moonshining involves the fermentation of the grain. It is through the fermentation process that the starches in the grain are broken down through enzyme action into sugars and then alcohol. In moonshining, the fermenting mixture is referred to as "mash." Mash is generally composed of grain (usually corn), water, sugar and malt or yeast. The moonshiner selects the corn carefully and discards any discolored or mildewed grains. He then changes the starch of the corn into sugar obtaining what is called "corn malt." This is accomplished by wetting the unground corn with warm water and keeping it warm until it sprouts in four or five days. The sprouting process can be accelerated by burying the corn (in sacks) in a manure pile. The added warmth of the oxidation generally cuts the sprouting time in half.

After the corn sprouts, it is dried and ground into a course meal called "chop." The chop is then mixed in mash barrels, usually made of poplar or oak, with the other ingredients used. If it is a straight chop and water mash (usually one bushel of sprouted corn to ½ barrel of water) then it could take as long as ten to fourteen days, depending on the temperature. If sugar is added, the time is cut to as little as three to four days. The addition of sugar also greatly increased the alcohol yield of the mix but would result in a change in flavor of the resulting whiskey. During the fermentation process, the barrels would be kept warm by burying them, packing them with straw or leaves or bringing them indoors. After several days of rolling and bubbling, the moonshiner would then thin out the mash by adding warm water and rye malt or yeast. This would then turn the "sour mash" into "sweet mash" for the purpose of distillation in a few more days. After the mash is fully fermented, it is a soupy yellow mixture with approximately a 10% alcohol content and is referred to as "still beer" or just beer. The beer mixture must be distilled in a short time or it will go sour.

The third step in the manufacturing of moonshine is the distillation of the mash. It is through this method that the alcohol is separated from the mash and other impurities. The distillation of mash is accomplished in three stages. First, the mash is heated, then the alcohol is vaporized, removed, and finally condensed. The distillation process can be used to separate the alcohol from the mash because the boiling point of alcohol is 176°F, while water boils at 212°F. Thus by heating the mash to 176°, the alcohol would be vaporized and the water and other impurities left behind.

The distillation process took place in what is referred to as a still. Though there are many variations on the exact structure, all stills consist largely of a heating drum or cooking pot, a neck for carrying the vapors away from the pot and a worm (copper tubing) for the cooling of the vapors.

The distillation procedure (referred to as making a run) would begin by straining the fermented mash through a cloth or bedsheet and into the cooking pot. The cooking pot was usually a copper container often shaped like a large kettle with a round lid and long spout. Heat would be applied to the container to heat the mash to 176°F. Once the mash begins to cook the lid would be put on and sealed with a paste of flour and water. The cooking is done at a constant even heat as the mash cannot cook too fast or too slowly. When the alcohol begins to vaporize, the only place for it to go is into the long spout where it is carried into the worm. The worm is a long system of tubing (usually copper) that is either placed in a container of cold water or has cold water running over it to cool the vapors from the cooking mash. The condensation is then collected in a container for another run. The first run of the mash is called "singling" and produces a murky whiskey full of impurities and excess water. To remove these, the moonshiner would repeat the distillation process on the liquid, this run is referred to as the "doubling run". Before the doubling run could be initiated, the moonshiner would have to thoroughly clean the still and all of the connections to remove any sour odors. The doubling run was made slower than the first and at a lower temperature to insure the removal of as many impurities as possible.

Many moonshiners eliminated the need for a doubling run by using what is known as a "thumper keg". This thumper keg was situated between the cooking pot and the condensing worm. The vapor from the cooking pot would be forced into the bottom of the thumper keg, which was half filled with beer. The vapor would rise through the beer and exit the keg at the top through a connecting pipe and enter the worm for cooling. This process of filtering the vapors through the beer removes almost as much of the impurities as the doubling run.

The final end product of the doubling run (or thumper-keg run) ranged from as high as 190 proof (at the beginning of the run) to a low of 70 proof (toward the end of a run) and now had to be mixed with branch water for the desired consistency. Some moonshiners would also age their whiskey in charred oak barrels (bourbon) or by adding ground charcoal or hickory chips. Unless the whiskey was for personal consumption, the aging of the brew was generally kept to a minimum.

# THE DECLINE

As discussed earlier, the art of moonshining declined considerably during the Prohibition era. Greed and expediency replaced the pride and care that formerly was taken in manufacturing whiskey as the quantity of the liquor produced began to matter more than the quality. However, even after the decline in craftsmenship, the moonshiners in the hills of northern Georgia continued to ply their trade, producing huge quantities of illicit whiskey. As late as the mid 1960's Dawson and Lumpkin counties were considered to be the major producers of moonshine not only in the state of Georgia but nationwide. (Dabney: 1974). According to local law enforcement officials, ex-moonshiners and current moonshiners three major developments have led to the recent decline and possibly the eventual demise of moonshining in these areas. They are: (1) The drastic increase in cost of the raw materials needed to manufacture moonshine (2) the introduction of marijuana and other drugs as an alternative cash crop and (3) the encroachment of civilization on even the most remote areas of southern Appalachia.

Because profit is now the primary motive in moonshining the first two factors combine to draw the greedy quick-buck moonshiner into other areas of exploitation. Over the last twenty years the cost of sugar and copper has risen so dramatically that the moonshiner must now charge a price for his product that is comparable to legal liquor. With most of the northern counties in Georgia having gone "wet" in recent years store brands are available to most of the population. Thus competition with "legal" liquor has forced the price down to such a degree that the profit is minimal.

With the large federal crackdown on drugs in Florida a considerable amount of drug traffic has moved into the hills of northern Georgia. (Newsweek: 1982). Backwoodsmen who formerly used secluded areas to run moonshine are now using these areas to grow marijuana or as landing strips for drug deliveries. According to local Georgia Bureau of Investigation officers, small planes equipped with bladder bags of fuel fly in from several Central American countries loaded with drugs (usually cocaine) and unload their cargo in secluded mountain airstrips. Drug trafficking is far more profitable than moonshining as a recent load of cocaine discovered in Gilmer County was valued at $500,000,000 with a possible street value of 1.5 billion dollars after being properly (or improperly) cut. The enormous profits to be gained from drug operations has drawn many shiners away from their traditional stills despite the potentially harsher penalties.

The final major development that is bringing about the end of moonshining, and probably the biggest factor, is the encroachment of civilization. Increased development has been spearheaded by the large population increases in many of the rural areas. Much of the increase is a result of the migration of "northerners" and Floridians into the area. These groups have not been exposed to the tradition of moonshining and so do not view it as an acceptable livelihood. They have also had the influence of relaxing many of the prohibitions regarding lawful liquor sales thus increasing competition for the moonshiners. These new residents are also less tolerant of "good-old-boy" law enforcement techniques which often allowed many of the shiners to engage in their work unhindered by the threat of arrest.

The large influx of new people has resulted in the intrusion of building developments into many remote areas. These new developments have also brought about the improvement of transportation methods to gain access to these communities. All of which are limiting the amount of secluded land for moonshine operations. These aforementioned factors have contributed to a sense of hostility between many of the "locals" and the new "fornerrs".

While moonshining has declined considerably in recent years, (only 2,477 gallons were confiscated by law enforcement officials in 1980) it has not disappeared totally from the scene. Many local families run a small still for their own personal consumption. Local law enforcement officials are usually aware of most of them and leave them alone as long as it doesn't develop into a "business". As one Dawson county deputy told me, "How can I arrest them folks for what I used to do when I was younger?" This attitude of tolerance and empathy is still very widespread amongst the local populace. Most feel that as long as you're not hurting anyone what you do is your business and no one else's. This individualism is a reflection of the attitudes of their pioneering ancestors that led them to settle in such remote areas to begin with. Unfortunately for them there are no new frontiers to retreat to and the onslaught of the "civilized" world is upon them.

## REFERENCES

Carr, Jess, *The Second Oldest Profession.* Englewood Cliffs, New Jersey: Prentice Hall, 1972

Coulter, E. Merton, *Georgia: A Short History.* Chapel Hill: University of North Carolina Press, 1933

Dabney, Joseph, *Mountain Spirits.* Lakemont, Georgia: Copple House Books, Inc., 1974

Hofstadter, Richard and Michael Wallace, *American Violence.* New York: Alfred A. Knopf, Inc., 1970

Kellner, Esther, *Moonshine: Its History and Folklore.* New York: Weathervane Books, 1971

Morgan, Edmund, *The Birth of the Republic.* Chicago: University of Chicago Press, 1956

*Newsweek,* "Gun, Grass and Money: America's Billion-Dollar Marijuana Crop". October 25, 1982, pp. 36-43.

Powell, Levi, Who Are These Mountain People. New York; Exposition Press, 1966

Randolph, Vance, *The Ozarks.* New York; The Vanguard Press, 1931

Trevelyan, G. M., *History of England: The Tudors and the Stuart Era.* Garden City, New York; Doubleday Anchor Books, 1952

Whitelock, Dorothy, *The Beginning of English Society.* Baltimore, Maryland; Penguin Books, 1966

Wildson, Charles, Backwoods America. Chapel Hill: University of North Carolina Press, 1935

Wiltse, Henry, *The Moonshiners,* Chattanooga, Tennessee: Times Printing Company, 1895

www.ingramcontent.com/pod-product-compliance
Lightning Source LLC
Chambersburg PA
CBHW051052160426
43193CB00010B/1157